Understanding
Othello

The Greenwood Press "Literature in Context" Series
Student Casebooks to Issues, Sources, and Historical Documents

UNDERSTANDING
Othello

A STUDENT CASEBOOK TO ISSUES, SOURCES, AND HISTORICAL DOCUMENTS

Faith Nostbakken

The Greenwood Press
"Literature in Context" Series
Claudia Durst Johnson, Series Editor

GREENWOOD PRESS
Westport, Connecticut • London

Library of Congress Cataloging-in-Publication Data

Nostbakken, Faith, 1964–
    Understanding Othello : a student casebook to issues, sources, and
historical documents / by Faith Nostbakken.
        p.   cm.—(The Greenwood Press "Literature in context" series, ISSN
      1074–598X)
    Includes bibliographical references and index.
    ISBN 0–313–30986–8 (alk. paper)
    1. Shakespeare, William, 1564–1616. Othello—Examinations—Study guides.
2. Shakespeare, William, 1564–1616. Othello—Sources.   3. Shakespeare,
William, 1564–1616—Stage history.   4. Literature and history—Sources.
5. Tragedy.   6. Muslims in literature.   7. Blacks in literature.   I. Title.
II. Series.
PR2829.N65   2000
822.3'3—dc21   00–022334

British Library Cataloguing in Publication Data is available.

Copyright © 2000 by Faith Nostbakken

Library of Congress Catalog Card Number: 00–022334
ISBN: 0–313–30986–8
ISSN: 1074–598X

First published in 2000

Greenwood Press, 88 Post Road West, Westport, CT 06881
An imprint of Greenwood Publishing Group, Inc.
www.greenwood.com

Printed in the United States of America

The paper used in this book complies with the
Permanent Paper Standard issued by the National
Information Standards Organization (Z39.48–1984).

10 9 8 7 6 5 4 3 2 1

For my parents,
who continue to teach me more than they know,
and for Dan, Sylvia and Hans, Joy and Phillip,
and two small wonders, Andreas and Mathias.

Contents

Acknowledgments

In the sequence of events between the inception and the completion of this book, a number of people played important roles, and I wish to recognize and thank some of them here. I extend my gratitude to the editors at Greenwood Press for inviting me to write a second book in their "Literature in Context" series; to my family and friends who supported me in my decision to undertake this project in spite of debilitating chronic health problems; to the very generous family who quietly supplied the funds for a new computer system allowing me to use voice-activated software to compensate for disabling pain in my arms; to the patient few who initially helped me set the technology in motion; to Rick Bowers for reading each chapter as I wrote it, for responding with valuable insights and enthusiasm, and for offering a bit of delightfully serendipitous and timely research; to all my good people—the great host of them—who occasionally took me to the library or brought the library to me, who patiently listened to me either formulate ideas for this book or apply the wisdom and relevance of *Othello* to numerous other conversations, and who not only encouraged me throughout this endeavor but who began that noble work of encouragement before I ever received an invitation to write this book, and who now continue to keep me company along the journey.

Introduction

Identified by many scholars as one of Shakespeare's "great" tragedies, along with *Hamlet*, *Macbeth*, and *King Lear*, *Othello* follows a traditional tragic pattern, tracing the central character's fall from greatness and bringing together qualities of nobility with choices that lead to inevitable suffering. *Othello* is also, however, one of Shakespeare's most emotionally compelling plays. The momentum with which the devastating series of events unravels creates a breathless sense of chaotic turmoil that captivates viewers almost as much as it drives the characters. Iago's revelations beginning in the first scene and recurring throughout the play provide the audience with a disturbing burden of foreknowledge from which there is virtually no relief. Perhaps this combined intensity of dramatic action and audience involvement explains *Othello*'s widespread, enduring appeal. Records from the play's first performances in 1604 to the present indicate its ongoing popularity over centuries of changing cultural fashions, political assumptions, and social expectations.

But *Othello* has generated almost as much controversy as it has popularity. In spite of the straightforward action of the plot, Shakespeare's character development and his presentation of difficult issues make for an extremely complex play that raises a number of artistic, moral, and social questions. While some call Othello

Shakespeare's most heroic tragic character, others call him the least. Iago's crucial role sparks some of this debate, for it is not easy to see Othello's behavior and choices independent of Iago's relentless villainy. The domestic focus of the plot also generates a level of critical discomfort. Some suggest that *Othello*'s movement away from public scenes to the intimacy of the bedroom diminishes the play's tragic scope and undermines the important promise of restored social order that typically compensates for the loss of greatness at the end of Shakespeare's other, more public tragedies. Artistic questions, therefore, revolve around the meaning of tragedy as it is dramatized in *Othello* and the consistency between characters' motives and actions. Moral questions center on the portrayal of good and evil, and social questions arise from the play's treatment of race, violence, gender, and justice.

All these questions emerge from a variety of contexts. This casebook is designed, first, to draw attention to relevant questions, and, second, to address them by exploring their many contexts in order to offer multiple ways of understanding *Othello* from historical and modern perspectives. The study is organized both chronologically and topically, beginning with an analysis of *Othello* that examines the dramatic contexts of its origin and discusses the play's source material and literary elements. The subsequent chapters open more broadly onto the historical context within which *Othello*'s topics and concerns first found an audience. Three historic chapters begin with single questions that connect attitudes and values in Shakespeare's time with issues in the play. A chapter on race and religion explores the nature of identity, asking, "Who are you?" as a means of considering Renaissance English views toward Venetians, Turks, and Moors within and beyond the play. In a chapter on love and marriage, the question that implicitly challenges a number of *Othello*'s characters—"How do you love?"— becomes the avenue of inquiry into disparate and contradictory views about love, marriage, and gender in the sixteenth and seventeenth centuries. A third chapter on war and the military attaches historic relevance to concerns about military rank and status in *Othello* with the question, "What is your occupation?" Information on Renaissance controversies in each of these chapters provides both background and insight into relationships and conflicts within the play.

The four centuries since Shakespeare wrote *Othello* have bred new generations of the play's admirers and critics, new interpretations of its artistic merit, and new ideas about its social commentary. The chapter on performance and interpretation traces this development chronologically with a survey of *Othello*'s theater and film history and an overview of various critical approaches to the play. This analysis points to the close interaction between art and the various cultural contexts within which it finds expression. For example, at times in English and American history, prejudice against blacks made it impossible for actors, audiences, or critics to conceive of Othello as a tragic black hero married to a white woman. At other times in spite of racial prejudice, actors challenged accepted cultural standards, risking public outrage by daring to cast Othello as a black man. As a living art form, drama is sensitive to the values and assumptions of each place and time in which it is performed and reinterpreted. *Othello*'s stage and critical history indicates that its continued popularity and controversy emerge sometimes in its ability to reflect dominant political and social attitudes and sometimes in its capacity to question those accepted viewpoints.

The final chapter in this casebook expands the focus of discussion to explore how *Othello* might reflect and challenge perspectives on contemporary stories, including both factual events recorded in newspaper headlines and fictional plots drawn from a variety of storylines in poetry, short stories, and a novel. This portion of *Understanding* Othello invites readers to recognize relationships between the themes and characters in Shakespeare's tragedy and issues or topics appearing in "real-life" drama or other literature. Identifying such relationships can stimulate fresh observations about the play, raise awareness about current events, and refine analytical thinking to give personal opinion a sharper edge.

Documents, in both full and excerpted form, added to every chapter directly connect *Othello* to the wide variety of contexts presented throughout this study, including dramatic and literary approaches, theatrical and cultural perspectives, social and political angles, and historic and modern viewpoints. The following list indicates the range of materials represented:

an Italian narrative source for *Othello*

travel journals

a royal proclamation

Elizabethan marriage conduct books

Renaissance military manuals

dramatic criticism

actors' and directors' diaries and journals

newspaper articles

editorials

a president's national address

poetry

speeches from other plays

passages from short stories and a novel

performance photographs

an illustration of a sixteenth-century Moor

Sections or subsections of each chapter also conclude with "Questions for Written and Oral Discussion." These questions vary in purpose, scope, and degree of difficulty. Some are direct and specific, addressing the content and relevance of selected documents. Many call for a more complex level of inquiry and comparison by indicating possible points of intersection between *Othello* and the various documents included. Others offer opportunities for exploration beyond the materials within this study, making suggestions for library and Internet research that could form the basis of individual or class projects. Some questions give very explicit instructions, for example, about how to divide into groups to debate a particular topic, while others are more general, allowing for an effective or comfortable approach to be determined by participants or teachers guiding the choice of assignments. Often one topic includes a series of related questions. It may not be necessary or practical to address all the questions at once or to reach independent conclusions about each one of them. Primarily, these sets of questions are intended to stimulate ideas and generate fruitful written or oral discussion. All of them are designed to engage both the intellect and the imagination. Some topics encourage statements or arguments that require thoughtful analysis and evidence; others allow for creative artwork, video cameras, music, performance, and numerous opportunities to enter into characters—either historic or fictional—and respond to issues from their perspectives.

As a student casebook in a "Literature in Context" series, *Understanding* Othello strives toward an interdisciplinary approach to the play. By examining its diverse contexts, this study attempts to discourage vague, narrow, or simplistic generalizations about *Othello* and invites even those who are encountering the play for the first time to recognize and enjoy the many factors contributing to *Othello*'s long and ongoing history. Even beginners can participate in the life of the play by drawing on the experience and expertise of others, making personal discoveries, and adding a voice to conflicting observations, interpretations, and opinions that continue to sustain *Othello* as a popular and controversial work of art.

All quotations from *Othello* throughout this book come from the Signet Classic version: William Shakespeare, *Othello*, Alvin Kernan, ed. (New York: Penguin Books, 1998).

1

Dramatic Analysis

This first chapter explores various elements that contribute to *Othello*'s dramatic power and appeal. As a Renaissance playwright, Shakespeare wrote within a tradition that included ancient classical theories of tragedy, themes and character types from early English medieval plays, and popular Elizabethan and Jacobean perceptions about the relationship between the theater and the world. This theatrical tradition clearly illuminates aspects of *Othello*. The main source of the play's plot is another important influence. Shakespeare borrowed a simple Italian murder story and reshaped it by developing more psychologically complex characters, incorporating stage conventions, and adding details from recent history. Finally, considering *Othello* as a text reveals rich poetic and structural patterns that indicate the play's merit not only as a stage script but also as a literary work of art. The following examination of traditions, conventions, sources, and poetic and thematic elements aims to increase awareness and understanding of the many factors and conditions that influenced Shakespeare's dramatic craft and specifically the composition, performance, and publication of *Othello*.

TRAGEDY AND THE POPULAR TRADITION

To speak about tragedy is no easy matter because the term can be vague and broad or very personal. However, to speak of it as a form of English drama in the sixteenth and seventeenth centuries begins to narrow the focus to certain expectations, patterns, and assumptions. Shakespeare's tragedies, we might suggest, usually include a central hero, develop some form of conflict, perhaps involving ambition, revenge, or family strife, and unfold the drastic consequences of choices that lead to suffering and loss, most often culminating in death. These general observations describe the bare structure of a tragic plot and even provide the basic outline of *Othello*. But knowing more about the theories and elements contributing to this dramatic form allows for more meaningful discussion about the way Shakespeare combines and works them into the particular story of Othello's fall from greatness as it involves and affects characters around him.

ARISTOTLE

Greek philosopher Aristotle's definition of tragedy (c. 330 B.C.) became influential among Renaissance dramatists and literary critics and has continued to guide and shape an understanding of tragedy as a literary form. His theory concentrates on dramatic structure: (1) identifying plot as the most important element, (2) describing the central character as one who is neither wholly good nor wholly evil and whose fall results from an error in judgment, (3) suggesting that the hero eventually realizes his error and its consequences when it is too late to change, and (4) indicating that the audience responds with a combination of fear and pity to a story about a character who elicits their sympathy. The following excerpt develops some of these ideas by distinguishing tragic form from other plots and indicating how the differences affect an audience's involvement.

FROM ARISTOTLE, *THE POETICS* (c. 330 b.c.)
(*Aristotle's Theory of Poetry and Fine Art*, Trans. S. H. Butcher,
London: Macmillan, 1907)

[Tragedy] should . . . imitate actions which excite pity and fear, this being the distinctive mark of tragic imitation. It follows plainly, in the first place, that the change of fortune presented must not be the spectacle of a virtuous man brought from prosperity to adversity: for this moves neither pity nor fear; it merely shocks us. Nor, again, that of a bad man passing from adversity to prosperity: for nothing can be more alien to the spirit of Tragedy; it possesses no single tragic quality; it neither satisfies the moral sense nor calls forth pity or fear. Nor, again, should the downfall of the utter villain be exhibited. A plot of this kind would, doubtless, satisfy the moral sense, but it would inspire neither pity nor fear, for pity is aroused by unmerited misfortune, fear by the misfortune of a man like ourselves. Such an event, therefore, will be neither pitiful nor terrible. There remains, then, the character between these two extremes—that of a man who is not eminently good and just, yet whose misfortune is brought about not by vice or depravity, but by some error or frailty. (45)

Shakespeare did not simply adopt Aristotle's ancient principles as a rigid formula for his tragedies. In fact, with the growing Renaissance interest in humanism, individualism, and self-expression, the psychology of characters often became more important than Aristotle's emphasis on plot or action. In *Othello*, for example, the longest and—in many ways—most crucial scene is 3.3, which involves virtually no external action but focuses on Iago's careful manipulation of words to poison Othello's mind, turning his love into irrational suspicion and horrified jealousy. Shakespeare creates almost as much fascination and horror about this internal transformation as its external consequences.

However, Aristotle's description of a tragic hero provides a valuable measure for considering Othello's title role, especially in relation to two other important characters, Iago and Desdemona. According to Aristotle's views, Othello cannot be viewed as a tragic hero if he simply becomes a victim of Iago's "vice or depravity" or if his drastic change from devotion to brutality against Desdemona robs him of all sympathy. Neither of those scenarios would stir a response of both pity and fear. To be a truly tragic figure, Othello must bear some blame for his misfortune through his own "error or frailty"—perhaps his willingness to let Iago's lies awaken or stir his own private misgivings so that he becomes unwilling or unable to seek the truth from other reliable sources. Any discussion of tragedy in *Othello* should evaluate the extent of the main character's responsibility for his actions and the degree of pity or fear his actions evoke. And yet the experience of Shakespeare's play moves beyond Aristotle's theories about the central hero. Desdemona's suffering, for example, cannot help but draw a share of the audience's pity and fear towards her and, in some way, affect responses to Othello. Furthermore, Iago's powerful villainy inevitably complicates any easy assumptions about other characters' responsibility for their actions.

ENGLISH MEDIEVAL DRAMA

Desdemona's suffering and, even more so, Iago's villainy suggest that Shakespeare was influenced not only by classical Greek theories of tragedy but also by early English drama which enacted the battle between good and evil, opposites that Desdemona and Iago often appear to represent. Moreover, Iago's villainy closely resembles actions of certain characters in medieval plays popular in the fourteenth and fifteenth centuries. These plays, known as miracle plays and morality plays, had religious or moral themes. Miracle plays were organized as a series or cycle of scenes or short dramas about biblical characters and were performed annually by medieval English communities to celebrate the story of Christian salvation. The devil figured prominently in several scenes, including the temptation of Adam and Eve in the Garden of Eden and Christ's conquering of hell by his death and resurrection. The devil in this religious drama had a reputation not only for his evil motives but for his cunning deception and manipulation, his ability to feign goodness in order to achieve his own desires.

In *Othello*, many references associate Iago with the devil. Plotting to mislead Othello with lies about Desdemona's infidelity, Iago explains how he will cloak his intentions in friendly terms:

> Divinity of hell!
> When devils will the blackest sins put on,
> They do suggest at first with heavenly shows,
> As I do now. (2.3.350–353)

When Othello finally realizes the magnitude of Iago's deception, he comments on the similarities between Iago and the devil, saying, "I look down towards his feet—but that's a fable. / If that thou be'st a devil, I cannot kill thee" (5.2.282–283). Like the devil in earlier English miracle plays, Iago is a powerful stage figure, full of energy, malice, and dark ambitions.

Contemporary with miracle plays, medieval morality plays also included an evil character known as the Vice figure. Initially, morality plays contained many characters that represented various vices and other characters that represented virtues. As personified moral abstractions, these characters had names such as Pride and Infidelity, or Humility and Peace. Virtues struggled against vices to win the soul of the main character, known as Everyman or Mankind, a representative of the human race.

As allegories designed to offer moral encouragement and instruction, morality plays continued to be performed as late as the 1560s when English secular drama began to emerge and increase in popularity. In the later morality plays, however, one Vice figure began to dominate as the main evil tempter identified by certain set or "stock" characteristics. Typically, he practiced skilled deception amongst other characters while displaying honesty and truth in revealing his intentions to the audience. Similarly, while representing the power of darkness venturing to destroy goodness, he light-heartedly engaged the audience with his wit, humor, and obvious delight in his harmful schemes.

This Vice figure influenced stage villains that began appearing in secular English drama. Iago, commonly regarded as Shakespeare's most villainous villain, demonstrates many traditional Vice-like qualities: hypocrisy, cunning, and pleasure in tormenting others, as well as an intimate, open relationship with the audience whom he addresses frequently throughout the play. Like the Vice figure, he seems to enjoy evil for evil's sake, and the reasons for his destructive behavior often pale in comparison to their effects. Unlike the Vice figure, however, Iago is not a personified abstraction. He is a character who demonstrates psychological realism, meaning that he displays thoughts, behaviors, and relationships that are complicated and unpredictable yet somehow humanly possible and believable. Consequently, he finds his place and power in a tragedy of well-rounded, convincingly complex characters.

THE STAGE MACHIAVEL

Another type of stage villainy reflected in Iago comes from the secular rather than the sacred dramatic tradition. A figure known as "the stage machiavel" became popular in English plays in the late sixteenth century as the writings of Italian political adviser, Niccolò Machiavelli, began to spread across Europe and reach England. Early English views of Machiavelli were based not on an accurate assessment of his ideas or philosophy but instead on a hostile misinterpretation of his intentions. Machiavelli was a realist who advised state leaders to separate politics and religion, to make pragmatic decisions, and, if need be, to use both threats and appearances as effective tools of leadership. The English, however, saw his recommendations not as valid political options but as a manifestation of evil qualities such as atheism, immorality, self-interest, and cynicism. This perception became exaggerated on the stage where atheists, schemers, and horrifying villains came to be recognized and identified as "stage machiavels." Iago, as a consummate plotter and schemer who sometimes appears to be in control of everyone's actions and responses on stage, would likely have struck Shakespeare's audiences as the same type of cynical and self-serving character that Machiavelli represented in England.

Without doubt, the tragic dimension and characterization in *Othello* demonstrate Shakespeare's dramatic skill and his insight into human strengths and weaknesses. But the play's structure, plot, and thematic vision also reflect a broader set of traditions that contributed to Shakespeare's art, including a heritage of classical and medieval influences, a mixture of sacred and secular values and perspectives, and a contemporary context in which theaters were becoming vital places for expressing and responding to politics and popular culture.

OTHELLO'S ITALIAN SOURCE

While Shakespeare worked within a diverse dramatic tradition and experimented with its assumptions, he rarely wrote an original play that was not based on a previous narrative or poetic source. His main source for the plot of *Othello* is a novella by Italian author Giraldi Cinthio and appears in his collection, *Gli Hecatommithi* (meaning "A Hundred Tales"). Published in Venice in 1565, the Italian narrative clearly provides Shakespeare's inspiration for his play. In Cinthio's tale, a Moor marries a Venetian lady, "Disdemona," against her parents' wishes and the two travel to Cyprus where the Moor is appointed as Venetian military commander. The Moor's Ensign (Iago's counterpart) is a wicked, deceitful man, while the Captain (Cassio's counterpart) is a good friend to the Moor and Disdemona. The Ensign lies to the Moor about Disdemona's alleged affair with the Captain, and Disdemona's handkerchief becomes the main evidence against her. Conspiring together, the Ensign and the Moor attempt unsuccessfully to murder the Captain and then violently murder Disdemona in her bed. As a short summary, this synopsis sounds very much like *Othello*'s plot.

There are, however, significant details in Cinthio's novella that do not appear in Shakespeare's play. In the Italian story, for example, the marriage between the Moor and Disdemona lasts harmoniously for some time before the two depart for Cyprus. The wicked Ensign is motivated solely by his own love for Disdemona and spurred to revenge by her unwillingness to reciprocate his advances. The handkerchief falls into the Captain's possession because the Ensign deliberately steals it, rather than simply taking advantage of a moment when Disdemona misplaces it. The Moor bribes the Ensign to persuade him to kill the Captain and then the Moor and Ensign devise a plan together to kill Disdemona while making it appear an accident. The Moor later blames the Ensign for Disdemona's death, and a battle of mutual revenge between the two men ends the story as one man exposes the guilt of the other, neither admitting his part, and both eventually facing death which the storyteller announces as the moral conclusion to their crimes.

Partly because these details are left out of *Othello* and because conditions of impending warfare in Cyprus are added, reading Cinthio's story and reading or watching Shakespeare's play are two completely different experiences. From a practical perspective, some of the changes involve the natural effect of transforming narrative into drama. Shakespeare compresses time in order to adapt Cinthio's tale to a two- or three-hour performance. He omits passages that would not work well on stage and turns paragraphs of description into the dialogue and monologue of character interaction and self-revelation.

Apart from such practical alterations, however, Shakespeare's choices suggest other creative intentions and artistic results. In his hands Cinthio's straightforward, moralistic tale becomes an emotionally intense drama of manipulation, self-deception, and suffering for which no moral conclusions offer comfort. Othello is a much nobler man than Cinthio's Moor and Iago is a much more complex villain. The quality of Desdemona's love is both more beautiful and more difficult to understand. The war-like atmosphere that Shakespeare adds to the play heightens the tension and atmosphere of inevitable doom. In short, while Shakespeare uses a narrative source for *Othello*, he does not remain limited by its limitations nor bound by its logic and purpose. Instead he reshapes it, turning relatively flat characters into well-developed tragic heroes, villains, and victims, raising the level of desperation, tightening the threads of the plot, complicating the narrative's moralistic tone with questions about motivation and with agonizing barriers of misunderstanding, thus demanding greater emotional involvement from his audiences and readers.

The following excerpts from Cinthio's novella reveal some parallels and differences between the Italian narrative and Shakespeare's tragedy. The first passage [1] describes how the marriage between the Moor and Disdemona begins; the second [2] explains the Ensign's wicked character and motivation for his villainy; the third [3] narrates a conversation between the Ensign and the Captain which Shakespeare develops into a crucial scene in *Othello*; the fourth [4] reveals the Moor and the Ensign plotting Disdemona's murder; and the fifth [5] records the story's violent conclusion.

FROM GIRALDI CINTHIO, *GLI HECATOMMITHI*, DECADE 3,
NOVELLA 7 (1565)
(*The New Variorum Shakespeare. Othello*, Ed. Horace Howard
Furness, Vol. 6; Philadelphia: J. B. Lippincott Co., 1886)

[1] There once lived in Venice a Moor, who was very valiant and of a
handsome person; and having given proofs in war of great skill and pru-
dence, he was highly esteemed by the Signoria of the Republic. . . .
   It happened that a virtuous lady of marvellous beauty, named Disdemona, fell in love with the Moor, moved thereto by his valour; and he,
vanquished by the beauty and the noble character of Disdemona, returned her love; and their affection was so mutual that, although the
parents of the lady strove all they could to induce her to take another
husband, she consented to marry the Moor; and they lived in such harmony and peace in Venice that no word ever passed between them that
was not affectionate and kind. . . . (377)

[2] Now amongst the soldiery there was an Ensign, a man of handsome
figure, but of the most depraved nature in the world. This man was in
great favour with the Moor, who had not the slightest idea of his wickedness; for, despite the malice lurking in his heart, he cloaked with proud
and valorous speech and with a specious presence the villainy of his soul.
. . . This man had likewise taken with him his wife to Cyprus, a young,
and fair, and virtuous lady; and being of Italian birth she was much loved
by Disdemona, who spent the greater part of every day with her.
   In the same Company there was a certain Captain of a troop, to whom
the Moor was much affectioned. And Disdemona, for this cause, knowing
how much her husband valued him, showed him proofs of the greatest
kindness, which was all very grateful to the Moor. Now the wicked Ensign, regardless of the faith that he had pledged his wife, no less than of
the friendship, fidelity, and obligation which he owed the Moor, fell passionately in love with Disdemona, and bent all his thoughts to achieve
his conquest; yet he dared not to declare his passion openly, fearing that,
should the Moor perceive it, he would at once kill him. He therefore
sought in various ways, and with secret guile, to betray his passion to the
lady; but she, whose every wish was centred in the Moor, had no thought
for this Ensign more than for any other man; and all the means he tried
to gain her love had no more effect than if he had not tried them. But
the Ensign imagined that the cause of his ill success was that Disdemona
loved the Captain of the troop; and he pondered how to remove him
from her sight. The love which he had borne the lady now changed into
the bitterest hate, and, having failed in his purposes, he devoted all his
thoughts to plot the death of the Captain of the troop and to divert the

affection of the Moor from Disdemona. After revolving in his mind various schemes, all alike wicked, he at length resolved to accuse her of unfaithfulness to her husband, and to represent the Captain as her paramour. But knowing the singular love the Moor bore to Disdemona, and the friendship which he had for the Captain, he was well aware that, unless he practised an artful fraud upon the Moor, it were impossible to make him give ear to either accusation; wherefore he resolved to wait until time and circumstance should open a path for him to engage in his foul project. (378–379)

[3] . . . [O]ne day [the Ensign] took occasion to speak with the Captain when the Moor was so placed that he could see and hear them as they conversed. And whilst talking to him of every other subject than of Disdemona, he kept laughing all the time aloud, and, feigning astonishment, he made various movements with his head and hands, as if listening to some tale of marvel. As soon as the Moor saw the Captain depart, he went up to the Ensign to hear what he said to him. And the Ensign, after long entreaty, at length said, 'He has hidden from me nothing, and has told me that he has been used to visit your wife whenever you went from home, and that on the last occasion she gave him this handkerchief which you presented to her when you married her.'

The Moor thanked the Ensign, and it seemed now clear to him that, should he find Disdemona not to have the handkerchief, it was all true that the Ensign had told to him. . . . (383)

[4] Then [the Moor and the Ensign] consulted of one means and another—poison and daggers—to kill poor Disdemona, but could resolve on nothing. At length the Ensign said, 'A plan comes to my mind, which will give you satisfaction and raise cause for no suspicion. It is this: the house in which you live is very old, and the ceiling of your chamber has many cracks; I propose we take a stocking, filled with sand, and beat Disdemona with it till she dies; thus will her body bear no signs of violence. When she is dead we can pull down a portion of the ceiling, and thus make it seem as if a rafter falling on her head had killed the lady. Suspicion cannot rest on you, since all men will impute her death to accident.'

This cruel counsel pleased the Moor, and he only waited for a fitting time to execute the plot. . . . (386)

[5] On the following day Disdemona was buried, followed to the grave by the universal grief of the people. But Heaven, the just regarder of all hearts, willed not that so wicked a deed should go unpunished. Ere long the Moor, whom Disdemona had loved more than her own life, began to feel such sorrow at her loss that he went wandering about as one

bereft of reason, searching in every part of the house. And reflecting in his thoughts that the Ensign had been the cause that he had lost, with Disdemona, all joy in life, he conceived so deep a hatred to that wicked man he could not bear to set eyes on him, and had it not been for his fear of the inviolable justice of the Signoria of Venice, he would have slain him openly. But being unable to do this with safety, he deprived him of his rank, and would not allow him to remain in his Company; whereat such an enmity arose between the two that no greater or more deadly can be imagined.

The Ensign, that wickedest of all bad men, now turned his thoughts to injuring the Moor; and seeking out the Captain . . . he said to him, ' . . . if you will come with me to Venice, I'll tell you who the malefactor is, whom I dare not mention to you here for many reasons; and I will bring you proofs.' . . .

The Signoria of Venice, when they heard of the cruelty inflicted by barbarians upon a lady of their city, commended that the Moor's arms should be pinioned in Cyprus, and he be brought to Venice, where, with many tortures, they sought to draw from him the truth. But the Moor, bearing with unyielding courage all the torment, denied the whole charge so resolutely that no confession could be drawn from him. But, although by his constancy and firmness he escaped death, he was, after being confined for several days in prison, condemned to perpetual banishment, in which he was eventually slain by the kinsfolk of Disdemona, as he merited. The Ensign returned to his own country, and, following up his wonted villainy, he accused one of his companions of having sought to persuade him to kill an enemy of his, who was a man of noble rank; whereupon this person was arrested and put to the torture; but when he denied the truth of what his accuser had declared, the Ensign himself was likewise tortured to make him prove the truth of his accusations; and he was tortured so that his body ruptured, upon which he was removed from prison and taken home, where he died a miserable death. Thus did Heaven avenge the innocence of Disdemona; and all these events were narrated by the Ensign's wife, who was privy to the whole, after his death, as I have told them here. (387–389)

QUESTIONS FOR WRITTEN AND ORAL DISCUSSION

1. Discuss whether and how Othello conforms to Aristotle's model of a tragic character. Is it possible to see Othello instead simply as Iago's victim or as Desdemona's brutal victimizer with few redeeming qualities? If either of these views seem potentially valid, how does that affect your understanding of the play as a tragedy? To what extent is Othello responsible for his own actions? What is his "error or frailty"?

Argue your position in a short essay or divide into three groups and debate the issue, considering how the word "misfortune" describes Othello's circumstance. One group will defend him as a tragic figure, the second will portray him as an unwitting victim of deception, and the third will describe him as insufficiently tragic because his horrible behavior is more convincing than his virtues or noble stature.

2. Discuss whether and how *Othello* inspires pity and fear. Find specific examples of scenes or characters that evoke these responses and consider whether one of these responses seems more common or compelling than the other does. Do the experiences of both Othello and Desdemona inspire pity and fear? If so, what balance is achieved between the two characters? Does your response to Desdemona make your reaction to Othello more or less sympathetic? How does their relationship influence your understanding of the play as a tragedy?

3. An important aspect of tragedy for Aristotle involves the hero's eventual realization of his error when it is too late to change. Does Othello demonstrate such awareness at the end of the play? If so, when and how? Does his decision to kill himself seem appropriate, foolish, or excessive? Explain why and suggest how your response determines your view of the tragedy in Othello's story and your attitude towards him.

4. Aristotle believes that a tragic hero is a character somewhat "like ourselves." Does Othello remind you at all of yourself in his weakness or his error? Although you may not imagine reacting with such extreme behavior as he does, can you see yourself foolishly accepting one person's word over another's because it confirms your own suspicions? Have you ever allowed envy or jealousy to destroy a good relationship? Have you ever been an "Iago" figure or been tempted by one? Have you ever been a "Desdemona" figure suffering because others have misrepresented your actions and intentions or because you have had faith in people who do not merit your trust? Write a personal account that describes such a situation—real or imagined— and the outcome of your choices. Does this exercise change the way you respond to Othello, Iago, or Desdemona? Does either Othello or Iago seem more or less of a monster?

5. English medieval plays dramatized the battle between good and evil in religious or moral terms. Discuss how that same battle is enacted in *Othello*. Even if the play does not offer a simple moral conclusion, is there a moral element to the central conflict and its consequences? Explain how or why. Is it useful to describe the characters' decisions and actions as moral or immoral? Why or why not?

6. Some scholars observe clear parallels between *Othello*'s main characters and morality play stock figures. Desdemona represents virtue or goodness, Iago is vice or evil personified, and Othello is the "Everyman" figure whose soul is caught between the other two. Does this reading of the play seem valid or useful? Does it increase your understanding of the interaction between the characters or does a "morality play" reading impose conditions that are too simplistic or limiting to reflect accurately the characters' internal and external struggles? Explain your position.

7. Do you think that the many references to Iago as "devil" in *Othello* are meant to characterize him as something other than human or simply to reinforce his evil motives? Does his power to harm others seem believably human or supernatural? Support your answer with examples from the play.

8. Why do you think Iago is one of Shakespeare's most memorable villains? Considering the stage tradition of villainy—including the devil, the morality Vice, and the "stage machiavel"—make a list of the qualities that characterized a villain in medieval and Renaissance drama. Describe how Iago represents some of these qualities and provide examples. Are there ways he does not fit the stereotype? How do you respond to Iago? Emotionally or intellectually? With horror or with admiration? Or with a confusing mixture of reactions? Try to explain why.

9. Using Iago as your central example, address the following question: "Why are the 'bad guys' sometimes most interesting and entertaining to watch?"

10. Compare how the marriage begins in Cinthio's story with the way that it begins in *Othello*. Note both similarities and differences, and offer your own ideas about the reasons and results of Shakespeare's changes. In what ways does Shakespeare make his play more dramatic than his narrative source?

11. Compare and contrast Cinthio's Ensign and Shakespeare's Iago. Why do you suppose Shakespeare significantly changed the motives for Iago's actions from Cinthio's story? What is the effect of Iago revealing his own intentions rather than having a narrator describe them?

12. Read Cinthio's paragraph in which the Moor watches the Ensign and the Captain in conversation. Consider how closely Shakespeare follows this source in creating the similar "handkerchief scene" in *Othello* (Act 4.1). What is the effect of Othello's comments on the dialogue, and of us—as readers and audience members—being able to hear what Iago and Cassio say to each other? Why is this scene so important in the play?

13. The murders of Cinthio's Disdemona and Shakespeare's Desdemona are quite different. Why might Shakespeare make his scene less violent and exclude Iago from the action? In two small groups, dramatize the death scenes from the play and the novella, including the action that follows the murder. You may need to shorten speeches and simplify the conclusions in the interest of time. Then hold a class discussion, identifying as many differences between the two as you can, making suggestions about why Shakespeare alters his source, and drawing some conclusions about the dramatic, artistic, moral, or emotional effects of his revisions.

14. Several notable characters in *Othello*, including Roderigo, Brabantio, and Bianca, have no counterparts in Cinthio's tale. Write an essay about *one* of these characters in which you explain his or her significance in the play and suggest why Shakespeare might have included the character. How does the presence of one of these three contribute to the plot, the portrayal of other characters, or the development of certain themes?

15. Imagine you are Shakespeare planning to write a new play and have just discovered Cinthio's tale as a possible source. Write a journal entry or series of notes about why you think the plot would make a good play, how you will use it, what changes you intend to make, and your reasons for doing so.

SUGGESTED READINGS

Bratchell, D. F. *Shakespearean Tragedy*. New York: Routledge, 1990.

Bullough, Geoffrey, ed. *Narrative and Dramatic Sources of Shakespeare*. Vol. 7. London: Routledge, 1973.

Hyman, Stanley Edgar. *Iago: Some Approaches to the Illusion of His Motivation*. New York: Atheneum, 1970.

Leech, Clifford. *Tragedy*. London: Methuen, 1969.

Margeson, J.M.R. *The Origins of English Tragedy*. Oxford: Clarendon Press, 1967.

Raab, Felix. *The English Face of Machiavelli, A Changing Interpretation*. London: Routledge, 1964.

Scragg, Leah. "Iago—Vice or Devil?" *Shakespeare Survey* 21 (1968): 53–66.

Spivak, Bernard. *Shakespeare and the Allegory of Evil: The History of a Metaphor in Relation to His Major Villains*. New York: Columbia University Press, 1958.

POETIC AND DRAMATIC PATTERNS

As a literary work of art in printed form, *Othello* reveals many layers of meaning that may not be immediately apparent to an audience member attending a stage production for the first time. Yet even in performance, as producers and actors deliberately work with the pattern and repetition of words, Shakespeare's poetry can unconsciously—if not consciously—add to the audience's emotional, psychological, and intellectual response. Studying the words on the page, therefore, draws attention to Shakespeare's skill as a poet and dramatist, allowing for greater awareness of the connection and tension between words and images, images and characters, and characters and themes. *Othello* is both poetry and drama, the two complementing each other.

BLANK VERSE

The main form of poetry in Shakespeare's plays is blank verse: unrhymed lines of ten syllables with an unaccented syllable followed by an accented syllable. This poetic pattern is called iambic pentameter, "iambic" referring to the rhythm and "pentameter" identifying the number of accented syllables per line. Blank verse closely approximates the rhythm of natural speech, bringing together the sound and sense of poetry and prose.

Conventionally, Shakespeare uses blank verse for noble or upper-class characters or for speeches that express seriousness or dignity. He reverts to prose for characters of low stature or for humorous exchanges. In *Othello*, however, there are many irregularities in the verse form, and frequent shifts between poetry and prose do not always reflect a character's status or the tone of the scene. The Duke, for example, speaks in both blank verse and prose, as do Iago and Roderigo. In part, these inconsistencies may reflect errors or difficulties in transmitting Shakespeare's original lines from stage script into printed text because of complications and imperfections in the seventeenth-century printing process. Nevertheless, *Othello* includes some of Shakespeare's greatest poetry, much of it spoken by Othello himself, expressing the grandness of his adventures, the nobility and authority of his character, the strength of his passions, and the convictions of his soul. Not surprisingly, perhaps, when Othello endeavors to demonstrate and maintain his noble stature or self-control, he speaks in blank verse, but when he sinks into the beast-like rage and frenzy of jealousy, he speaks in prose or utters short, exclamatory phrases, such as "Goats and monkeys!" (4.1.263)

IMAGERY

Figurative language contributes to patterns created in the play's poetry. Images woven into similes and metaphors help to develop some of *Othello*'s themes. Iago's frequent references to webs and snares, for example, draw attention to the deception and manipulation with which he entraps his victims. In observing Cassio's courtesy to Desdemona, he says to himself, "He takes her by the palm. Ay, well said, whisper! With as little a web as this will I ensnare as great a fly as Cassio" (2.1.165–167). A little later, Iago continues to unfold his devious plot against Desdemona, saying,

> So will I turn her virtue into pitch,
> And out of her own goodness make the net
> That shall enmesh them all. (2.3.360–362)

Iago's images increase the sense of power he has over other characters.

Recurring animal imagery also intensifies the play's conflict. References to animals and monsters articulate the contrast between people and beasts, and then add to the atmosphere of darkness and violence as Iago and Othello begin to act more like beasts than human beings. Believing Iago's lies about Desdemona and seeing himself as a cuckold—a man who allegedly develops horns on his forehead as a sign that his wife has committed adultery—Othello adopts some of Iago's metaphors.

Iago: Would you bear your fortune like a man.

Othello: A horned man's a monster and a beast.

Iago: There's many a beast then in a populous city,
     And many a civil monster. (4.1.63–66)

These images of beasts and monsters, goats and monkeys, dogs and toads enrich the play as they convey its growing impression of irrationality, chaos, and disaster.

IRONY

Irony is another important literary technique that adds texture and meaning to the linear action of the plot. Irony derives from the difference between seeming and being or appearance and reality, crucial distinctions in *Othello*. Often verbal irony results from a character saying one thing while intending another. When Iago begins to explain the night brawl between Cassio and Roderigo, he says to Othello, "I had rather have this tongue cut from my mouth / Than it should do offense to Michael Cassio" (2.3.220–221). Nothing could be further from the truth as Iago's earlier speeches have indicated. In fact, much of what Iago says to other characters is ironic. He acts concerned for their well-being while endeavoring to destroy them.

Irony works not only at a verbal level but also at a dramatic level in that the audience knows far more about characters' circumstances than many of the characters do about themselves. Again, Iago crafts much of this irony by revealing his intentions to the audience while concealing his plans from his victims. When Cassio says of Iago, "I never knew / A Florentine more kind and honest" (3.1.38–39), the audience knows otherwise. When Othello accepts Iago's story about Desdemona's unfaithfulness, the audience knows otherwise. When Othello believes he is acting justly in demanding Cassio's death and murdering his own wife, again the audience knows otherwise. Only Iago seems to know more than the audience as he informs them step-by-step about what will happen next, but when he eventually loses control of his own schemes, then the audience knows before he does that he has been trapped by his own web of deceit. Dramatic irony is thick throughout *Othello*, often making viewers feel like Iago's accomplices, perhaps creating feelings of guilt and, at the same time, heightening anxiety and horror as the tragedy unfolds.

STAGE CONVENTIONS

The effect of irony in *Othello* is closely related to the use of certain stage conventions. Conventions are aspects of stage activity that may not appear convincingly realistic but that actors and audiences accept as part of the play's dramatic illusion. Some important conventions are based on the way characters speak to each other and to the audience. In "dialogue," two or more characters converse together while the audience seemingly overhears. But in an "aside," a character addresses the audience while the other characters on stage appear not to hear. And in a "soliloquy," a single character speaks alone to the audience—either deliberately addressing them or appearing to think aloud. In the absence of a narrator explaining the story, these conventional forms of dramatic communication are essential in developing character, revealing and unfolding the plot, and giving the audience a much broader understanding of motives and action than any individual character may have.

The convention of asides and soliloquies in *Othello* focuses primarily on Iago who achieves his dominance on stage partly through his many speeches directed at the audience and unheard by other characters. He provides viewers with a burden of knowledge that traps them as much as it does the other characters. What the audience knows it cannot change or control. That is part of the irony; that is the power of the tragedy.

Another convention that is less obvious but also important in creating the specific tragic intensity of *Othello* is Shakespeare's use of two simultaneous time schemes, referred to as "double time." On the one hand, the play's action seems to take place within a very short period. Act 1 dramatizes events on the night that Othello and Desdemona marry and Othello is ordered to lead Venetian military fleets to Cyprus. Once the setting shifts to Cyprus, the rest of the drama appears to happen within two days. On the first night the street brawl plotted by Iago results in Cassio's dismissal from office. The next morning Cassio is already pleading through Desdemona to be reinstated and Iago begins tempting Othello to false assumptions about Desdemona and Cassio. By that evening Othello is in his bedchamber murdering his wife. The speed with which these events take place adds to the atmosphere of turmoil and the emotional momentum of the plot.

On the other hand, characters make comments that suggest a second, longer timeframe for the action. When Emilia retrieves Desdemona's handkerchief as it falls, she says, "My wayward husband hath a hundred times / Wooed me to steal it" (3.3.291–292), an unlikely exaggeration if Iago's request is part of a plan to destroy a marriage that is only a few days' old. Bianca also implies a lengthier period of time in Cyprus when she confronts Cassio, saying, "And I was going to your lodging, Cassio. / What, keep away a week? Seven days and nights?" (3.4.171–172). Moreover, Iago's success in deceiving Othello would seem completely ludicrous if there were only a day or two for Desdemona to commit adultery and for Othello to believe "That she with Cassio hath the act of shame / A thousand times committed" (5.2.208–209). The implied longer timeframe gives credibility to the tragic sequence of events. Thus, while the existence of a double time scheme might raise the question of inconsistency from a realistic perspective, the result is theatrically effective rather than confusing. As a convention that helps to create *Othello*'s dramatic illusion, the double time scheme allows for the impact of suspense and tension, as well as for the development of powerful doubts and convictions that are central to the life of the play.

CHARACTER

Literary and dramatic conventions such as image patterns, irony, dialogue, soliloquies, and asides all contribute to character development in the play. How characters speak and what they say reveal who they are, how they change, what their strengths and weaknesses are, and whether or not they appeal to audiences and readers as sympathetic. Equally as important in dramatic characterization is what characters do and how they interact with each other. Observing actions and relationships between characters helps to identify important patterns of connection and response that define *Othello*'s tragic plot and shape its overall dramatic structure.

One important way to identify or understand *Othello*'s characters and to recognize their complexity is to look for parallels and contrasts between various roles, behaviors, and relationships. Othello, for example, would seem to be the central character in the play as the title suggests, but Iago's actions appear more influential as he successfully preys on other characters and draws much attention toward himself in his intimacy with the audience. By comparison, then, Othello provides the play's emotional focus as a man of stature who rises and falls from greatness, while Iago is the intellectual focus as the manipulator who convinces his victims to act and respond in certain ways. From one angle, their relationship is that of opposites, hero and villain. From another angle, the changes that Othello undergoes throughout the play turn him and Iago into partners in crime, reflecting rather than contrasting each other at certain points. Their relationship is professional and personal; it involves contradictory qualities of trust and distrust, deception and honesty, disbelief and confidence, hatred and admiration. How they share center stage becomes one of the most fascinating and disturbing aspects of characterization in the entire play.

Othello and Desdemona's relationship is also fascinating and disturbing. Their love for each other initially seems like a force that can withstand all trials. Their response to each other, as well as their united stand against opposition, reveals a shared level of passion and commitment that seems like a mutual strength but that soon begins to expose individual weaknesses or lapses in judgment that open the way for tragic consequences. Determining what is admirable or blameworthy, whether traits of boldness and commitment are strengths or weaknesses in either character becomes more difficult as the conflict intensifies. Attempting to understand both characters requires careful examination of the way they behave toward each other.

Interaction or connection between groups on stage also contributes to character development. In particular, the number of triangular relationships suggests an intentional dramatic pattern that illuminates individual roles and traits by drawing attention to comparisons and contrasts. While Othello, Iago, and Desdemona form the most obvious triangular connection of central characters and the source of primary conflict, other similar groups of three characters mirror or challenge the dynamics of this trio. Othello, Cassio, and Desdemona, for example, begin as a compatible group, their relationship based on love and friendship. When Iago turns that positive connection into an imaginary "love triangle," the outcome exposes not only his malicious motives, but also character traits of the three people caught in his web who appear either too trusting or not trusting enough. A third "pseudo love triangle" involving Othello, Roderigo, and Desdemona allows the audience to see courtship, seeming courtship, romance, and self-delusion demonstrated in yet another configuration. The conflict in the relationship between Othello, Desdemona, and Brabantio also contributes to this broad structure of overlapping triangular connections. The complex layers of stage interaction between these various groups sow the seeds of tragedy because of the friction between different characters' hopes and expectations and the limitations in their ability to understand each other and themselves.

Important patterns of connection also exist along gender lines. The many relationships between pairs of male characters invite questions about how each pair portrays the two individuals involved and what one pair reveals about another. Again, Othello and Iago form the dominant pair, and how they respond to each other says much about their own values or goals and their feelings toward each other. Other pairs include Othello and Cassio, Othello and Brabantio, Iago and Cassio, and Iago and Roderigo. The combination of military rank and social status, as well as personal competition or friendship, defines these relationships and develops individual character traits. The female connection between Desdemona and Emilia demonstrates a level of personal intimacy that is free of the professional distinctions in the male relationships, but is complicated by class distinctions and compromised by Emilia's divided loyalty as Iago's wife and Desdemona's serving lady. Adding Bianca to the list of female characters suggests another triangular relationship that draws attention to the gender conflict around romance, love, and marriage in *Othello*. Three couples that represent various connections between men and women in romance or marriage include Othello and Desdemona, Emilia and Iago, and Cassio and Bianca. By portraying similarities and striking differences between these couples, Shakespeare shapes his characters, dramatizing diverse attitudes that form each relationship and exposing contrasts in the level of respect or commitment in each.

Looking at characters in pairs, triangular associations, or parallel groups draws attention to important relationships and roles in the play: relationships such as friendship, leadership, and marriage; and roles such as heroes, villains, lovers, husbands, wives, and victims. The combination and interaction of these relationships and roles not only add to the depth and dimensions of *Othello*'s characters, but also shape the play's dramatic structure of balance and opposition.

THEME

A theme is a main idea that is expressed or portrayed in literature. A play as rich as *Othello* has many potential themes because
the characters are complex, their motives mixed, their relationships complicated, and their conflicts intense and diverse. Image
patterns, repeated words or phrases, and suggestive speech or action provide clues about the main ideas or themes in *Othello*.
Meaning accumulates around many recurring images, such as animals and monsters, webs and weaving, wit and witchcraft, food
and drink, money and property, devils and hell, angels and heaven,
and whiteness and blackness. In general, all these recurring images
reflect ways in which characters value themselves and others, and,
by so doing, indicate broader ideas about how the best and worst
qualities of humanity combine to lead to tragedy. Each image pattern, however, focuses on more specific thematic concepts. Webs
and witchcraft, for example, emphasize the destructive and malicious powers of deception and entrapment. References to food
and drink and money and property have the effect of devaluing
the heart and soul of humanity, suggesting that love is nothing
more than lust, or that the end—whether it be money, ambition,
or personal gain—can justify the means, whatever cruel and inhuman actions are required. Certainly these are the values Iago
lives by, and his philosophy tends to poison—though perhaps not
entirely destroy—higher human principles or values other characters accept and demonstrate.

Some image patterns work together to contribute to a variety of
themes in *Othello*. Whiteness and blackness draw attention to the
central conflict between good and evil that is also reinforced by
references to angels and devils and heaven and hell. But the colors
white and black also raise awareness about the contrast that *Othello* presents between innocence and guilt and justice and judgment. Although white and black are both visible and symbolic
opposites, ironically the action in *Othello* challenges those clear
distinctions. The fact that Iago and Desdemona are both white
characters undermines assumptions that white simply represents
goodness or innocence. Likewise, Othello's black skin is symbolically misleading. Initially, Othello appears as a noble, just, and
honorable man and, in spite of his poor judgment and violent
behavior, he concludes as the tragic hero, appealing again to jus-

tice and honor by killing himself as punishment for his murder of Desdemona. The imagery of whiteness and blackness, therefore, points to a variety of thematic possibilities about how *Othello* portrays not only good and evil and innocence and guilt, but also appearance and reality.

Many single words have thematic significance in the play including those mentioned above, as well as the following: love, jealousy, revenge, power, temptation, honesty, honor, reputation, integrity, control, and deception. Each word represents some aspect of *Othello*'s meaning. However, the challenge we face in experiencing and understanding the play is not simply to identify key words but also to articulate the importance of those words by developing them into specific statements. The word "love" can generate different statements about the play's meaning. One theme, for example, can be expressed this way: "*Othello* portrays the vulnerability of love by demonstrating how quickly and disastrously it falls prey to misunderstanding, temptations, and self-doubt." Another relevant theme might focus on the aspect of sacrifice rather than vulnerability in love: "*Othello* reveals the tragic potential of sacrifice in love by dramatizing two extreme interpretations of what that sacrifice means." These statements about love indicate themes that provide the basis for a valid argument or perspective on the play. *Othello* has many possible meanings, and key words or image patterns can stimulate observations that do not simply address what happens in the play but offer answers to much more valuable and interesting questions, such as "What is the play about?" or "How does it affect you?"

Further discussion of *Othello*'s structure and characters, imagery and themes appear in the final section of Chapter 5, "Currents of Criticism."

QUESTIONS FOR WRITTEN AND ORAL DISCUSSION

1. Choose one speech by a main character or several speeches within a scene and identify the image patterns. What similes, metaphors, or word associations can you find? How do they contribute to character development or the play's thematic significance?

2. Find examples of irony in *Othello*. Distinguish between verbal irony—when a character says the opposite of what he or she means—and dramatic irony—when the audience knows more than one or more of the characters. What effect does irony have on your involvement as an

audience member? How does it affect your view of the play's tragedy? Why do you suppose Shakespeare makes Iago the center of the irony, and how does that choice of character and plot development influence your response to Iago and the other characters?

3. Many comments about Othello are made before he appears on stage. Identify some of these comments, discuss what impression they initially create, and explain how they compare with the main character when he does appear. Why might Shakespeare introduce Othello in this way? What effect does this beginning have on your reaction to Othello and to others around him early in the play?

4. Choose a scene or part of a scene in *Othello* that includes dialogue between characters, as well as asides or soliloquies. Write notes or draw diagrams to indicate where you would place the characters to create the dramatic illusion of believable stage interaction. Which characters are meant to hear each other and which are not? When is the audience directly addressed? Act 4.1 might be an interesting choice in the section where Othello watches Iago, Cassio, and Bianca. You may want to act out a scene rather than simply diagram it to help you appreciate the effect of combining dialogue, asides, and soliloquies.

5. Referring to the heading "Character" in this section, consider how contrasting and connecting various characters allows you to understand or see them more clearly. Write a formal response or hold an informal discussion that addresses one of the questions listed here.

   a) Discuss how Shakespeare's portrayal of the relationship between Othello and Iago reveals positive or negative traits of each character.

   b) How do Othello and Desdemona's attitudes toward each other help to develop and reveal their character traits and create the play's conflict?

   c) How does the triangular relationship between Iago, Othello, and Desdemona establish comparisons and contrasts between the three characters?

   d) Choose two of the triangular relationship in *Othello* and compare them, explaining how one affects your understanding of the other, of the characters in each, and of their contribution to the play's tragedy.

   e) Choose one of the male relationships and discuss how military rank and social status, as well as friendship or competition, contribute to it. Alternatively, compare two male relationships, indicating how they are similar or different and what each reveals about the characters involved.

f) What is the nature of the relationship between Desdemona and Emilia, and how is that female connection like or unlike one or more of the male relationships?

g) What kind of triangular relationship can you see between the three women, Desdemona, Emilia, and Bianca? What connects and distinguishes each woman from the other?

h) How does Iago and Emilia's marriage illuminate the marriage between Othello and Desdemona?

i) How does Cassio and Bianca's relationship compare to either Iago and Emilia's marriage or Othello and Desdemona's relationship?

j) Iago's primary aim is to deceive and harm others. Who are his victims, how does he relate to them, and what similarities or differences exist in the ways they are victimized?

6. Write an essay about one of the relationships or roles in *Othello* mentioned in the discussion of "Character": leadership, friendship, marriage, heroes, villains, victims, lovers, husbands, wives.

7. Choose an image pattern listed in the discussion of "Theme" and explain how that pattern helps to develop one of the themes in the play, using examples to support your position.

8. Decide what seems to be the most important theme to you in *Othello* and write a short essay explaining your choice.

9. Choose one or two of the words included under the heading "Theme" in this section and write as many possible themes for *Othello* as you can. Find a partner who has agreed to focus on the same word or words, and compare your statements once you have written them. Discuss what you learn from each other's observations and how your effort to find more than one theme from a single word affects your appreciation of *Othello*'s layers or levels of meaning.

SUGGESTED READINGS

Elliott, G. R. *Flaming Minister: A Study of "Othello" as a Tragedy of Love and Hate*. New York: AMS Press, 1965.
Wine, Martin. *Othello: Text and Performance*. London: Macmillan, 1984.

Related questions (especially #8 to #11) and further suggested readings appear at the end of Chapter 5, which explores some modern literary, historical, and dramatic approaches to *Othello*.

2

Historical Context:
Race and Religion

The full title of Shakespeare's tragedy, *Othello, The Moor of Venice*, draws attention to identity as a significant element in the play. The title identifies the main character not only in the most typical and obvious fashion—by naming him—but also by announcing two other distinguishing features: race and place. Both aspects are crucial to Othello's characterization and to the conflict that defines the plot. In fact, Othello is referred to as "the Moor" long before his name is even mentioned or he appears on stage. And Venice is his adopted home, the play's chief setting, although the action shifts to Cyprus after the first act. Who Othello is as "the Moor of Venice" becomes his tragedy of gain and ultimate loss.

If the question of identity—"Who are you?"—is answered with specific details such as name, place, and corresponding values, beliefs, and religion, it is also determined by answering negatively with details about "who you are not." Differences matter. Othello, for example, is *not* a Venetian by birth and therefore he both belongs and does not belong to the city. He belongs because he is Venice's military general, chief defender of the city, and he is a Christian, sharing a common religion with Venetian citizens. However, he is also a stranger from a strange country, a foreigner and an outsider. Tension exists between the differences that set him apart and the qualities that allow him to play a respected and vital role in the city's public life. Cassio, too, is an outsider, although less of a stranger than Othello, for he is a European gentleman, a citizen from the neighboring Italian city of Florence rather than from the mysterious and unfamiliar continent of Africa. Shakespeare explores the positive and negative impact of identity by dramatizing many degrees of difference between various characters distinguished by their rank and status, and by their physical places of origin, adoption, or conquest.

First of all, however, Shakespeare invites his audiences into the imaginary world of the stage that is separate from and yet connected to their daily lives. They enter a story that is not their own but that involves them mentally and emotionally with strangers—fictional characters—whose joys and sufferings nevertheless matter for the duration of the play. It is important to remember that Shakespeare was writing for English audiences in the early seventeenth century and that his imaginary world reflected and responded to issues, attitudes, and concerns of the time. Just as identities in the play are defined by differences as well as similarities, the responses of English audiences would have been affected by their own sense of identity as a nation, as men and women, and as individuals who were similar to and different from Shakespeare's characters.

Setting influences the relationship between audiences and the story enacted on stage. Venice, the backdrop for *Othello*, is an Italian city, and Shakespeare's English contemporaries had mixed views of Italy as a nation that was in many ways different from their own. It was, for example, Catholic rather than Protestant, but like England it was still part of Christianized Western Europe as opposed to non-Christian states and empires in the Far East. Venice, in particular, was seen as a key protector of Christianity from Eastern threats of Islam, as well as a central contact point, geographically, for trade and international relations from the west to the east and the south.

Cyprus, the second important setting in the play, exists not as a separate, independent place, but as a military outpost of Venice in the eastern Mediterranean. This island has an assigned governor rather than an established government or social order of its own. It is defined by war rather than peace. Compared to Venice, then, it is one step further away from England and their recognizable civilized world and one step closer to the alien Islamic culture of the Turks. Geographically, in fact, Cyprus is just off the coast of Turkey and a great distance from either Venice or England. Symbolically, the island represented the farthest fortress of the Christian world, the last stronghold guarding it from the Ottoman Empire to which Turkey belonged. The Turkish threat to overtake Cyprus in *Othello* had specific historical parallels in the 1570s. Furthermore, the Turks represented a great adversary to Western Europe, both because the Ottoman Empire was militarily powerful and because their Islamic religion was antagonistic to Christianity. English audiences watching the play as well as the Venetian characters within it considered Turkey an incomprehensible place whose citizens were enemies with incompatible differences and hostile intentions.

Othello's difference from Venetian characters surrounding him and from Turks that threaten in the background is defined especially and primarily by his color and race as a Moor. Shakespeare makes much more of these distinguishing features than his fictional source, Cinthio's story. That Shakespeare's main character is black rather than white is repeatedly emphasized throughout the play and would have been visually conspicuous through black masks or makeup used on stage. It is almost impossible to approach this aspect of identity in the play without viewing it through the history of racial prejudice and conflict that has unfolded from the seventeenth century to the present. As Chapter 5, "Performance and Interpretation," will indicate, racial sensitivities since Shakespeare's time have made *Othello* extremely controversial. However, to put the play in its own time can broaden our understanding of it as we explore attitudes towards the race and religion of Africa expressed by Shakespeare's contemporaries and presented in other English plays. Examining historical circumstances and viewpoints allows us to consider how Shakespeare develops this central character, how Othello defines his own identity, how other characters see him, and how his difference on stage might have been perceived by the play's original English audiences.

The degrees of difference between Venetians and Turks, Europeans and Moors, Christians and Muslims, and the complex, varied attitudes of English people in the late sixteenth and early seventeenth centuries towards these other nations, races, and religions provide a rich context from which to approach Shakespeare's tragedy.

Brief Chronology of Historic Events Surrounding *Othello*

1554	First black men brought to England following African trade expedition.
1558	Elizabeth I becomes Queen of England.
1570	Turks attack Cyprus; city of Nicosia captured on Sept. 9.
1571	City of Famagusta in Cyprus surrenders to Turks on Aug. 2.
	Battle of Lepanto between Turks and European Holy League on Oct. 7; Turks defeated.
1589	George Peele writes *The Battle of Alcazar*, a play with a black villain.
1593–1594	Shakespeare writes *Titus Andronicus*, a tragedy with a black villain.
1599	Lewis Lewkenor translates into English Gasper Contareno's *The Commonwealth and Government of Venice* (1543).
1600	Moorish ambassadors from Morocco visit England for six months.
	John Leo Africanus's *The History and Description of Africa* first published in English.
1601	Elizabeth I issues her second royal proclamation against Blacks living in England.
1603	Queen Elizabeth dies; James VI of Scotland becomes King James I of England.
	Richard Knolles's *The Turkish History* published and dedicated to King James; King James's poem "The Lepanto" (1591) first printed in England.
1604	*Othello* written and first performed.
1611	Thomas Coryat's travel journal *Coryat's Crudities* first published.

THE VENETIAN

ENGLISH VIEWS OF ITALY

Venice, as Shakespeare portrays it in *Othello*, is a relatively late sixteenth-century setting based on a combination of factual accounts and fictional perceptions of Italy that were still popular and accepted in England in the early seventeenth century. Unlike England, Italy did not have a cohesive national identity but instead was composed of several loosely associated city-states, including— among others—Venice, Florence, and Rome. Each city-state had its own separate government and its own reputation. Rome, for example, was home to the Pope and Catholicism. Therefore, following the Reformation, it represented an antagonistic political and religious force against Protestantism in England and elsewhere in Europe. It was also the site of classical Roman history and civilization for which there was growing appreciation and interest during the "Renaissance" or "rebirth" of European culture from the fifteenth to the seventeenth century. Florence was the home of Machiavelli, the political philosopher whom the English loved to hate because they considered his writing immoral and unchristian. But Florence was also recognized as one of the most beautiful cities in Europe. Venice had perhaps the most favorable reputation as a city-state renowned for its justice, peace, and good government. But it was also known for the decadence of its pleasures, especially its sexual liberties. Each city-state encouraged a specific set of positive and negative responses from foreigners observing or visiting from abroad.

As a whole, Italy was perceived as a place of classical learning, history, and art, as well as contemporary refinement, wealth, and economic power. The English traveled there to study and to trade. Italy was also considered a place of violence, corruption, and treachery, fascinating to read about yet dangerous to experience firsthand. Venice stood apart but also shared this mixed review. It was greatly admired throughout Europe. England in particular identified with Venice as another seaport concerned with commercial success, safe trading routes, and peaceful government. Other aspects of the city-state, however, were judged as damaging, unattractive, or immoral. Shakespeare draws from the diverse perspectives around him and incorporates into his drama some of the contradictory views that comprised English attitudes towards Italy during the Renaissance and especially following the religious divisions of the Reformation that began in the early sixteenth century.

ENGLAND'S POLITICAL RELATIONSHIP WITH VENICE

In the 1570s England began increasing its trade in the Mediterranean and consequently developed closer relations with Venice as a competitor and commercial contact. During Elizabeth I's reign until 1603 diplomatic ties remained informal. However, when James VI of Scotland succeeded as the new monarch, James I of England, Venice became the first Italian city-state to which a regular ambassador was appointed. Political relations became more formal in 1603 and state correspondence provided regular accounts of the city's culture and commerce. Ambassadors from Venice also began coming to England in 1603. King James offered them an initial royal welcome, complete with dramatic entertainment from the King's Men, the acting company for which Shakespeare wrote his plays. Shakespeare composed *Othello* shortly after James's ascent to the throne at a time when renewed political relations may have increased England's interest in Venice.

THE MYTH OF VENICE

Scholars have described a prevailing historical view of this northern Italian city-state as "the myth of Venice" because attitudes represented an ideal rather than a realistic picture of the place and its people. "Myth," in this context, does not indicate an entirely false perspective. Instead, it suggests a set of beliefs that reflect historic truths while exaggerating the best and ignoring or dismissing the worst details. Thus, the myth of Venice was an unbalanced rather than nonfactual representation. It grew out of firsthand accounts of travelers visiting Venice, as well as Italian books and treatises that were exported and translated into other European languages including English. Familiarity with the myth sheds light on the relationship between *Othello*'s setting and its plot development.

Central to the myth was a recognition of Venice's political stability and longevity. Reportedly, the city had lived at peace for over a thousand years, suffering neither revolt from within nor invasion from without. Although this period of peace may be exaggerated, no authority would dispute Venice's success and sophistication for many centuries as an independent political organization. The city gained a reputation as "the Virgin City" by avoiding both conquest and division while governments all across Europe suffered continual attacks and civil unrest. Venice's achievement was attributed to its republican form of government, its laws and constitution, its citizens' emphasis on the public good, and its accomplishments in trade and commerce.

Venice was a republic with a mixed form of government based on a complex constitution and system of voting. Political philosophers who saw the city as a model society admired the balance of powers among the Duke, the Senate, and the larger voting body called the Great Council. Although not every male resident of Venice had voting privileges, the republican government was still considered an effective compromise between alternative systems, each with its own inherent dangers. Monarchy, for example, could lead to tyranny. Aristocracy ran the risk of becoming a corrupted oligarchy in which a few people gained and abused power. Pure democracy held the potential for confusion, revolution, and revolt. According to the myth of Venice, good government required a mixed form that combined aspects of these three systems by involving the one, the few, and the many. Political peace existed because no single person could become too powerful and because public wisdom depended not only on a series of checks and balances, but also on the good will and consensus of individuals who put the city's interests before their own.

Secondly, Venice prized its laws and impartial system of justice. The fact that many people were elected to participate in various levels of government meant fewer opportunities for individuals to exercise control or use personal influence. Furthermore, the law was highly valued and held to be above the people who made it so that even foreigners or residents without voting rights were given an open hearing in legal decisions that affected them. While the system was fair, it was also severe. Harsh punishments were dispensed without favor or mercy. This combination of consistency and impartiality gave Venice a reputation as a just city.

A third element of the myth is related to conditions of justice and peaceful government. Because of and as a result of its political stability, Venice allowed its people a great degree of liberty and freedom. Far more religious tolerance for Protestantism existed here than in Rome or in other Italian city-states. Venetians were also more accepting of foreigners and outsiders. Because local wealth depended on a thriving merchant economy, foreigners were expected and welcomed as part of the city's successful trading business abroad. Consequently, the city was very cosmopolitan. People from a variety of races and places mingled in the streets. Furthermore, Venetians felt that hiring outsiders for key military roles ensured peace by providing a safeguard against power abuse or uprisings that might result if one of their own citizens were chosen as commanding officer. Othello's status in Shakespeare's play as an outsider with military leadership was not an uncommon historical occurrence. His position as "the Moor of Venice," as a stranger who partly belonged and partly did not, reflected one aspect of the myth of Venice.

Shakespeare's establishment of the Venetian setting at the beginning of *Othello* illustrates other elements of the myth that would have been familiar to English audiences. The view of the city-state as an orderly, peaceful place finds voice in Brabantio's response to his rude awakening by Iago and Roderigo in the first scene: "What tell'st thou me of robbing? This is Venice; / My house is not a grange" (1.1.102–103). Venice, he suggests, is a civilized society, not a site for violence and night intruders. The republican system of government is also represented in 1.3 with the emergency meeting of the Duke and Senators to consider the imminent Turkish invasion of Cyprus. The Senators appear as respected members of a council whose joint wisdom exposes the Turks' deceptive attempt to divert attention to Rhodes. The consultation leads to concrete decisions about how to forestall the invasion by sending out a fleet of ships and delegating naval authority to the Moor, an accomplished military officer.

The domestic dispute between Brabantio and Othello that interrupts the council meeting dramatizes the accepted view of Venice's rational, unbiased, and severe justice system. No rash decisions are made until the council hears from each affected party: Brabantio as a respected Senator; Othello as an accused outsider as well as a valued military figure; and Desdemona as a young woman presumably under her father's authority and supervision. Brabantio, the Duke, and Othello all appeal to both the severity and impartiality of the law. When Othello requests Desdemona as his witness, he says,

If you do find me foul in her report,
The trust, the office, I do hold of you
Not only take away, but let your sentence
Even fall upon my life. (1.3.117–120)

Ultimately, when the council finds that no crime has been committed, Brabantio grudgingly accepts the cause of the public good over his own personal grievance, saying, "I have done. / Please it your Grace, on to the state affairs" (1.3.187–188). Act 1 establishes Venice as an organized and just society, at least at a formal, public level. Iago and Roderigo offer another perspective, but while everyone remains in Venice, order prevails over chaos, and harmony over dissent. Only once the setting shifts to Cyprus do discord and chaos begin to escalate beyond formal attempts to maintain peace and control.

THE DARK SIDE OF VENICE

Although the myth of Venice presented the city as an ideal place to be admired and emulated, other negative views of the city-state were equally widespread in England. Just as the positive version of Venice exaggerated, simplified, or ignored aspects of the truth, so too the darker side of Venice gained acceptance without necessarily reflecting a balanced view of the facts. England's favorite metaphor of Venice as "the Virgin city," for example, apparently did not seem inconsistent with a darker view that saw the model city as a place of sexual license, immorality, political intrigue, corruption, and greed. The most relevant aspects of this reputation in *Othello* are the domestic and sexual relationships between men and women and the self-serving corruption practiced by characters such as Iago and Roderigo.

Venice was renowned for its courtesans and its jealous husbands. Courtesans were prostitutes serving an upper-class clientele. Some were reportedly wealthy and sophisticated women themselves, and although contemporary accounts greatly exaggerate their presence in the city, a conservative estimate puts their

numbers at a relatively high level of between five and ten percent
of the entire population of 150,000 to 200,000 people (McPherson,
43). Their prominent role in the leisure and pleasure of the city
and their apparent acceptance or tolerance by public authorities
gave Venice a reputation for immoral sexual license. Bianca is
Shakespeare's courtesan whose character he develops much more
fully than his source in Cinthio's story. Her presence adds an obvious Venetian flavor to the play, but her response to Cassio's behavior towards her perhaps challenges English notions about
courtesans as wicked and untrustworthy women.

Venetian women, in general, were understood to be deceptive.
Husbands, on the other hand, were known for their jealousy, violence, and treachery. Both generalizations became accepted stereotypes which Iago articulates in *Othello* when he refers to
Desdemona as a "super-subtle Venetian" and suspects practically
every man and woman on stage of being unfaithful, adulterous, or
promiscuous. That Desdemona does not fit the Venetian stereotype of infidelity and deception indicates Shakespeare's willingness
to do more than simply cast Italian caricatures on stage. Jealousy,
however, is a prevalent theme throughout the play which English
audiences would have accepted as an appropriate topic for a story
set in Venice.

Iago speaks for and enacts the corruption and intrigue English
people expected in Venice and other Italian settings. In the first
scene he implies the practice of political prejudice, as opposed to
impartiality, by suggesting that friendship gained Cassio the title
of lieutenancy while Iago's own attempts at persuasion and influence failed. As a model of self-interest rather than public duty, he
appeals to Roderigo's self-interest as well. Iago's advice to Roderigo to "put money in thy purse" expresses ambition and greed that
foreigners identified with Venice's wealthy merchant economy.
Iago is revengeful, scheming, and manipulative. His dominance in
Othello emphasizes generally the dark side of humanity, but more
specifically the dark side of Venice. Although Iago achieves his destructive success in the less civilized setting of Cyprus, he is a true
native of Venice and belongs there in a way that Othello, the outsider, does not. References to Iago as a villain and a devil throughout the play reflect not only popular figures from English morality
plays but common views of Venice as a place of plotters and
schemers. Ironically, English people admired Venice as a just city

but also judged it as a corrupt, dangerous place. *Othello* reflects both viewpoints.

THEATRICAL AND LITERARY TRADITION

The double perspective of idealism and suspicion that colors the setting and characters of *Othello* should be seen in context not only of Italian myth and history but also of England's theatrical and literary tradition. Italy was an extremely popular setting for drama in Shakespeare's time, and Shakespeare himself uses it for a number of plays including *The Merchant of Venice*, *Romeo and Juliet*, and *The Taming of the Shrew*. Fellow playwrights such as Ben Jonson, John Marston, and Cyril Tourneur were also attracted to Italy. More than Shakespeare, they emphasized Italy's darker side that they found represented in Italian novellas and in prevailing English attitudes. These attitudes grew out of fear and distrust of Machiavelli's political views and, even more so, Roman Catholicism which posed a continuous threat to England's parliamentary government and official Protestantism. Many English plays during the reigns of both Elizabeth I and James I portrayed Italy as a place of deception, atheism, violence, horror, murder, eroticism, passion, and revenge. The plots were often gruesome and the characters stereotypical villains. Likewise, contemporary prose writers such as Roger Ascham depicted the horrors and degradation of Italy.

Unlike some of his fellow literary artists, Shakespeare appeared more interested in portraying complex characters with credible motives and with responses that sometimes questioned rather than confirmed Italian stereotypes. But although Iago may be less violent than his counterpart in Cinthio's original novella and more complicated and fully developed than similar Italian figures in other English plays and stories, Shakespeare's audiences would have been familiar with Iago's variety of villainy. The stage machiavel was a common dramatic figure (see Chapter 1). In general, Italy attracted playwrights and other English writers not so much as a realistic and historical setting but as a place distanced by differences that allowed the imagination to explore and create. Accurate geographical, social, and political details were not a priority. Myth, generalizations, and common opinions were more influential than facts in shaping a literary and dramatic concept of Italy that included contradictory attitudes and perceptions.

The remainder of this section on Venice includes documents from sixteenth- and seventeenth-century writers who reflected and influenced views of Venice and Italy in their time. Their blend of idealism and criticism is apparent in the selected excerpts. Spelling has been regularized and modernized for clarity.

A SOURCE FOR THE MYTH OF VENICE

Gasper Contareno (also commonly spelled Contarini), a Venetian churchman and aristocrat, was a primary source of the myth of Venice for Europeans beyond Italy. His book about Venetian government, *The Commonwealth and Government of Venice*, glorified its virtues. Published in 1543, it was one of the most widely read books about Venice throughout Europe and helped to foster admiration for an ideal vision of the Venetian republic. In 1599 Lewis Lewkenor translated Contareno's book into English, adding an introduction that further praised the excellence and success of Venetian society. The following excerpts describe the political system operating in this Italian city-state. A lengthy passage from Lewkenor's introduction [1] summarizes the key political elements developed in greater detail by Contareno. Keep in mind Lewkenor's use of "the Virgin city" metaphor as you read [2] Contareno's description of Venice. The final selections explaining [3] the use of foreigners or strangers as military leaders and [4] the authority of captains sent to maritime provinces in time of war have particular relevance in *Othello*. Think about Othello's title and authority as you read these passages.

FROM GASPER CONTARENO, *THE COMMONWEALTH AND GOVERNMENT OF VENICE*, TRANS. LEWIS LEWKENOR
(The English Experience Facsimile No. 101, London: 1599; New York: Da Capo Press, 1969)

[FROM LEWKENOR'S INTRODUCTION]

[1] [I]n the person of the Venetian prince, who sitting at the helm of this city shineth in all exterior ornaments of royal dignity; (nevertheless both he and his authority, being wholly subjected to the laws) they may see a strange and unusual form of a most excellent Monarchy.

Then what more perfect and lively pattern of a well ordered Aristo-cratical government can there in the world be expressed, than that of their Council of Pregati or Senators, which being the only chief and prin-cipal members of all supreme power; yet have not any power, mean, or possibility at all to tyrannize, or to pervert their Country laws.

Lastly if they desire to see a most rare and matchless precedent of a Democracy or popular estate, let them behold their great Council, con-sisting at the least of 3000 Gentlemen, whereupon the highest strength and mightiness of the estate absolutely relyeth, notwithstanding which number all things are ordered with so divine a peaceableness, and so without all tumult and confusion, that it rather seemeth to be an assem-bly of Angels, than of men.

In fine, whithersoever you turn your eyes, they shall not encounter anything but objects of admiration; their justice is pure and uncorrupted: their penal Laws most unpardonably executed: their encouragements to virtue infinite: especially by their distribution of offices & dignities, which is ordered in such so secret, strange, and intricate a sort, that it utterly overreacheth the subtlety of all ambitious practices, never falling upon any but upon such as are by the whole assembly allowed for men of greatest wisdom, virtue and integrity of life. . . . (Sig. A2r–A2v)

And lastly, though not least to be wondered at, they have . . . preserved this royal City of theirs this 13 hundred years since the first foundation thereof, in an estate so perpetually flourishing & unblemished, that though sundry & mighty kings and Emperors being enamored with her beauty and goodliness, have with marvellous endeavour and multitude of armies sought to possess themselves of so fair and precious a prey: yet have they hitherto kept her like a pure and untouched virgin, free from the taste or violence of any foreign enforcement. (Sig. A3r–v)

I yet entreat them that shall read this discourse, to entertain this fa-mous Commonwealth with all friendliness and favor, if in no other re-gard, yet in this; that the rest of the whole world honoreth her with the name of a Virgin, a name though in all places most sacred & venerable, yet in no place more dearly and religiously to be reverenced, than with us, who have thence derived our blessedness, which I beseech God may long continue among us. (Sig. A4r)

[FROM CONTARENO'S BOOK]

[2] This is that rare and excellent thing, wherein *Venice* seemeth to shine, and to surpass all antiquity, for though it is apparent that there hath been many commonwealths, which have far exceeded *Venice* as well in empire and greatness of estate, as in military discipline and glory of the wars: yet hath there not been any, that may be paragoned with this

of ours, for institutions & laws prudently decreed to establish unto the inhabitants a happy and prosperous felicity, the proof whereof is made manifest by the long continuance thereof in such security and happiness, which when I consider with myself, I am wont greatly to wonder at the wisdom of our ancestors, at their industry, the virtue of their minds, & their incredible love and charity towards their country. (5–6)

[3] But now this their [military men's] continual frequentation of the continent and divorcement, as it were from the civil life, would without doubt have brought forth a kind of faction different and disjoined, from the other peaceable Citizens, which partiality and division would in time have bred civil wars and dissensions within the City. . . . To exclude therefore out of our estate the danger or occasion of any such ambitious enterprises, our ancestors held it a better course to defend their domin-ions upon the continent, with foreign mercenary soldiers, than with their homeborn citizens, & to assign them their pay and stipend out of the tributes and receipts of the Province, wherein they remained: for it is just, and reasonable, that the soldiers should be maintained at the charge of those in whose defence they are employed, and into their warfare, have many of our associates been ascribed, some of which have attained to the highest degree of commandment in our army, & for the exceed-ingness of their desserts been enabled, with the title of citizens & gen-tlemen of *Venice*. . . . The Citizens therefore of *Venice*, for this only cause are deprived of the honors belonging to wars by land, and are contented to transfer them over to strangers. (130–132)

[4] Besides these Captains of the Galleys, there is a Legate over the whole navy, who hath full and whole authority over the same, and over the particular Captains of every Galley. He (as a Lieutenant general of the army, if the Captain general be not present) hath power of life and death, and authority to direct the navy whither it shall please him.

This magistrate is commonly created in time of peace, and hath in his hands the charge of the Galleys of war: but if the occasions of the com-monwealth do so require, and that there be a great navy indeed to be set out, then there is appointed & proposed over the whole navy a Cap-tain general with high and preeminent authority not only over the same, but also over all maritime provinces in manner as great, as that the Ro-man Dictator was wont to have, save only that this in all things obeyeth the authority of the Senate, and the decrees of the commonwealth. Nev-ertheless his power is singularly great, as well over the navy, Legates, captains and Lieutenants of the same, as also over all governors and mag-istrates, that have government or superintendence in any of the Islands or maritime places; in so much that when the Captain general of the navy shall come to any City, the clergy is presently to meet him with solemnity, and the keys of the gates and castles are to be delivered unto him. The authority of all the other governors for that time ceaseth: and whosoever in whatsoever cause may appeal from any other magistrate to the Captain general: who only if it shall so please him, may administer justice, dispose of the public money, and alone himself exercise the office and authority of all the rest. There is among the Venetians no magistrate of higher power, and therefore he, but seldom and upon most urgent occasions created: for not rashly but upon most weighty & grounded consideration, is this mighty dignity, investing a private citizen with so great and absolute an authority committed to anyone. (136–137)

AN ENGLISH TRAVELER IN VENICE

Thomas Coryat, seventeenth-century English traveler, recorded and published his observations for others to read. Although his tour to Italy began several years after Shakespeare wrote *Othello*, Coryat's journals reflect the mixed, even contradictory English views of Italy that began circulating decades earlier. In a detailed account of his stay in Venice, Coryat devotes much attention and praise to the city's system of government and elaborate architecture. The following excerpts, however, have been chosen to demonstrate how Coryat combines an ideal image of Venice with its darker reputation. In [1] and [5], Coryat praises Venice using the popular metaphor of the Virgin city. By contrast, he also describes with disapproval and wonder [2] the famous courtesans or city prostitutes, and [3] the Mountebanks, who today might be referred to as "snake-oil salesmen," falsely claiming great knowledge about medical cures in order to sell useless remedies. Coryat's criticism [4] of violent lawlessness in the city streets seems inconsistent with the mythic view of Venice as a model of peace and justice. Consider whether and how these inconsistencies and contradictions also appear in *Othello*. Compare, for example, Coryat's description of Venetian mountebanks with Brabantio's accusation that Othello has enchanted Desdemona with magic. Think of Shakespeare's portrayal of women while reading Coryat's account of wives, husbands, and courtesans. Similarly, consider *Othello*'s street scenes in context of [4] Coryat's report of street brawls in Venice.

FROM THOMAS CORYAT, *CORYAT'S CRUDITIES* (1611)
(Vol. 1; Glasgow: James MacLehose and Sons, 1905)

[1] Though the incomparable and most decantated majesty of this city doth deserve a far more elegant and curious pencil to paint her out in her colors than mine. For I ingenuously confess mine own insufficiency and unworthiness, as being the unworthiest of ten thousand to describe so beautiful, so renowned, so glorious a Virgin (for by that title doth the world most deservedly style her) because my rude and unpolished pen may rather stain and eclipse the resplendent rays of her unparalleld beauty, than add any lustre unto it: yet since I have hitherto continued this slender and naked narration of my observations of five months' travel in foreign countries; this noble city doth in manner challenge this at my hands, that I should describe her also as well as the other cities I saw in my journey. . . . Therefore omitting tedious introductions, I will descend to the description of this thrice worthy city: the fairest Lady, yea the richest Paragon and Queen of Christendom. (302–303)

[2] But since I have taken occasion to mention some notable particulars of their women, I will insist farther upon that matter, and make relation of their Courtesans also, as being a thing incident and very proper to this discourse, especially since the name of a Courtesan of Venice is famoused over all Christendom. . . .

The woman that professeth this trade is called in the Italian tongue Cortezana, which word is derived from the Italian word cortesia that signifieth courtesy. Because these kind of women are said to receive courtesies of their favorites. . . . A most ungodly thing without doubt that there should be a toleration of such licentious wantons in so glorious, so potent, so renowned a city. For me thinks that the Venetians should be daily afraid lest their winking at such uncleanness should be an occasion to draw down upon them God's curses and vengeance from heaven, and to consume their city with fire and brimstone, as in times past he did Sodom and Gomorrah. But they not fearing any such thing do grant large dispensation and indulgence unto them, and that for these two causes. First, . . . [f]or they think that the chastity of their wives would be the sooner assaulted . . . (which of all the indignities in the world the Venetian cannot patiently endure) were it not for these places of evacuation. But I marvel how that should be true though these Courtesans were utterly rooted out of the City. For the Gentlemen do even coop up their wives always within the walls of their houses for fear of these inconveniences, as much as if there were not Courtesans at all in the City. So that you shall very seldom see a Venetian Gentleman's wife but either at the solemnization of a great marriage, or at the Christening of a Jew, or late in the evening rowing in a Gondola. The second cause is for that the revenues which they pay unto the Senate for their toleration, do maintain a dozen of their galleys, (as many reported unto me in Venice) and so save them a great charge. (401–403)

[3] I hope it will not be esteemed for an impertinence to my discourse, if I next speak of the Mountebanks of Venice, seeing amongst many other things that do much famous this City, these two sorts of people, namely the Courtesans and the Mountebanks, are not the least: for although there are Mountebanks also in other Cities of Italy, yet because there is a greater concourse of them in Venice than elsewhere, and that of a better sort and the most eloquent fellows; and also for that there is a larger toleration of them here than in other Cities . . . therefore they use to name a Venetian Mountebank . . . principal Mountebank of all Italy. . . . These Mountebanks at one end of their stage place their trunk, which is replenished with a world of new-fangled trumperies . . . after (I say) they are all upon the stage, the music begins. . . . This music is a preamble and introduction to the ensuing matter: in the meantime while the music plays, the principal Mountebank which is the Captain and ring-leader of all the rest, opens his trunk, and sets abroach his wares; after the music hath ceased, he maketh an oration to the audience of half an hour long, or almost an hour. Wherein he doth most hyperbolically extol the virtue of his drugs and confections. . . . Though many of them are very counterfeit and false. Truly I often wondered at many of these natural Orators. For they would tell their tales which such admirable volubility and plausible grace, even extempore, and seasoned with that singular variety of elegant jests and witty conceits, that they did often strike great admiration into strangers that never heard them before: and by how much the more eloquent these Naturalists are, by so much the greater audience they draw unto them, and the more ware[s] they sell. . . . I have observed marvellous strange matters done by some of these Mountebanks. For I saw one of them hold a viper in his hand, and play with his sting a quarter of an hour together, and yet receive no hurt; though another man should have been presently stung to death with it. (409–411)

[4] I observed one thing in Venice that I utterly condemned, that if two men should fight together at sharp openly in the streets, whereas a great company will suddenly flock together about them, all of them will give them leave to fight till their hearts ache, or till they welter in their own blood, but not one of them hath the honesty to part them, and keep them asunder from spilling each other's blood: also if one of the two should be slain they will not offer to apprehend him that slew the other (except the person slain be a Gentleman of the city) but suffer him to go

at random whither he list, without inflicting any punishment upon him.
A very barbarous and unchristian thing to wink at such effusion of Christian blood, in which they differ (in my opinion) from all Christians. The
like I understand is to be observed in Milan and other cities of Italy. (413–
414)

[5] It is a matter very worthy the consideration, to think how this noble
city hath like a pure Virgin and incontaminated maid . . . kept her virginity
untouched these thousand two hundred and twelve years (for so long it
is since the foundation thereof) though Emperors, Kings, Princes and
mighty Potentates, being allured with her glorious beauty, have attempted to deflower her, every one receiving the repulse: a thing most
wonderful and strange. In which respect she hath been ever privileged
above all other cities. For there is no principal city of all Christendom
but hath been both oppugned and expugned since her foundation . . .
only Venice, thrice-fortunate and thrice-blessed Venice, as if she had been
founded by the very Gods themselves, and daily received some divine
and sacred influence from the heaven for her safer protection, hath ever
preserved herself . . . free from all foreign invasions to this day. (415–416)

. . . [A]nd so at length I finish the treatise of this incomparable city,
this most beautiful Queen, this untainted virgin, this Paradise, this
Tempe, this rich Diadem and most flourishing garland of Christendom.
(427)

AN ENGLISH WRITER'S DESCRIPTION OF ITALY

Roger Ascham, a trained classical scholar and educator, reflects
some common English prejudices against Italy in his book *The
Schoolmaster*, a grammar guide and teaching text for young boys.
Note how morality plays an important part in his criticism of Italy's
negative influence on England. *Cires* (or Circe), whom he mentions, is a mythological temptress or sorceress who destroyed men
in her presence. How does this classical allusion add to the tone
of Ascham's complaints?

FROM ROGER ASCHAM, *THE SCHOOLMASTER* (1570, 1572)
(Ed. Edward Arber, London: Archibald Constable & Co., 1909)

If some yet do not well understand, what is an Englishman Italianated, I
will plainly tell him. He, that by living, and traveling in *Italy*, bringeth
home into England out of *Italy*, the Religion, the learning, the policy, the
experience, the manners of *Italy*. That is to say, for Religion, Papistry or

worse: for learning, less commonly than they carried out with them: for policy, a factious heart, a discoursing head, a mind to meddle in all men's matters: for experience, plenty of new mischiefs never known in England before: for manners, variety of vanities, and change of filthy living. These be the enchantments of *Cires*, brought out of *Italy*, to mar men's manners in England; much, by example of ill life, but more by precepts of fond books, of late translated out of *Italian* into English, sold in every shop in London, commended by honest titles the sooner to corrupt honest manners: dedicated over boldly to virtuous and honourable personages, the easilier to beguile simple and innocent wits. (78–79)

I was once in Italy myself: but I thank God, my abode there, was but ix. [nine] days: And yet I saw in that little time, in one City, more liberty to sin, than ever I heard tell of in our noble City of London in ix. year[s]. . . . I learned, when I was at *Venice*, that there it is counted good policy, when there be four or five brethren of one family, one, only to marry: and all the rest, to welter, with as little shame, in open lechery, as Swine do here in the common mire. (83–84)

Our Italians bring home with them other faults from Italy, though not so great as this of Religion, yet a great deal greater, than many good men will bear. For commonly they come home, common condemners of marriage and ready persuaders of all other to the same: not because they love virginity, nor yet because they hate pretty young virgins, but, being free in Italy, to go whither so ever lust will carry them, they do not like, that law and honesty should be such a bar to their like liberty at home in England. (84–85)

QUESTIONS FOR WRITTEN AND ORAL DISCUSSION

1. The idealism expressed in the myth of Venice depended, in large part, on the way writers and travelers described the city-state. Reading Lewis Lewkenor's introduction to Gasper Contareno's *The Commonwealth and Government of Venice*, make a list of positive words he uses to refer to Venice. Does he rely on hyperbole or exaggeration? Find examples. Look for similar examples of idealism in *Coryat's Crudities*, especially in selections [1] and [5]. Describe the tone used by Lewkenor and Coryat.

2. Lewkenor praises Venice's republican government. What does he see as the source of success? How does he describe the distribution and balance of powers among the different levels of government?

3. Discuss the significance of "the Virgin city" as a metaphor for Venice. What connotations does the word suggest? What other related titles

or adjectives do Lewkenor, Contareno, and Coryat also use for the city? Why did Venice gain a reputation as a Virgin city? What, according to Contareno's section [2], makes Venice different from other cities or commonwealths?

4. Research the history of Venice in several other sources and write a short paper that discusses the myth of Venice in relationship to the facts on record.

5. Examine Shakespeare's presentation of Venice in Act 1 and compare it to the ideal descriptions provided by Lewkenor, Contareno, and Coryat. What are the positive or ideal aspects of Shakespeare's setting? Are there negative details as well?

6. Contareno discusses the use of "foreign mercenary soldiers" in Venice [3]. What reasons does he give for this practice? Why does Venice not rely on its own citizens to lead them in times of war? Describe Othello's position in Venice as a "mercenary" or hired soldier.

7. Contareno also describes the great authority given to captains over islands and other maritime provinces under Venetian control [4]. How does he explain and justify this practice? Does it seem consistent with the republican balance of powers and supremacy of law described earlier? How and why or why not?

8. Consider Othello's role as captain of the Venetian navy and governor over the island of Cyprus. What parallels exist with Contareno's account of Venetian history? Discuss the relationship between Othello's status as foreigner and as military leader in Venice. How do these two positions affect his authority and acceptance among the Venetians?

9. What is Coryat's opinion of the courtesans in Venice? How does he compare their presence to the treatment of Venetian wives? What conclusions does he make about the acceptance of courtesans, and what do these conclusions suggest about the citizens and government of the city?

10. How does Shakespeare's Bianca compare to Coryat's courtesans? Do you view her more positively or negatively after reading Coryat's account? Why?

11. Is Bianca a sympathetic character or not? Write a short essay defending your position, using evidence from the play, or write a monologue or diary entry from Bianca's point of view that would portray her as sympathetic or unsympathetic, according to your position.

12. What is the occupation of a Mountebank? Why do you suppose Coryat mentions mountebanks in connection with courtesans? What are the similarities?

13. Reread the accusations and defense between Brabantio and Othello in 1.2 and 1.3. How many references can you find to magic, witchcraft, enchantment, and mountebanks? How does Brabantio assume that his daughter has been enchanted away from him? What evidence does Othello use in his own defense? Is there more than one reason that the council ultimately accepts Othello's cause?

14. Coryat refers to mountebanks as "natural Orators." What does he mean by this? Discuss whether a similar title might fit Othello? Is he a "natural Orator"? Is he a mountebank? Can he be one and not the other? Explain.

15. Hold a mock trial with Othello as the accused and Brabantio as the accuser. Remember that Venice is noted for its justice and impartial legal system. Assign lawyers to each party and a judge to oversee the trial. Call witnesses, including Iago, Roderigo, Desdemona, and Cassio. Allow for examination and cross-examination. Those in the class without specific roles can act as jury in determining the final decision. In a fair trial, should the fact that Othello is required on state business influence the outcome? Your final decision may or may not be consistent with the council's decision in the play, but try to use specific evidence from *Othello* to establish the position and credibility of each participant.

16. Coryat criticizes the violence of the street brawls he witnessed. There are a number of street scenes in *Othello*, as well, and several are violent or potentially so. Find two examples and discuss the cause of the violence. What or who restores peace? What damage is done? Is the time of day significant in any way? Is justice or injustice most apparent? Are any patterns established in the causes, participants, and outcomes?

17. Consider Othello or Cassio as a traveler in Venice. How might either one describe the place? How would either account compare with Coryat's description?

18. What specific influences does Roger Ascham feel Italy has on English people? Given that Ascham's complaints reflect some commonly held views in England, how does Shakespeare's portrayal of Venice as an Italian city compare to contemporary generalizations? Does *Othello* lean more towards the idealism of the myth of Venice or the negative stereotypes of danger, immorality, and villainy that were also popular? Use evidence from the play to answer these questions.

THE TURK

Although no Turks appear in *Othello*, the Islamic Ottoman Empire of Turkey plays a significant role in defining the identities of Shakespeare's characters by adding a public, political context of war to the otherwise primarily domestic plot of love and jealousy. Act 1 and the beginning of Act 2 establish this public setting and indicate Othello's essential position as a gifted military leader in Venice. References to "the Turks" also reinforce connections between race and religion because the Ottoman Empire was not only one of the largest world powers in the sixteenth century but also the center of Islam, a faith that clashed with Christianity and that was violent in its attempts at conversion. The political and religious aggression of the Turks (also known as the Ottomites) fostered great anxiety and fear in Western Europe as they successfully expanded their control on land and at sea in the 1400s and 1500s, taking territories from Christian states and imposing Islam on conquered peoples.

Several important battles in 1570 and 1571 finally resulted in Western European victories but reaction remained ambiguous. On the one hand, there was a sense of relief and celebration; on the other hand, many people still saw the Turks as a menace and potential threat for years to follow. Original audiences watching *Othello* in 1604 and shortly thereafter would have been aware of this history and its continuing effect on the public mood and international relations. This understanding would have influenced their response to the play in ways that are perhaps lost on us as modern audiences and readers unfamiliar with the context. Today we can appreciate the seventeenth-century mood more fully by exploring the factual events Shakespeare clearly refers to as he shapes his fictional plot.

VENICE AND THE TURKS

Venice had an uneasy relationship with Turkey. Although the two political powers had warring religions, they were also trading partners in the Mediterranean. Moreover, Venice paid the Ottoman Empire an annual sum to ensure its position as a Western state exchanging valuable goods in the East. Ambassadors traveled freely between Venice and Constantinople, Turkey's capital. Ironically, while Turkey helped sustain the Venetian economy in this way, a growing Eastern Empire also endangered Venetian peace and independence. Gradually, in fact, Ottomite goals of expansion became an increasing hazard and, by the mid-sixteenth century, Venice had already lost several garrison islands protecting its Mediterranean trade routes. Rhodes, the island mentioned in *Othello*, had been overtaken long before Cyprus became a Turkish target. Contrary to Shakespeare's plot, therefore, Rhodes was no longer a possible victim of Eastern aggression but rather a Turkish fortress where enemy forces gathered before declaring war on Cyprus.

In the summer of 1570 the Ottomites launched their attack on Cyprus, Venice's richest and most profitable outpost. This war and a subsequent battle at Lepanto between the Turks and a Western Christian alliance in 1571 provide the specific public background and tone for *Othello*. While Venice conventionally represented peace and stability in European thought, Cyprus recalled conditions of war against an enduring, powerful enemy. The potential Ottoman threat in *Othello* dies at the beginning of Act 2 when the Turkish military is drowned at sea but the sense of political danger and of public insecurity remains and adds to tensions as the private tragedy of Othello and Desdemona unfolds. All references to the Turks are ominous, and any deliberate identification with them is a strong accusation of barbaric behavior. For example, when Othello commands order after the drunken night riot in the streets of Cyprus, he attempts to disgrace the guilty participants by invoking the name of the common enemy:

> Why, how now, ho? From whence ariseth this?
> Are we turned Turks, and to ourselves do that
> Which heaven hath forbid the Ottomites?
> For Christian shame put by this barbarous brawl! (2.3.168–171)

War and a cosmic clash of world religions—"us" versus "them," Christians versus Moslems, civilized versus uncivilized people—inform the understanding of honor and integrity in the public realm of *Othello* and also translate into judgments about the characters' private behavior. As Shakespeare's historical references suggest, Cyprus is a more likely setting for cruelty and violence than for love.

THE WAR AT CYPRUS, 1570

When the Turks invaded Cyprus, they focused their military energies on two major centers, Nicosia, the capital, and Famagusta, the primary seaport which was also the seat of the Venetian governor. Under the leadership of General Mustafa Pasha, the Ottomites easily captured Nicosia on September 9, 1570. Famagusta, however, had a stronger defense and remained under siege for a year until August 1, 1571. As the first city fell and later when the second finally surrendered, the Turks enacted great violence and brutality against the citizens of Cyprus and more notably against the Venetian governor of Famagusta, Marcantonio Bragadino, whom they tortured to death. Perceived as war crimes, this news outraged Venetians who were by then preparing for naval battle in hopes of regaining control over this crucial island and reestablishing their diminishing economic strength.

THE BATTLE OF LEPANTO, 1571

Venice did not have sufficient military and naval power to confront the Turks alone, nor did the Italian city desire war as much as it wanted to restore peaceful trade relations with Turkey. But some states in Western Europe were becoming increasingly concerned about Ottomite aggression and the spread of Islam. On May 25, 1571, Venice joined with Rome and Spain in a Holy League whose combined power might be capable of challenging the Eastern enemy. This Catholic Holy League began gathering its fleet of war galleys under the leadership of Don Juan of Austria, half-brother to the King of Spain. Meanwhile, the Turks consolidated their navy at Lepanto, a port in the Gulf of Corinth at the south end of Greece which was then part of the Ottoman Empire. Sailing war gallies over to the Gulf, the alliance of Western states engaged in an historic naval conflict with the Ottomites on October 7, 1571, an encounter later known as the Battle of Lepanto. The Holy League gained a resounding victory over the Turks, destroying or capturing most of its galleys and significantly diminishing the Ottomites' naval capability. When the losses and gains were tallied, more than half the Turks had been killed, others taken as prisoners. The Holy League saw its success as a great triumph for Christianity and Western Europe after decades of living under the threat of Eastern violence and expansion.

Historians recognize the Battle of Lepanto as a significant turning point in sixteenth- and seventeenth-century politics but also as an event that had less impact than potential. Having achieved a notable victory, the West could have used its combined power to attempt to regain lost territories and increase its own influence over the Ottoman Empire. However, conflicting goals within the Holy League led to divisions that prevented any further success. Venice never did regain Cyprus but instead negotiated a private treaty with Turkey, independent of the Holy League, in which Venice agreed to pay an even larger annual fee for continued Eastern trade. Spain and Rome saw this betrayal as Venetian self-interest and the Western alliance lost its military unity and momentum. Nevertheless, the defeat seriously crippled Turkish naval power, ambition, and confidence. The Ottomites were no longer the reigning sea power in the Mediterranean and Venice maintained peaceful trade relations in the East for the next seventy years.

KING JAMES I AND LEPANTO

Success at Lepanto inspired an outpouring of art, both visual and literary, in Western Europe. One possible reason for Shakespeare's inclusion of historical references to the Mediterranean wars of 1570–1571 in *Othello* is that England's King James I had written a heroic poem about the Battle of Lepanto. Composed when he was a young prince in Scotland, "The Lepanto" was published several times and had been printed for the first time in London in 1603 at the time of James's succession to the English throne a year prior to *Othello*'s first appearance on stage. The popularity of King James's poem likely heightened public awareness of and interest in recent Mediterranean history and its impact on the balance of powers in the East and West. Furthermore, the acting company for which Shakespeare wrote and performed came under the patronage and support of King James and became known as the King's Men when James rose to the throne. Shakespeare may have been responding to raised public awareness of Cyprus and Lepanto after 1603. He may have also been consciously addressing a topic of specific interest to the new patron of his acting company, King James himself.

While the Turkish wars never gain a place of prominence in *Othello* overshadowing the tangled web of Iago's intrigue, Othello's emerging jealousy, and Desdemona's innocent death, they reflect the concerns of the time and therefore assume greater relevance in the play's tone and character development than a modern audience might expect. Ultimately, Othello condemns himself with his own sword, as judge and offender, recognizing that he has become like a Turk, the terrible enemy of Christian humanity he originally meant to oppose:

> Set you down this.
> And say besides that in Aleppo once,
> Where a malignant and turbaned Turk
> Beat a Venetian and traduced the state,
> I took by th'throat the circumcised dog
> And smote him—thus. (5.3.346–351)

The following documents record two English perspectives on the Mediterranean wars in 1570–1571. The first is an excerpt from Richard Knolles's narrative history of the conflict at Cyprus. The second comes from King James's poetic celebration of the victory at Lepanto. Together these documents provide the details of action and the mood of conquest current when *Othello* was written and performed. Spelling and punctuation have been regularized and modernized throughout.

CYPRUS UNDER ATTACK

Richard Knolles's *The Turkish History* was dedicated to King James and published in 1603, the year James became England's monarch. Knolles's two-volume history is considered a probable source for *Othello*. Shakespeare's main fictional source, Cinthio's Italian novella, was written before the Mediterranean wars took place and *The Turkish History* was the most recent, available record of the conflict. Shakespeare focuses primarily on the fiction and devotes relatively little attention to historical details, even significantly altering obvious facts by having the Turks drown at sea before battle. However, some references are reasonably accurate, such as the estimated size of the Turkish fleet at two hundred galleys, mentioned in 1.3. These details suggest that Shakespeare knew more than he chose to include, adding only what strengthened the tone and development of the main plot.

The following excerpts from Knolles's history explain the close connection between religion and war for the Turks, their cruelty as conquerors, and the internal dissension that initially weakened the Christian allies before their ultimate victory. As you read this narrative, keep in mind the significance of Cyprus at the time of the invasion and its continued symbolic power more than thirty years later when Shakespeare wrote *Othello*. This small island represented profound political and religious consequences for Western Europe because many felt that if Cyprus fell to the Turks, the rest of Europe would soon follow. Whether such a conquest ever would have happened is less important than the fact that in 1570 European Renaissance people saw Cyprus as a place where western civilization collided with eastern barbarianism for an outcome that would affect the entire known world.

FROM RICHARD KNOLLES, *THE TURKISH HISTORY*, ABRIDGED
BY MR. SAVAGE, VOL. 1 (1603)
(London: Isaac Cleave, 1701)

Being now at Peace with all the world, [Selim II, Fifth Emperor of the Turks] purposed to erect several Charities . . . but at the same time was very much puzzl'd and perplex'd within himself, how to endow and maintain them. . . . Wherefore the new Emperor calling a Council, to consult what measures to take, in order to find out Revenues to support what he has so piously design'd, it was at last, after a long debate, resolv'd, notwithstanding the late Treaty with the *Venetians*, to invade and subdue the most fertile and flourishing Island of *Cyprus*. In pursuance hereof, the *Turks* made most mighty preparations both by Sea and Land, pretending for Cause, that those Islanders had harbour'd and encourag'd Pirates, which robb'd and destroy'd their Pilgrims, as they were sailing to *Mecca*. . . . In the meantime the State of *Venice* knowing themselves too weak to resist so powerful an Enemy, dispatch'd Ambassadors to all the Courts in *Europe*, either to desire their assistance, or to stir them up against the Infidels; but they all excus'd themselves, except the King of *Spain*, the Pope, the Duke of *Savoy*, the Duke of *Urbin*, the Duke of *Florence*, and the Knights of *Malta*. . . . (325)

Mustafa hearing of the Christians' proceedings, us'd his utmost endeavour to carry the City [Nicosia] by storm, but being again most valiantly repuls'd, he caus'd Letters to be shot into the Town, to persuade the Citizens to surrender, with wonderful promises of kindness, if they would comply; and on the contrary, most grievously threatening them, if they continu'd obstinate. . . . These resolute *Turks* getting up early the next morning, mounted the said Towers, without opposition, putting to the Sword all the Defendants. . . . The Besiegers being by this means in possession of the Walls, became quickly Masters of the whole City; into which they pour'd like a mighty Torrent, killing and destroying after a most inhumane manner the Inhabitants of all Ages and Sexes. Nay, the slaughter was so great, that 15,000 are said to have lost their lives therein. Thus this rich and populous City of *Nicosia* became a prey to the Infidels on the 9th of *September*, who carried away thence, in Money, Plate, Jewels, and other Riches, to the value of 20,000 Millions of Ducats. (326–327)

Mustafa being thus unexpectedly got into possession of that important place, march'd to *Famagusta*, which he likewise summon'd, causing the Heads of the Governour and the most eminent Citizens of Nicosia to be exposed to the view of the Inhabitants, hoping thereby to fright 'em into compliance with his haughty demands; but finding that the Soldiers and Burghers were resolved to defend themselves to the last extremity, notwithstanding his cruel menaces and fair pretences, and understanding moreover that the Confederate Fleet was near at hand, he drew off his Army and retreated to the Neighbouring Villages, where he put his men into quarters of refreshment during the following Winter. (327)

In the meantime the Confederates passing between the two Islands of *Rhodes* and *Caprathos*, heard by their Advice Boats, that *Nicosia* was lost, and *Famagusta* besieged, whereupon they holding a Council of War, it was therein very much press'd by *Columni* and *Zani*, to go and fight the Enemy; but which *Auria* the *Spanish* Admiral most strongly oppos'd, alleging that the Enemies' Fleet was far stronger than theirs, which had been greatly weaken'd by the late raging Pestilence, that the Season of the year was far advanced, and that they had no Harbours to protect them in case of any misfortune. This disagreement among the Christian Admirals, prevented an Engagement; for *Auria* tacking about, went back to *Messina*, *Columni* to *Italy*, and *Zani* to *Candie*, and from thence to *Corfu*; *Pial* also the *Turkish* Admiral having had notice of the Christians' departure, return'd to *Constantinople*, leaving seven great Galleys behind him to block up the Harbour of *Famagusta*. (328)

Neither was the miserable usage of the unfortunate *Bragadin* the last act of the *Bassa*'s cruelty; for he commanded all the Nobility, Burghers and

Soldiers of that City to be horribly massacred. Thus that fruitful and flourishing Island of *Cyprus* was brought under the subjection of the *Turkish*
Emperor.

But whilst the Confederates were coming together, the whole Island
of *Cyprus* was lost, several other Islands plunder'd, and many Towns
taken. (332)

On the other side, the *Turks* were not idle, for having had information
that the Confederates were join'd, and that they were coming towards
'em, they held a Council of their chief Commanders, to consult whether
they should give the Christians battle or decline it; but at length, such as
believed it dangerous to fight, being over-balanced by those of the contrary opinion, it was concluded that they should put themselves in a line
of battle, and engage the Confederates, to which they were rather in-
clin'd, for that famous Pirate *Caracoza*, who had been sent to get intelligence of their numbers was returned, and reported that the Enemies'
whole fleet consisted but of 110 Galleys; whereas the *Turks* had 250
Galleys, 50 Galliots and 20 *Brigandines*, besides other smaller Vessels.
This prodigious Navy of the Infidels being plac'd in the form of a half
Moon went proudly forth to meet the Christians. (334)

In this overthrow the Christians kill'd above 30,000 of the Infidels, sunk
and burnt 40 of their Galleys, took 161 great Galleys, 60 lesser Vessels,
and above 3000 Prisoners, besides an incredible booty of all sorts of
Riches. (337)

VICTORY AT LEPANTO

King James's heroic poem copies the style of classical epic poetry
in idealizing and glorifying war. The poem establishes a universal,
cosmic context by depicting the Battle of Lepanto as a conflict between good and evil in which the Christian God or Jehovah supports the Holy League of Western Europe while Satan leads the
Turks. War, in this light, is not simply violent but holy, and victory
leads naturally to worship. Shakespeare makes no specific reference to this poem or the Battle of Lepanto in *Othello*. He does,
however, draw clear distinctions between Turks and the characters
of the play, who are all assumed to be Christian. Consider how
Shakespeare dramatizes these contrasts as you read the following
selections from King James's poem. Remember also that James was
still a teenager when he wrote it.

FROM KING JAMES VI & I, "THE LEPANTO OF JAMES THE SIXT,
KING OF SCOTLAND," IN *HIS MAJESTY'S POETICAL EXERCISES
AT VACANT HOURS* (1591)
(Edinburgh: Robert Walde-grave, 1818)

I sing a wondrous work of God,
   I sing his mercies great,
I sing his justice here-withall
   Power'd from his holy seat.
To wit, a cruel Martial war,
   A bloody battle bold,
Long doubtsome fight, with slaughter huge
   And wounded manifold.
Which fought was in LEPANTO'S gulf
   Betwixt the baptiz'd race,
And circumsized Turban'd Turks
   Rencountering in that place. (ll. 1–12)

JEHOVAH also hath balances,
   Wherewith he weighs aright
The greatest and the heaviest sins,
   With smaller faults and light,
These grace did move him for to take,
   And so he weighed in Heaven,
The Christian faults with faithless Turks,
   The balance stood not even,
But swayed upon the faithless side:
   And then with awful face,
Frowned God of Hosts, the whirling Heavens
   For fear did tremble apace,
The stayest Mountains shuddered all,
   The grounds of earth did shake,
The Seas did bray, and PLUTO'S Realm
   For horror cold did quake. (ll. 400–415)

Now up now down on either side,
   Now Christians seemed to win,
Now overthrown, and now again,
   They seemed but to begin.
My pen for pity cannot write,
   My hair for horror stands,
To think how many Christians there

Were killed by Pagan hands.
O Lord throughout this Labyrinth
  Make me the way to view,
And let thy holy three-fold Spirit
  Be my conducting clue:
O now I spy a blessed Heaven,
  Our landing is not far:
Lo good victorious tidings comes
  To end this cruel war. (ll. 792–807)

But all this time was Venice Town
  Revolving what event
Might come of this prepared fight,
  With doubtsome minds and bent:
They long'd, and yet they durst not long
  To hear the news of all,
They hoped good, they feared the evil,
  And guessed what might befall:
At last the joyful tidings came,
  Which such a gladness bred,
That Matrons grave, and Maids modest,
  The Market place bespread:
Anon with cheerful countenance
  They dress them in a ring,
And thus the foremost did begin
  Sign all the rest to sing. (ll. 905–915)

CHORUS VENETUS.

Sing praises to our mighty God,
  Praise our deliverer's name, . . .
The faithless snares did compass us,
  Their nets were set about,
But yet our dearest Father in Heaven,
  He hath redeemed us out.
Not only that, but by his power,
  Our enemies' feet they slayed,
Whom he hath trapped, and made to fall
  Into the pit they made:
Sing praises then both young and old,
  That in this town remain,
To him that hath relieved our necks,
  From Turkish yoke profane. (unnumbered lines)

QUESTIONS FOR WRITTEN AND ORAL DISCUSSION

1. In *Othello*, Shakespeare offers no explanation for the Turkish invasion of Cyprus. According to Richard Knolles's historical account, what purpose and reason did the Turks have for their attack?

2. From a Turkish perspective, Western Europe was the enemy, but for Knolles, Shakespeare, and other Europeans, the Turks represented the common adversary. Find examples in Knolles's account that express this European bias. Can you identify specific words that emphasize the cruelty and other negative qualities of the Ottomites?

3. Knolles describes a Council of the Turks similar to the Council of Venice in 1.3 of *Othello* preparing for war and trying to estimate the opponent's strength. Compare the two accounts, noting common elements. Choose from the following suggestions:

   a) Write a dramatic scene for the Turkish Council, deciding before you begin whether to portray the group negatively as the enemy or more neutrally or positively as a military power simply fighting for its safety and beliefs.

   b) Divide into two small groups, one to present the Turks as enemies, the other to cast the group as a legitimate Council responsibly conducting a war. Perhaps dramatize these short scenes for the class and then discuss what techniques—language, gestures, lighting, even costumes, and props—helped to set the tone and guide the audience to respond according to your intentions.

   c) Enact the initial portion of *Othello*'s 1.3 that addresses the Turkish invasion, considering the concerns presented in earlier parts of this question. How, for example, do Shakespeare's language and characterization present the Venetian Council in a favorable light? How would your decisions about staging and delivering lines contribute to that positive impression?

4. Historically, disagreements arose among the allies of the Holy League defending the interests of Western Europe. One instance appears in Knolles's account and another is mentioned earlier in this chapter's discussion of the Battle of Lepanto. Pretend you are one of the Christian Admirals or a naval recruit on board one of the war galleys and write a diary account or monologue that describes the conflicts within the alliance. What is your tone and concern: Fear that lack of unity will strengthen the enemy and threaten your safety? Anger and frustration that others disagree with you? Belief and hope in the common cause despite the friction? Conclude by suggesting how this imaginative exercise affects or changes your perception of heroes and en-

emies in general and more specifically in Richard Knolles's narrative or *Othello*.

5. The poem of King James's youth, "The Lepanto," celebrates the cause and outcome of the Battle of Lepanto in 1571. How does he turn a one-day battle involving fewer than 150,000 men into a much more significant event? Find specific examples. What words or phrases create the tone of celebration? How does he emphasize the evil of the Turks?

6. Discuss the term "Holy War." In your view, is holy war possible? Under what conditions? Does James's poem describe a holy war? If so, how?

7. Research the Ottoman invasion of Cyprus and/or the subsequent Battle of Lepanto. Write a short paper about this naval history, focusing on an aspect that most interests you such as events leading up to the conflict, the political impact of the attacks, naval weapons and war galleys used, military strategies employed. Include diagrams or maps as visual aids if they seem appropriate.

8. Look at a map of the Mediterranean region and identify key locations referred to in *Othello*: Venice, Rhodes, Cyprus, Turkey. Duplicate or draw this map and mark out the journey of Othello's company, as well as the likely path of the Turks.

9. Although history is not fulfilled in *Othello* because the Turks are drowned at sea before a war takes place, the fear of war and the need to exercise control and order continue throughout the play. Write a paragraph or two that explain how Shakespeare continually reminds audiences of this state of affairs and how these details affect the overall mood. Alternatively, write an imaginary report from a local citizen of Cyprus, describing your reaction to the arrival of the Venetians under Othello's command and the simultaneous news about the drowning of the Turks. Record your feelings about living as an inhabitant of a military outpost and about the behavior of the Venetian soldiers who have come to protect you.

10. Research the geography and landscape of Cyprus in travel guides or picture books and design several backdrops for *Othello*, possibly representing the arrival in 2.1, a citadel scene, and a street scene.

THE MOOR

Answers to questions of identity in *Othello*—"Who are you?" and "Where do you belong?"—are shaped partly by the two influences already discussed in this chapter: the dual setting of Venice and Cyprus as places of peace and war, and the background of anti-Christian barbarianism represented by the Turks. Even more important to the central conflict, however, is the fact that Othello is a solitary black man amongst a cast of white characters. This is the most striking feature of identity in the play, one that cannot be ignored visually and that is very deliberately addressed by many characters, including Othello himself. Iago and Roderigo begin Act 1 by verbally attacking the absent Othello with racial insults, calling him "an old black ram," "the thick lips," and "a Barbary horse." Yet when Othello appears, he is a noble character, generous and well-respected for his authority. Desdemona professes to love him for these virtues and declares her indifference to the color of his skin, but by remaining loyal to him, she ultimately becomes the victim of his rage and jealousy. In the crucial temptation scene in Act 3 where the seeds of violence are planted, even Othello considers his marriage to a white Venetian unnatural as his doubts draw him towards Iago's prejudices and stereotypes about black men.

The tragic movement of the play addresses, among other issues, concerns of race. What does it mean to be a black Moor in a white European society? What happens when a black man has authority over white men or chooses to marry a white woman? These questions point to the distinctions and conflicts presented in Othello's character between his personal power and public authority and between his Christian religion and non-European heritage. Because *Othello* stands alone in its time as the only play in which a black character is the central tragic hero, it invites consideration of cultural standards and perceptions in the early seventeenth century. Shakespeare may have allowed some of his characters to reflect current prejudices, but he was also certainly challenging common conventions. Exploring facts and myths about race and blackness during Shakespeare's time can help us re-examine our own views about Othello's identity in the play and our sympathies toward him as a man who is both a victimizer and a victim.

MORO DI
CONDI-
TIONE.

Print of a sixteenth-century Moor from Cesare Vecellio's *De gli habiti antichi, et moderni* (Venice, 1590). By Permission of the Folger Shakespeare Library.

DEFINITION AND SYMBOLISM

The meaning of the word "Moor" and the symbolism of blackness in the sixteenth and seventeenth centuries provide an important context for racial attitudes in *Othello*. Most accurately, a Moor
was an inhabitant of Northern Africa including Morocco, as well as
parts of Algeria and Mauritania, a broad region also known as Barbary in the sixteenth century. Some Moors were considered to be
light-skinned, tawny, or white, while others were identified as
"blackamoors." Europeans, however, were not precise in their use
of the word "Moor." They equated it with "Negro" but also occasionally referred to Ethiopians, North American Indians, Asians,
and Arabs as Moors. In vague popular terms, then, Moors could
apparently represent many people outside of Christianized Europe
whose skin color may have contributed to their difference. Like the
Turks, "Moors" were considered threatening because of their religion; they were either "infidels" practicing Islam or "heathens" following no recognizable faith at all. Predominantly, however, Moors
came to represent African people in general, although evidence
suggests that Europeans sometimes distinguished between the true
Moors of Morocco and Mauritania and other African natives who
were perceived to be more savage or primitive.

Africa, according to European perception and myth, was a place
characterized by both barbarianism and exoticism, inhabited by
wild beasts and by people with enviable riches and strange customs. What Europeans knew, they did not necessarily understand.
What they did not know, they feared or viewed with wonder.
Among their many images of Africans or black Moors, two common
beliefs are relevant in *Othello*. First, black people were considered
sensual, lustful creatures, more beast than human. Nakedness and
the practice of polygamy that some European voyagers witnessed
in parts of Africa contributed to this perception. Iago is Shakespeare's key spokesperson for this viewpoint in his use of animal
imagery to describe Othello. Second, Africans were judged to be
extremely jealous, a belief that grows to tragic proportions in the
play. As common racial assumptions in Shakespeare's time, these
European views marked Moors or blackamoors of Africa not simply
as different but as inferior and less civilized than the way that Europeans saw themselves.

Blackness has its own ancient symbolism which simply helped

to confirm European Renaissance prejudices about the inferiority of Africans. Black is the color of night, typically a time of danger, uncertainty, and fear compared to daylight clarity. For centuries in the literature and philosophy of a predominantly white culture, black has represented many negative qualities and forces including evil, ugliness, sin, the devil, damnation, hell, and death. In England's medieval sacred drama, popular in the fourteenth and fifteenth centuries, and in secular court performances of the early sixteenth century, a black face indicated the forces of darkness. White and light were signs of goodness and beauty. This traditional symbolism influenced perceptions about people who were naturally black or dark-skinned. While some theorists blamed the condition on the hot African climate where black people lived, others offered a Biblical explanation, suggesting that blackness was the result of God's curse on Noah's son Ham in the *Genesis* story of the Great Flood. Although these interpretations were not compatible, consistent, or provable, they prejudged an understanding of blackness as an undesirable contrast to preferable qualities of the color white.

These were common attitudes and popular beliefs in England in the century leading up to Shakespeare's composition of *Othello*, and the symbolic contrast between white and black informs the struggle between good and evil, beauty and ugliness, virtue and vice throughout the play. Shakespeare, however, resists the temptation simply to equate outward appearances with inward realities. In fact, much of the conflict and tension that engages the audience results from the way appearances and realities keep shifting and overturning expectations. Whiteness and goodness do not always coincide; nor does blackness stand solely for evil.

ENGLAND'S RELATIONSHIP WITH AFRICA

History, as well as traditional symbolism and popular opinion, affected the dramatic image of Moors in Elizabethan and Jacobean England. Prior to 1550 England had virtually no direct contact with Africa and relied on ancient classical legends for its understanding of the dark, unknown continent. By the 1550s, however, trade relations began to develop between England and northwestern Africa, resulting in first-hand accounts, maps, and stories by merchants, explorers, and voyagers who challenged or enlarged on the fantastical, improbable details of legend. Two consequences of developing trade are that black people began to appear in England for the first time and that international political relations began to influence popular views of Moors. Motivated by economics and politics, England began to practice slavery but also saw their trade connection with African non-Christians as a potential source of power and protection from European Catholics who threatened their Protestant government.

Following a west African trade expedition to Guinea in 1554 a sea merchant brought to London five black men whom he instructed in the English language and used as interpreters in further trade missions. This early English voyage marked the arrival of black people in England. During the fifty years between this significant beginning and the first performance of Shakespeare's *Othello*, the black population in England increased to the point that Queen Elizabeth I issued an edict or proclamation in 1599 and again in 1601 demanding that black African residents be deported from the country. By all indications the black minority was small and the Queen's statement appeared relatively ineffective but her concern reflects a negative racial bias undoubtedly shared by many of her subjects.

At the same time, however, trade with Northern Africa grew and economic ties with the Moors became more important to England's prosperity. In the 1550s only a few independent merchants risked piracy and other dangers for personal wealth. But by 1600 governments had become involved and an entire embassy from Morocco journeyed to London for a six-month stay designed to strengthen diplomatic and economic relations with England. The public reacted to this group of Africans with a mixture of curiosity, suspicion, and prejudice. As noblemen sent by their king, these Moors were granted enough respect for a private meeting with the queen. As foreigners with an unfamiliar culture and Muslim religion, however, they were criticized and shunned. Regarded as "infidels" or non-Christians, they were not treated with the same respect as ambassadors from other Christian European states although they likely inspired more interest and attention.

Initial audiences of *Othello* may have remembered this diplomatic visit and most certainly would have seen or heard about other Moors in England, some who were tawny and others who were black-skinned. Slavery was only beginning to take root with the birth of the English empire and, consequently, although black people were subject to prejudice and stereotype, they were not immediately identified as slaves. Blacks in Shakespeare's England were potentially servants, slaves, political ambassadors, or trading partners. By the late seventeenth century when slavery was well-established, it might have been extremely questionable to present a noble black hero on stage. In the early part of the century, however, it was merely unusual, and its exoticism and originality quite possibly helped to ensure the play's attention and success.

One key political concern affecting English perceptions of Moors was the relationship between Moors and Spain in the context of intense Spanish hostility to England. The Moors had conquered Spain in the eighth century and maintained control with their Islamic culture and religion until 1492. This history made the Moors appear similar to the Turks as anti-Christian threats to Europe. However, after 1492 the Moors lost their power in Spain to the Catholics and either returned to Africa or stayed and converted to Christianity. When England began to trade in Africa, Spain was already there as its chief competitor. More importantly, under Elizabeth I's reign from 1558 to 1603, Spain actively supported an attempt to replace the Protestant queen in England with a Catholic monarch. Spain's Catholic threat, therefore, began to be recognized as greater than an Islamic threat from African Moors. The English defeat of the Spanish Armada in 1588 was an important victory in the conflict between Protestants and Catholics, but the Moors continued to play a potentially important role in support of England. One apparent purpose of the embassy from Morocco to London in 1600 was to consider a formal alliance between England and African Moors against Spain.

Nothing ever came of these negotiations and when Queen Elizabeth died in 1603, English relations with Spain improved dramatically with the new monarch, James I, so that a political agreement with the Moors no longer seemed necessary. However, half a century of history preceding Shakespeare's play indicates that attitudes to the Moors were connected not only to interest sparked by legends and tales of English voyagers but to much larger complicated international concerns for England's safety, peace, and economic growth. In the Renaissance, religion and politics were linked. Catholics were enemies of Protestants and non-Christians were enemies of Christians but alliances were flexible, reflecting the greatest threat and greatest need for support. England's relations with the Moors suggest a pragmatic willingness to compromise religious principles for economic wealth and political strength but the uneasy connection was typically marked by suspicion, self-interest, and a sense of superiority.

THEATRICAL TRADITION

Shakespeare's unusual portrayal of a black stage hero had direct and indirect influences in current travel literature and occurred within a theatrical tradition which demonstrated a growing fascination with Africa and black people. In 1600 John Leo Africanus's *The History and Description of Africa* was published in English for the first time. Not only did this three-volume history provide more extensive and accurate information about Africa with less bias and prejudice than any previous source but the writer's life also paralleled details of Othello's, suggesting Shakespeare's knowledge of and dependence on this newly translated history. In the same year a twelve-volume collection of works compiled by another travel writer made available stories and travel journals from previous decades and helped to inspire interest in Africa for English playwrights seeking new material for their plays. Africa appealed to the dramatic imagination as an exotic, savage, strange world that could either contrast or expose conflicts and values familiar to English audiences.

Although black-masked figures already had a history in early court performances and street pageants, playwrights began developing a specific type of black character for the public stage in the 1580s more than fifteen years before Shakespeare wrote *Othello*. In 1589 George Peele's *The Battle of Alcazar* was the first English drama to focus attention on a black man. The Moor in this play is a complete villain combining the qualities of the Vice figure in earlier medieval drama, the symbolic connection between blackness and evil, the Machiavellian model of treachery, and the prejudices against Moors and Muslims emerging in the historical activity of the late sixteenth century. A stage stereotype began to gain acceptance and popularity following Peele's play so that when audiences saw a black character, they expected and usually discovered a villain with few or no redeeming qualities. Shakespeare demonstrated his own interest in this character type by including a villainous Moor in *Titus Andronicus*, a tragedy written a decade before *Othello*.

Othello, therefore, stands in stark contrast to this dramatic tradition by dignifying a black Moor and creating as the central villain a white man, Iago. While audiences would have been ready to equate blackness with some form of evil, Shakespeare dares to overturn these expectations. Questions still spark debate today, however. Does Othello's eventual shift to jealousy and violence simply delay the identification of blackness with evil until later in the play, or does Iago's success in darkening Othello's humanity help to reinforce sympathy for the tragic hero who happens to be a black Moor? Regardless of the answers, Iago's dominance as a white Venetian villain is enough to challenge the stereotypical contrast between black vice and white virtue that was popular and accepted on the Elizabethan and Jacobean stage.

The remainder of this section includes excerpts from a travel journal, a royal proclamation, and plays that reveal information about and attitudes towards Moors in Shakespeare's time. Spelling has been regularized and modernized throughout.

JOHN LEO AFRICANUS AND THE PEOPLE OF AFRICA

John Leo Africanus was a Moor born on the Spanish island of Granada and raised in Barbary in Africa. He traveled extensively throughout Africa working with merchants and diplomats until he was captured by Christian pirates (likely Venetians), taken to the Pope in Rome, converted to Christianity, and freed from slavery because of his nobility and education. His book, *The History and Description of Africa*, written in Italian in the 1550s and translated into English in 1600, is considered a source for *Othello* because of apparent parallels between the author and Shakespeare's tragic hero. John Pory, the translator of Africanus's work, begins the English edition with a biography of the writer's life with which Shakespeare was quite possibly familiar. The portion included below reveals some similarities between Africanus and Othello. Watch for these connections, considering them in light of Othello's description of his past in 1.3. Of particular significance is the shared Christianity of Africanus and Othello which made them more acceptable to Europeans than Moors who practiced Islam. Pory's introduction also offers a definition of African people, describing the two kinds of Moors and revealing that the connection between race and religion was more complex than the popular English dramatic stereotype of Moors as evil black heathens.

The passages from Africanus's own writing following Pory's introduction balance observations about the virtues and vices of African people. Qualities mentioned include honesty and jealousy, simplicity and savagery. Consider whether you agree with his distinction between virtues and vices and whether you think his account of African people is fair-minded relative to commonly held attitudes in Renaissance Europe.

FROM JOHN LEO AFRICANUS, *THE HISTORY AND DESCRIPTION OF AFRICA* [1600], TRANS. JOHN PORY, VOL. 1
(New York: Burt Franklin, 1896)

TO THE READER
[INTRODUCTION BY JOHN PORY]

Give me leave (gentle Readers) if not to present unto your knowledge, because some perhaps may as well be informed as myself; yet to call to your remembrance, some few particulars, concerning this Geographical History, *and* John Leo *the author thereof.*

Who albeit by birth a Moor, *and by religion for many years a* Mahumetan: *yet if you consider his* Parentage, Wit, Education, Learning, Employments, Travels, *and his conversion to Christianity; you shall find him not altogether unfit to undertake such an enterprise; nor unworthy to be regarded.*

First therefore his Parentage *seemeth not to have been ignoble: seeing . . . an Uncle of his was so Honorable a person, and so excellent an Orator and Poet; that he was sent as a principal Ambassador, from the king of* Fez, *to the king of* Tombuto. . . .

Neither wanted he the best Education *that all* Barbary *could afford. . . . So as I may justly say (if the comparison be tolerable) that as* Moses *was learned in all the wisdom of the* Egyptians; *so likewise was* Leo, *in that of the* Arabians *and* Moors. . . .

Moreover as touching his exceeding great Travels, *had he not at the first been a* Moor *and a* Mahumetan *in religion, and most skilfull in the languages and customs of the* Arabians *and* Africans, *and for the most part travelled in* Caravans, *or under the authority, safe conduct, and commendation of great princes: I marvel much however he should have escaped so many thousands of imminent dangers. And (all the former notwithstanding) I marvel much more, however he escaped them. For how many desolate cold mountains, and huge, dry, and barren deserts passed he? How often was he in hazard to have been captived, or to have had his throat cut by the prowling* Arabians, *and wild* Moors? *And how hardly many times escaped he the Lion's greedy mouth, and the devouring jaws of the Crocodile? . . . Besides all which places he had also been at* Tauris *in* Persia: *and of his own country, and other* African *regions adjoining and remote, he was so diligent a traveller: that there was no kingdom, province, signory, or city; or scarcely any town, village, mountain, valley, river, or forest, &c. which he left unvisited. . . .*

But, not to forget His conversion to Christianity, *amidst all these his busy and dangerous travels, it pleased the divine providence, for the discovery and manifestation of God's wonderful works, and of his dreadful and just judgments performed in* Africa . . . *to deliver this author of ours, and this present Geographical History, into the hands of certain* Italian Pirates, *about the isle of* Gerbi, *situate in the gulf of* Capes, *between the cities of* Tunis *and* Tripolis *in* Barbary. *Being thus taken, the Pirates presented him and his Book unto* Pope Leo the tenth: *who esteeming of him as of a most rich and invaluable prize, greatly rejoiced at his arrival, and gave him most kind entertainment and liberal maintenance, till such time as he had won him to be baptized in the name of* Christ, *and to be called* John Leo, *after the Pope's own name. And so during his abode in* Italy, *learning the* Italian *tongue, he translated this book thereinto, being before written in* Arabic. *Thus much of* John Leo. (4–7)

Moreover this part of the world is inhabited especially by five principal nations, to wit, by people called Cafri or Cafates, that is to say outlaws, or lawless, by the Abassins, the Egyptians, the Arabians, and the Africans or Moors, properly so called; which last are of two kinds, namely white or tawny Moors, and Negros or black Moors. Of all which nations some are Gentiles which worship Idols; others of the sect of Mahumet; some others Christians; and some Jewish in religion; the greatest part of which people are thought to be descended from *Cham* the cursed son of *Noah*; except some Arabians of the lineage of *Sem*, which afterward passed into Africa. (20)

[DESCRIPTION BY JOHN LEO AFRICANUS]

The manners and customs of the African people, which inhabit the desert of Libya.

• • •

For by reason of jealousy you may see them daily one to be the death and destruction of another, and that in such savage and brutish manner, that in this case they will show no compassion at all. . . . The liberality of

this people hath at all times been exceeding great. And when any trav-
ellers may pass through their dry and desert territories, they will never
repair unto their tents, neither will they themselves travel upon the common highway. (154)

The commendable actions and virtues of the Africans.

• • •

Moreover those [people] which inhabit Barbary are of great cunning &
dexterity for building & for mathematical inventions, which a man may
easily conjecture by their artificial works. Most honest people they are,
and destitute of all fraud and guile; not only embracing all simplicity and
truth, but also practicing the same throughout the whole course of their
lives. . . . Likewise they are most strong and valiant people, especially
those which dwell upon the mountains. They keep their covenant most
faithfully; insomuch that they had rather die than break promise. No nation in the world is so subject unto jealousy; for they will rather lose
their lives, than put up any disgrace in the behalf of their women. So
desirous are they of riches and honour, that therein no other people can
go beyond them. (183)

What vices the foresaid Africans are subject unto.

• • •

Those which we named the inhabitants of the cities of Barbary are somewhat needy and covetous, being also very proud and high-minded, and
wonderfully addicted unto wrath; insomuch that (according to the prov-
erb) they will deeply engrave in marble any injury be it never so small,
& will in no wise blot it out of their remembrance. So rustical they are
& void of good manners, that scarcely can any stranger obtain their familiarity and friendship. Their wits are but mean, and they are so cred-
ulous, that they will believe matters impossible, which are told them. So
ignorant are they of natural philosophy, that they imagine all the effects
and operations of nature to be extraordinary and divine. . . . Concerning
their religion, the greater part of these people are neither Mahumetans,
Jews, nor Christians; and hardly shall you find so much as a spark of
piety in any of them. They have no churches at all, nor any kind of
prayers, but being utterly estranged from all godly devotion, they lead a
savage and beastly life: and if any man chanceth to be of a better dispo-
sition (because they have no law-givers nor teachers among them) he is
constrained to follow the example of the other men's lives and manners.
. . . The Negros likewise lead a beastly kind of life, being utterly destitute
of the use of reason, of dexterity of wit, and of all arts. Yea they so behave
themselves, as if they continually lived in a forest among wild beasts. They
have great swarms of harlots among them; whereupon a man may easily
conjecture their manner of living: except their conversation perhaps be

somewhat more tolerable, who dwell in the principal towns and cities: for it is like that they are somewhat more addicted to civility. (185–187)

QUEEN ELIZABETH I'S ROYAL PROCLAMATION AGAINST BLACK PEOPLE IN ENGLAND

The following is Queen Elizabeth's second edict demanding that "Negroes and blackamoors" be removed from England in 1601. There is little evidence that Elizabeth's proclamation had much effect, and by *Othello*'s likely date of composition in 1604, a new monarch, King James, was on the English throne. However, Elizabeth's edict does establish an official view reflecting public sentiments current with Shakespeare's playwriting career. Try to identify the Queen's reasons for the deportation order, considering the influences of religion, politics, and economics in her mandate.

FROM ELIZABETH I, "LICENSING CASPER VAN SENDEN TO
DEPORT NEGROES" [DRAFT; CA. JANUARY 1601]
(*Tudor Royal Proclamations*, Ed. Paul L. Hughes and James F.
Larkin, Vol. 3, New Haven: Yale University Press, 1969)

Whereas the Queen's majesty, tendering the good and welfare of her own natural subjects, greatly distressed in these hard times of dearth, is highly discontented to understand the great numbers of Negroes and blackamoors which (as she is informed) are carried into this realm since the troubles between her highness and the King of Spain; who are fostered and powered here, to the great annoyance of her own liege people that which co[vet?] the relief which these people consume, as also for that the most of them are infidels having no understanding of Christ or his Gospel: hath given a special commandment that the said kind of people shall be with all speed avoided and discharged out of this her majesty's realms; and to that end and purpose hath appointed Casper van Senden, merchant of Lubeck, for their speedy transportation. . . .

These shall therefore be to will and require you and every of you to aid and assist the said Casper van Senden or his assignees to taking such Negroes and blackamoors to be transported as aforesaid as he shall find within the realm of England; and if there shall be any person or persons which be possessed of any such blackamoors that refuse to deliver them in sort aforesaid, then we require you to call them before you and to advise and persuade them by all good means to satisfy her majesty's pleasure therein; which if they shall eftsoons willfully and obstinately refuse, we pray you to certify their names to us, to the end her majesty may take such further course therein as it shall seem best in her princely wisdom. (221–222)

THE BLACK MAN ON THE ELIZABETHAN STAGE

George Peele's *The Battle of Alcazar* (1589) is a semi-historical play based on a war between Portugal and the Moors in 1578. The stage villain, Muly Hamet, is a black Moor who exercises great deception, manipulation, and cruelty. In the course of the play, he murders two brothers, as well as his uncle Abdilmelec who is the Moorish king of Barbary, and the Portuguese King Sebastian whom he lures into Africa only to savagely destroy him. In Muly Hamet, blackness becomes a metaphor for evil and the word "Moor" becomes synonymous with "barbarian." The passage quoted below begins the play as a Presenter provides a brief summary before the action begins. Notice how the language establishes Hamet as a villain and "tyrant king" prior to his appearance on stage and how his race becomes a part of that image.

FROM GEORGE PEELE, *THE BATTLE OF ALCAZAR* (1589)
(Malone Society Reprints, rpt. 1597; Charles Whittingham & Co.:
Chiswick Press, 1907)

Honor the spur that pricks the princely mind,
To follow rule and climb the stately chair,
With great desire inflames the Portingal
An honorable and courageous king,
To undertake a dangerous dreadful war,
And aid with Christian arms the barbarous Moor,
The Negro *Muly Hamet* that with-holds
The Kingdom from his uncle *Abdilmelec*,
Whom proud *Abdallas* wronged,
And in his throne instals his cruel son,
That now usurps upon this prince,
This brave Barbarian Lord *Muly-Molocco*.
The passage to the crown by murder made,
Abdallas dies, and [leaves] this tyrant king,
Of whom we treat sprung from the Arabian moor
Black in his look, and bloody in his deeds,

And in his shirt stained with a cloud of gore,
Presents himself with naked sword in hand,
Accompanied as now you may behold,
With devils coated in the shapes of men. (ll. 1–23)

Following the stage convention of black villainy that George
Peele made popular in *The Battle of Alcazar*, Shakespeare creates
a similar character in his first tragedy, *Titus Andronicus* (1593–
1594), a violent play whose black Moor, Aaron, is willing and eager
to maim, hurt, and destroy others. Titus Andronicus is a Roman
general and Aaron is the lover of a Roman prisoner, Tamora,
Queen of the Goths. Aaron's list of murders and other crimes is
long. The following lines from the play reveal how much pleasure
he receives from doing evil and how he identifies his villainy with
the color of his skin. Think about the qualities of both Othello and
Iago as you read Aaron's confessions.

FROM WILLIAM SHAKESPEARE, *TITUS ANDRONICUS* (1593–1594)
(*The Riverside Shakespeare*, Ed. G. Blakemore Evans et al., Boston:
Houghton, 1974)

[Aaron]: O how this villainy
Doth fat me with the very thoughts of it!
Let fools do good, and fair men call for grace,
Aaron will have his soul black like his face. (3.1.202–205)

[Lucius]: Art thou not sorry for these heinous deeds?
[Aaron]: Ay, that I had not done a thousand more.
Even now I curse the day—and yet I think
Few come within the compass of my curse—
Wherein I did not some notorious ill:
As kill a man, or else devise his death. . . .
But I have done a thousand dreadful things,
As willingly as one would kill a fly,
And nothing grieves me heartily indeed,
But that I cannot do ten thousand more. (5.1.123–144)

QUESTIONS FOR WRITTEN AND ORAL DISCUSSION

1. John Pory's introduction to Africanus's *The History and Description
   of Africa* provides information about the author's life. What qualities
   does Pory consider admirable in Africanus? How do these details com-

pare with Othello's character and his past? Find specific examples, referring especially to Othello's main speeches in 1.3.

2. Do you detect any prejudice in Pory's biography of Africanus and his description of the many types of African people? Pory distinguishes between tawny and black Moors; later in the eighteenth and nineteenth centuries, many people argued from their own prejudices that Othello was tawny or light-colored rather than black. Can you find evidence in the play that either supports or contradicts that interpretation of Othello's race?

3. Africanus identifies virtues and vices that he sees in African people. Make two lists, side by side, that summarize these virtues and vices in single words or phrases. Discuss with a partner or small group whether the virtues all seem positive or the vices all negative to you. Explain your position. Also, consider whether Africanus's description of these qualities seems balanced and fair-minded or simply inconsistent and contradictory. Explain your conclusions. Is it difficult for you as a modern reader to accept Africanus's account or can you appreciate it within its sixteenth-century context? Why or why not?

4. Consider the qualities which Africanus identifies that might also accurately describe Othello. Which virtues and vices does Shakespeare's character display and where in the play does he reveal them? Do you think Shakespeare intended these qualities to be associated with Othello's race or do you see them as aspects of human nature shared by other characters in the play? Provide examples.

5. Queen Elizabeth commanded the deportation of black people from England in 1599 and again in 1601. What reasons are included in her proclamation? How do religion, politics, and economics play a part in her decision? What does the fact that her order was largely ineffectual suggest to you about the attitudes and concerns of her loyal subjects?

   Can you identify any similar response from a modern political ruler in your country or elsewhere in the world where differences of race or religion pose a real or imagined threat to local or national identity? In Eastern Europe, perhaps, or South Africa before or after apartheid was abolished? Discuss why people find cultural or racial differences threatening. What actions or attitudes encourage prejudice? What responses help promote tolerance and acceptance?

6. Imagine yourself as an Elizabethan subject witnessing the six-month visit of the Moroccan embassy to England in 1600 to improve diplomatic and trade relations. Referring to information in this chapter, compose a response from one of the following perspectives:

a) As a person of significant political importance, how do you view England's national needs and expectations with respect to this visit and how do those issues affect your personal response to foreigners whose customs are very different from yours?

b) As a low-class or middle-class London observer, what is your reaction—curiosity, suspicion? How much are you influenced by facts and observations, as well as by myths, prejudices, and hearsay?

c) As an Elizabethan newspaper reporter looking for a good headline, how might you record the event?

7. Study excerpts included from *The Battle of Alcazar* and *Titus Andronicus* that represent black characters on the Elizabethan stage. Discuss what kind of stereotype they create and encourage. What specific references connect blackness and villainy?

8. Given the information provided in this chapter, what might the word "Moor" in the play's full title, *Othello, the Moor of Venice*, suggest about the main character's identity? Pretend you have attended the first performance of *Othello*. Individually or in pairs, compose and/ or dramatize your initial expectations about seeing a Moor in the title role and your response after seeing the play.

9. Symbolically, the colors white and black have a long history of representing good and evil, as well as other related positive and negative contrasts. Write an essay that discusses how the color symbolism works in the play, using specific references from the text as well as assumptions and traditions explained in this chapter.

10. Write an essay about race and Iago in the play. Consider what racial views he expresses, compared to other characters, and what his actions suggest about traditional expectations and theatrical representations of blackness in Shakespeare's time.

SUGGESTED READINGS

Barthelemy, Anthony Gerard. *Black Face, Maligned Race: The Representation of Blacks in English Drama from Shakespeare to Southerne*. Baton Rouge: Louisiana State University Press, 1987.

Beeching, Jack. *The Galleys at Lepanto*. New York: Charles Scribner's Sons, 1982.

Bouwsma, William. *Venice and the Defense of Republican Liberty: Renaissance Values in the Age of the Counter Reformation*. Berkeley: University of California Press, 1968.

D'Amico, Jack. *The Moor in English Renaissance Drama*. Tampa: University of Florida Press, 1991.

Finlay, Robert. *Politics in Renaissance Venice*. New Brunswick, NJ: Rutgers University Press, 1980.

Hale, J. R. *Renaissance Venice*. London: Faber and Faber, 1973.

Hunter, G. K. *Dramatic Identities and Cultural Tradition: Studies in Shakespeare and His Contemporaries*. Liverpool: Liverpool University Press, 1978.

Jones, Eldred. *The Elizabethan Image of Africa*. Charlottesville: The University of Virginia Press for The Folger Shakespeare Library, 1971.

———. *Othello's Countrymen: The African in English Renaissance Drama*. London: Oxford University Press, 1965.

Jones, Emrys. " 'Othello,' 'Lepanto' and the Cyprus Wars." *Shakespeare Survey* 21 (1968): 47–52.

Jordan, Winthrop D. *White Over Black: American Attitudes Toward the Negro, 1550–1812*. Chapel Hill: University of North Carolina Press, 1968.

Levith, Murray. *Shakespeare's Italian Settings and Plays*. New York: St. Martin's Press, 1989.

Lievsay, John L. *The Elizabethan Image of Italy*. Ithaca, NY: Cornell University Press, 1964.

Marrappodi, Michele, A. J. Hoenselaars, Marcello Cappuzzo, and L. Falzon Santucci, eds. *Shakespeare's Italy: Functions of Italian Locations in Renaissance Drama*. Manchester: Manchester University Press, 1993.

Marx, Robert. *The Battle of Lepanto, 1571*. Cleveland: World, 1966.

McPherson, David C. *Shakespeare, Jonson, and the Myth of Venice*. Newark: University of Delaware Press, 1990.

McWilliam, G. H. *Shakespeare's Italy Revisited: An Inaugural Lecture*. Leicester: Leicester University Press, 1974.

Tokson, Elliot H. *The Popular Image of the Black Man in English Drama, 1550–1688*. Boston: G. K. Hall and Co., 1982.

Vaughan, Virginia Mason. *Othello: A Contextual History*. Cambridge: Cambridge University Press, 1994.

3

Historical Context: Love and Marriage

The relationship between men and women in *Othello* is the center of emotional celebration and conflict, of joy and jealousy, of ultimate devastation. If we were to approach the play's characters with the question "How do you love?" we would discover a variety of answers. In the first act Desdemona attempts to guide the Duke's decision about her future by boldly insisting, "That I love the Moor to live with him, / My downright violence, and storm of fortunes, / May trumpet to the world" (1.3.243–245). In the final act when Othello confesses to the murder of his wife, he describes himself as "one that loved not wisely, but too well" (5.2.340). Emilia provides her own commentary throughout the play, saying generally of men's approach to women, "They are all but stomachs, and we all but food" (3.4.104), and particularly of Desdemona's marriage, "She was too fond of her most filthy bargain" (5.2.154). Cassio, Roderigo, and Iago also frequently profess and demonstrate their idealistic, ridiculous, or negative attitudes towards women, love, and marriage. As one of Shakespeare's most powerful love trage-dies, *Othello* explores the complex dynamics between men and women from a multitude of perspectives.

These perspectives give voice to some of the popular attitudes, debates, and controversies surrounding traditions and laws about love and marriage in sixteenth- and early seventeenth-century England. Literary conventions and social assumptions of that time did not always correspond; neither did public laws and private practices nor the standards of church and state. This chapter examines several dominant Renaissance ideals and customs, as well as persistent challenges and inconsistencies that complicated the harmony, value, and expectations of relationships between men and women. Considering *Othello* within this historical context can illuminate the play's tragedy and the way in which its characters address the enduring question of the heart: "How do you love?"

LITERARY CONVENTIONS

Literary conventions are styles, techniques, or forms of expression that writers and readers mutually accept and recognize as a means of addressing certain subjects. Two literary conventions that were current in the sixteenth century, the courtly love tradition and the formal debate about women, provide insight into Shakespeare's portrayal of love in *Othello*, for the play incorporates aspects of both conventions as it dramatizes gender roles and relationships.

The Courtly Love Tradition

Courtly love began as a medieval literary convention among eleventh-century French poets who wrote about knights seeking the love of beautiful ladies. The poetry, rather than reflecting reality, presented an idealized vision of romance in which the woman, as the object of love, was placed on a pedestal and worshipped from afar. The male worshipper in these courtly stories demonstrated gentlemanly behavior of courtesy, humility, and service but the expression of his ideal love was never meant to lead to marriage. In fact it was typically an adulterous longing or quest that was guaranteed—even intended—to be unfulfilled. By contrast, actual medieval marriages were seen primarily as business or economic alliances rather than romantic relationships.

The literary convention of courtly love eventually found its way to sixteenth-century England through the influence of Italian love poetry. English writers imported the sonnets of the Italian poet Petrarch and began to popularize the form in their own country, composing verses that depicted women as divine, angelic creatures praised for their purity and virtue, and desired for their perfection. The male lover, as speaker, exalted the goodness of the beloved woman in exaggerated language and often expressed a fatalistic willingness to die for love, believing that love's perfection could only be achieved in death. Shakespeare was one of the most renowned sonnet-writers in Elizabethan England, but although he adopted the poetic form and literary conventions of courtly love, he also adapted them. Many of his sonnets were addressed to a man rather than a woman and expressed the love not of romance but of friendship. Even his sonnets about women explored many sides of love relationships rather than simply idealizing perfection.

While courtly love is not the dominant view of relationships in *Othello*, it is integrated into some of the characters' language and attitudes. Othello's exaggerated descriptions of Desdemona's fairness, beauty, and goodness, using imagery of jewels, roses, and "alabaster" skin, echo the courtly tradition. Similarly, his misguided sense that love might be perfected in death recalls courtly idealism, not only in the murder scene, but earlier, in the reunion at Cyprus when he says to Desdemona, "If it were now to die, / 'Twere now to be most happy" (2.1.187–188). Cassio's polite courtesy towards Desdemona mirrors gentlemanly courtly behavior, whereas Roderigo's pursuit of her and his declared intention of drowning himself for love is a parody or mockery of the courtly convention because it appears so foolish and self-centered beside the passionate, mutual love of Othello and Desdemona. Shakespeare incorporates and explores these different aspects of the literary tradition without allowing tradition to dominate representations of love in the play.

The Formal Debate about Women

Because the courtly view of women was so overstated, unattainable, and unrealistic, its expression in the love sonnets perhaps encouraged an opposite perspective that articulated the degradation and hatred of women. Like the courtly ideal, these negative attitudes seemed to develop within a literary convention, not as poetry but as part of an intellectual debate conducted in printed pamphlets and engaged in a controversy about women by attacking or defending their gender in a formal, often satirical style. Some sixteenth-century scholars, for example, argued in favor of women

in one written discussion and against women in another, suggesting that their viewpoints were not necessarily personal opinions
but exercises meant to refine debating skills (Woodbridge 5). This
does not mean, however, that genuine expressions of misogyny or
hatred against women in Shakespeare's time did not exist, that
some women were not exploited or abused, or that others were
not assertive in voicing or demonstrating their strength and independence. Instead, the formal printed controversy indicates a conventional or stylized language for speaking about the position and
rights of women, just as there was a poetic courtly convention that
idealized and romanticized women.

   In *Othello*, some of the views articulated by Iago and Emilia
reflect the opposing attitudes about men and women that were
presented in the attacks and defenses of literary debates. Within
the play, however, the two characters do not necessarily argue simply for argument's sake. When Desdemona and Iago engage in a
witty exchange about the praise of women while waiting for news
of Othello's arrival in Cyprus in 2.1, their word game appears to
follow a conventional debating style. And yet many of Iago's remarks about women and his schemes against them throughout the
play seem genuinely hateful and destructive, while Emilia's comments and questions about men's motives, their jealousy, and their
abuse of women challenge the audience to see *Othello*'s male and
female characters in a thoroughly unconventional and deeply personal light. Shakespeare appeared willing and able to draw on the
literary traditions of formal debate, as well as romantic poetry, in
order to explore the complexity of love by including hostile and
ideal positions while raising questions about both.

MARRIAGE LAWS AND CUSTOMS

   Examining marriage laws and customs practiced in Shakespeare's England can also help to broaden our understanding of
the dynamics between men and women in *Othello*. Almost every
age, viewed through the lens of history, reveals elements of transition and change as widely-accepted, dominant values and beliefs
are subject to resistance, criticism, and challenges from dissenting
voices within society. Certainly, this observation appears to be
true of gender roles and expectations in sixteenth- and early
seventeenth-century England. Monarchy and patriarchy formed the

main political and social power structures and marriage provided the cornerstone of continuity for each. But within the boundaries of that social system, there were conflicting perspectives about the secular and sacred definitions of marriage, about the balance of individual rights and family expectations in arranging marriages, and about the duties and privileges of husbands and wives.

Patriarchy and Queen Elizabeth

In England's patriarchal system, men were granted supreme authority in politics, community, and family. This male-dominated hierarchy was part of a larger belief system known as the "chain of being," which saw God at the top, moving downward in succession to angels, people, animals, and plants. This official view of "natural" supremacy encouraged a set of parallel patterns that strengthened arguments for a patriarchal society. Just as God was Lord of all and Christ was head of the church, so were kings considered heads of state and fathers heads of households. Inheritances passed from father to son and the crown passed from king to prince. The family was seen as a miniature commonwealth mirroring the larger commonwealth or state of England, which, in turn, reflected a God-created universe. It is easy to see that in such a system, women played a necessary but secondary role, subject to their fathers, their husbands, their king, and their God.

Political history in the sixteenth century reveals the prominence of these patriarchal beliefs, but, at the same time, exposes the compromises and contradictions that both established and unsettled peace and order. During Henry VIII's reign (1509–1547), political unrest revolved around his desire for a divorce, his succession of six wives, and his break from the Roman Catholic Church to establish his own authority over the Protestant Church of England. As part of the Reformation, these revolutionary decisions stemmed from Henry's difficulty in producing a male heir to the throne who would satisfy the needs of patriarchy and monarchy. Edward, the only male heir, born to Henry's third wife, died as a young king. Edward VI's short kingship was followed by the stormy reign of his half-sister, known for her reputation as Bloody Mary, and then by the long, relatively peaceful government of his other half-sister, Queen Elizabeth I who reigned from 1558 to 1603.

Elizabeth's successful political leadership raised many questions

about the patriarchal system and its function in marriage and the
state. Although she identified herself in masculine terms as
"prince" of England, her position as a queen rather than a king
commanding obedience from her subjects contradicted the male-
dominated assumptions of hierarchy and order. Yet because she
was made head of state and governed with political wisdom, she
received the authority granted to her royal position. Early in her
reign, however, her advisors and subjects were determined to see
her married to an appropriate husband, partly because of the perceived need for an heir to continue the monarchy's political stability after her death and partly because of the traditional view that
women ought to be wives.

Elizabeth, however, resisted this move, recognizing the inconsistencies and dangers it posed. In marriage she would be considered
subject to her husband at the same time that she was queen or
"prince" over England. Refusing to compromise her political power
in this way, she declared herself to be married to the state and
simultaneously encouraged her subjects to view her as the Virgin
Queen. This contradictory language of marriage and virginity and
of male and female identity defined her public role until her death
in 1603. Although Shakespeare likely wrote *Othello* in 1604 at the
beginning of King James's rule, he was more familiar with Elizabeth's long reign. And that was a period when the most prominent
and powerful figure in the country challenged patriarchy's assumptions about gender, marriage, and authority while providing
dramatists with an unconventional model of female assertiveness.

Courtship and Union

Within this context of tension between the ideals of patriarchy
and the reality of a female head of state, other discrepancies and
conflicts existed between customs and laws about courtship and
marriage. These are more directly relevant to the love plot in *Othello*. The two issues of individual choice and parental consent that
stir up controversy about Othello's secret marriage to Desdemona
in Act 1 reflect friction between legal and traditional expectations
which Renaissance England inherited from its past and which was
not easily resolved in the unrest of Reformation politics.

One the one hand, the earlier medieval secular view of marriage
as an economic, social contract emphasized the parents' role in

arranging a match for their children and establishing positive financial conditions. One the other hand, the church, with its increasing influence prior to the Reformation, stressed the binding sacred power of two individuals consenting to a holy union before God without the need for parental influence. After Henry VIII broke away from the Roman Catholic Church and established the Protestant Church of England, conflicting secular and sacred views of marriage continued to coexist. Church or "canon" law remained the final arbiter and all that it required legally to make a marriage was the verbal pledge of a man and a woman to each other before witnesses, including the traditional words, "I do." Families, however, maintained a social, if not a legal, influence in directing their children's choices, and even the church firmly advised children to honor and obey their fathers and mothers.

Parental guidance was strongest in upper classes because the economic, social, and political outcome of a marriage was much more significant for people with rank and status. The tradition of parental consent was also stronger for daughters than for sons because in a patriarchal system, daughters were traditionally recognized as property, making their care and welfare dependent on their husbands' position. Into this mixture of laws and customs, of individual choice and family consent, there was a growing perception that marriage not only could have—but should have—love rather than economic or social gain as its most powerful binding force. Consequently, even when family guidance and approval were recognized and practiced, the feelings of the couple began to be a more important and respected pre-marital consideration.

How does a secret romantic marriage such as Othello and Desdemona's reflect or challenge this social context? It is important to remember that Shakespeare is dramatizing fiction rather than fact. Furthermore, he portrays a Venetian rather than an English marriage. Evidence also indicates both that Venetian daughters and wives had far less freedom than their English counterparts and that Venetian women had a reputation for cunning and deception. (See Chapter 2 on "Race and Religion," especially excerpted quotations from *Coryat's Crudities*.) However, English background also provides a way to explore *Othello*'s domestic conflict because Shakespeare and his audience would have shared an awareness of common practices and assumptions about courtship and marriage. Brabantio's outrage in Act 1 arises not only from his sense that

Desdemona's match is socially unsatisfactory for an aristocratic gentlewoman but also from his view that his fatherly duties and rights have been denied and that his daughter has betrayed him. Traditional patriarchal terms of male authority support his complaint. Iago further articulates this perception of Desdemona's offense by admonishing Brabantio, "Zounds, sir, y'are robbed! For shame" (1.1.83).

Nevertheless, when Othello and Desdemona independently testify to their mutual pledge of consent, the Duke and Senators acknowledge the validity of their marriage. Even Brabantio recognizes he has no recourse because the legally binding power of the marriage oath is greater than the tradition of parental consent or disapproval. Desdemona seems to acknowledge the patriarchal expectations of her gender by speaking respectfully of her divided obedience to father and husband. Yet her own assertiveness in the courtship, the secrecy of her marriage, and the choice of her mate all undermine the very traditions she claims to accept, suggesting unconventional female independence, albeit not an illegal union of husband and wife. Othello and Desdemona's eloquence about their love and the Duke and Senators' sympathy toward it tend to encourage the audience to favor the marriage and perhaps even judge Brabantio's cause as selfish, narrow-minded, and overly possessive. Still, his warning casts an ominous shadow over the unorthodox beginning of Othello and Desdemona's relationship as he says, "Look to her, Moor, if thou hast eyes to see: / She has deceived her father, and may thee" (1.3.287–288). Although the clash of values in Act 1 resolves temporarily in the face of public military demands, seeds of division have already been sown. And Iago is ready with his garden imagery (1.3.314–328) to reap whatever harvest of disasters he can from a secret marriage union initiated by passionate, romantic love and subject to societal reproach.

Husbands and Wives

In Shakespeare's England roles of husbands and wives were often addressed in sermons and domestic conduct books that expressed idealistic expectations and practical guidelines for marriage. These popular views invite attention in considering the two married couples in *Othello*, as well as the unmarried liaison between Cassio and Bianca. Within the male-dominated hierarchy of English patriarchy, not only were husbands traditionally granted supreme authority over their wives, but women were also regarded as the weaker sex, physically and morally. Both members of the marriage were expected to fulfil certain duties and responsibilities. The husbands' duties were primarily active and public, involving work outside the home and provision for the family's material needs. In contrast, the wives' responsibilities were more passive and private, including complete obedience to their husbands, as well as bearing and raising children and tending to domestic tasks. Once a woman became married, she surrendered all legal rights and property to her husband who assumed the control previously exercised by her father.

No doubt, because men were the chief authors of sermons and conduct books articulating these standards and because patriarchy depended on male supremacy, marriage texts often gave more attention to women's roles than to men's. A woman's virginity was considered her greatest virtue before marriage. After marriage her greatest virtue was her fidelity. She was repeatedly reminded to be silent and submissive. Conduct books and formal debates warned against women being too outspoken and becoming nagging "shrews," while the public harshly condemned adulterous wives, loose women, and unwed mothers. In contrast, a man's adultery was not judged with the same severity and a husband's honor depended more on his wife's faithfulness than his own. To be a "cuckold," that is, a man whose wife has cheated on him, was considered a source of intense shame and humiliation for the husband and an indication of his inability to exercise manly authority. These opposing sexual expectations of husbands and wives presented a double standard that some male writers even in Shakespeare's time began to acknowledge as discriminatory. And yet many others continued to uphold traditional sexual categories as part of the ideal and necessary model of gender relationships.

In fact, against traditional sixteenth-century views of spousal duties, virtues, and indiscretions, opposing perspectives began to emerge with the religious and political changes following the Reformation and during the "renaissance" or humanist revival with which it coincided. Historically, the pre-Reformation church viewed marriage as less admirable than a single celibate life but necessary for procreation and advisable to avoid the temptation of unlawful sexual relations. After the Reformation, leaders within the newly established Protestant church began to stress the dignity of marriage. A view of marriage that acknowledged the companionship or partnership of the relationship became more popular. The Puritans, a group within the Protestant church, even encouraged private morality and spiritual equality between husbands and wives. Simultaneously, the secular humanism of the Renaissance promoted individualism, recognizing, to a limited degree, the values of freedom and education for women as well as for men. Consequently, although the male hierarchy remained largely intact, women had a greater possibility of self-expression and self-assertion. Nevertheless, traditional assumptions of domestic hierarchy were not simply replaced by growing expressions of individualism and spiritual equality.

These inconsistent historical views of husbands and wives gave Shakespeare scope to explore the nature of male and female relationships in *Othello*. Two of the most fruitful questions to consider are to what extent Shakespeare's play reflects traditional patriarchal attitudes toward marriage and to what extent it challenges them. These questions require an examination of the domestic authority demonstrated by Othello and Iago; the submission demonstrated by Desdemona and Emilia; the companionship and personal independence reflected in both marriages; and the jealousy, suspected adultery, and sexual promiscuity that also involve the liaison between Cassio and Bianca. Woven into these many layers of relationships is the overriding question, "How do you love?" which each character answers with words and deeds that do not always correspond.

The poems and excerpted documents that comprise the remainder of this chapter help to draw connections between the literary conventions and social history of the English Renaissance and *Othello*'s dramatization of tragic love and jealousy. Spelling has been regularized and modernized throughout.

SHAKESPEAREAN LOVE POETRY

A sonnet is a fourteen-line poem with a fixed rhythm and rhyme scheme, typically addressing the topic of love. In the 1590s Shakespeare wrote 154 sonnets that adopted and experimented with the conventions of courtly love. He even included a sonnet in *Romeo and Juliet* (1595–1596), his love tragedy that preceded *Othello*. Shakespeare organized his sonnets into three four-line sections followed by a couplet (two rhymed lines) that often summarized or reversed the position presented in the previous twelve lines. This poetic structure contributes to the logical development and meaning of each sonnet as it addresses some aspect or view of love.

Of the two sonnets included below, 116 likely expresses one man's "love" or friendship for another man, while 138 obviously expresses the romantic love of a man for a woman in especially domestic terms. Both, however, use images to articulate a view of love that encourages comparisons with the relationship between Othello and Desdemona. Consider what Sonnet 116 says about love's constancy in the face of time, change, or "alteration." How does this argument for the "marriage of true minds" compare with the development of Othello and Desdemona's romantic love and the tragic conclusion of their marriage? In Sonnet 138, pay attention to what the speaker says about truth and lies and youth and age, and whether the poem reflects or challenges the behavior born of love between the main couple in *Othello*. Do these sonnets express the idealism or realism of love?

FROM WILLIAM SHAKESPEARE, SONNETS 116 AND 138
(c. 1590s)
(*The Riverside Shakespeare*, Ed. G. Blakemore Evans et al.,
Boston: Houghton, 1974)

SONNET 116

Let me not to the marriage of true minds
Admit impediments; love is not love
Which alters when it alteration finds,
Or bends with the remover to remove.
O no, it is an ever-fixed mark

That looks on tempests and is never shaken:
It is the star to every wand'ring bark,
Whose worth's unknown, although his highth be taken.
Love's not Time's fool, though rosy lips and cheeks
Within his bending sickle's compass come,
Love alters not with his brief hours and weeks,
But bears it out even to the edge of doom.
   If this be error and upon me proved,
     I never writ, nor no man ever loved. (1770)

SONNET 138

When my love swears that she is made of truth,
I do believe her, though I know she lies,
That she might think me some untutor'd youth,
Unlearned in the world's false subtilties.
Thus vainly thinking that she thinks me young,
Although she knows my days are past the best,
Simply I credit her false-speaking tongue;
On both sides thus is simple truth suppress'd.
But wherefore says she not she is unjust?
And wherefore say not I that I am old?
O, love's best habit is in seeming trust,
And age in love loves not t'have years told.
   Therefore I lie with her, and she with me,
     And in our faults by lies we flattered be. (1774)

A RENAISSANCE WOMAN'S VIEW OF MEN AND LOVE

Appearing within the formal debate about women that began long before Shakespeare wrote *Othello* and continued for years afterwards, the following document is a defense of women and simultaneously an attack against certain behaviors of men. Written by a woman identified as Jane Anger and addressed specifically to women readers, the text criticizes the abuses of false male lovers and often employs the metaphor of excessive appetite to describe how a man greedily seeks a woman's favor but easily tires of "the diet" she offers. Emilia's remark, "They are all but stomachs, and we all but food" (3.4.104), echoes the sentiments expressed in Anger's essay. As you read the excerpted passages below, consider the tone of Anger's writing and try to determine whether her arguments are fair-minded or one-sided. Apart from the food metaphor, do other comments recall the words of women or the behavior of the men in *Othello*?

FROM JANE ANGER, *JANE ANGER HER PROTECTION FOR WOMEN. TO DEFEND THEM AGAINST THE SCANDALOUS REPORTS OF A LATE SURFEITING LOVER, AND ALL THE OTHER VENERIANS THAT COMPLAIN SO TO BE OVER CLOYED WITH WOMEN'S KINDNESS*
(London, 1589. STC 644)

Our good toward [men] is the destruction of ourselves, we being well formed, are by them foully deformed: of our true meaning they make mocks, rewarding our loving follies with disdainful flouts: we are the grief of man, in that we take all the grief from man . . . [men's] stomachs [are] so queasy, as do they taste but twice of one dish they straight surfeit, and needs must a new diet be provided for them. We are contrary to men, because they are contrary to that which is good: because they are so purblind, they cannot see into our natures, and we too well (though we have but half an eye) into their conditions because they are so bad. . . . (Sig. B3)

. . . . If women breed woe to men, they bring care, poverty, grief, and continual fear to women, which if they be not woes they are worser.

. . . . There are men which are snout-fair, whose faces look like a cream-pot, and yet those not the fair men I speak of, but I mean those whose conditions are free from knavery, and I term those foul, that have neither civility nor honesty: of these sorts there are none good, none rich or fair long. . . . What shall I say? Wealth makes them lavish, wit knavish, beauty effeminate, poverty deceitful, and deformity ugly. Therefore of me take this counsel

> Esteem of men as of a broken Reed,
> Mistrust them still, and then you well shall speed. (Sig. B4)

. . . . I would that ancient writers would as well have busied their heads about deciphering the deceits of their own Sex, as they have about setting down our follies: and I would some would call in question that now, which hath ever been questionless: but [since] all their wits have been bent to write of the contrary, I leave them to a contrary vain, and the surfeiting Lover, who returns to his discourse of love. (Sig. C)

I have set down unto you (which are of mine own Sex) the subtle dealings of untrue meaning men: not that you should condemn all men, but to the end that you may take heed of the false hearts of all & still reprove the flattery which remains in all. . . . As men are valiant, so are they virtuous: and those that are born honorably, cannot bear horrible dissembling hearts. But as there are some which cannot love heartly, so there are many who lust incessantly, & as many of them will deserve well, so most care not how ill they speed so they may get our company. (Sig. C4)

THE CONSENT AND CONTRACT OF MARRIAGE

John Dod and Robert Cleaver's *A Godly Form of Household Government* (1598) is one of many handbooks on marriage written in England in the sixteenth and seventeenth centuries. The excerpts included below specifically address the terms of the marriage contract, outlining what constitutes a legitimate marriage and what potential miseries and dangers might result from a hasty or secret marital contract. Note the importance of mutual, voluntary consent between the engaged couple, as well as the rights and limitations of parents in approving or dissolving their children's marriages. As you read Dod and Cleaver's advice and explanations, consider the shocking disclosure of Othello and Desdemona's marriage in Act 1 and the various responses to it, especially Brabantio's.

FROM JOHN DOD AND ROBERT CLEAVER, *A GODLY FORM OF HOUSEHOLD GOVERNMENT: FOR THE ORDERING OF PRIVATE FAMILIES, ACCORDING TO THE DIRECTION OF GOD'S WORD* (London: 1598. STC 5383)

A Contract, is a voluntary promise of marriage, mutually made between one man and one woman, both being meet and free to marry one another, and therefore allowed so to do by their Parents.
. . . . [W]e call this promise of marriage, voluntary, because it must not come from the lips alone, but from the well-liking and consent of the heart: for if it be only a verbal promise, without any will at all, (and so mere hypocritical and dissembled) though it bindeth the party that promiseth, to the performance of his promise, made before God and man: yet if the Parents afterwards shall certainly know this, and that there was no will, nor unfeigned meaning at all in the party, neither yet is, but rather a loathing and abhorring of his spouse betrothed, though he be not able to render just and sufficient cause thereof, they may upon this occasion, either defer the day of marriage the longer, to see if God will happily change the mind of the party, or utterly break and frustrate the promise. . . . Wherefore this promise must be in this respect, at least, willing, and voluntary. For . . . if it be voluntary and unfeigned, it is enough, and fully sufficient, to make a true contract in the Lord. . . . Secondly, we call it voluntary, in respect of constraint and compulsion, contrary to a free

consent: for if either party be urged, constrained, or compelled, by great fear of their Parents, or others, by threatening of loss or preferment, of health, of limb, of life, or of any such other like, or by any other violent manner of dealing whatsoever, to yield their promise clean contrary to the motion of good liking of their hearts. This kind of promise, as it doth not bind the party to keep it: so it ought to be frustrated and broken by the Parents themselves, or by such masters as may and ought, to command and rule them in such cases. (116–121)

But if [a marriage contract] be mutual, then it doth mutually and inviolably bind both: so that in this regard, neither Parent, Magistrate, nor any other, can or ought to break it. For this being fully performed and accomplished, is one principal cause of making two one flesh. (123)

. . . [I]t is a calamity infernal . . . to be in company with those that a man would not be withall, and yet cannot be separated nor depart from them. Hereof cometh, as we do see in some marriages, so great ruins, so wicked and vile deed, as maims, & murders committed by such desperate persons, as are loath to keep, and yet cannot lawfully refuse, nor leave them: Therefore young folks ought not to be too rash and hasty in their choice, but to have the good advice and direction of their parents and trusty friends in this behalf, who have better judgment, and are more free from the motions of all affections, than they are. And they must take heed, lest following the light and corrupt judgment of their own affections and minds, they change not a short delectation and pleasure, into a continual sorrow and repentance. For we do learn, by great and continual use and experience of things, that the secret contracts made between those that be young do seldom prosper, whereas contrariwise, those marriages that are made and established by the advice of wise and religious parents, do prosper well. (151–152)

THE DUTIES AND RESPONSIBILITIES OF MARRIAGE

Edmund Tilney's *A brief and pleasant discourse of duties in Marriage, called the Flower of Friendship* was a popular conduct book on marriage, published in at least seven editions in England between 1568 and 1587. Tilney organizes his book in the form of a dialogue or conversation involving several male and female characters, some of whom represent prominent historical figures in the sixteenth century, such as Erasmus, the influential humanist thinker. Within the general debate about marriage, the first half of the narrative addresses a husband's specific virtues and responsibilities, while the second half considers a wife's parallel virtues and duties. Although the main argument stresses conventional Elizabethan values, characters occasionally disagree with one another, raising questions about accepted ideals of marital harmony. Consequently, the discussion includes seemingly incompatible references, such as the equality or friendship of spouses and the authority of the husband, or the importance of honesty and the value of pretending or dissembling.

The following selections have been chosen for their potential relevance to the diverse attitudes and behaviors toward marriage as dramatized in *Othello*. The excerpts [1] define what constitutes marital equality, [2] describe the husband's duties in relation to his wife's, [3] warn against the dangers of jealousy, [4] provide reasons supporting the husband's domestic authority, and [5] explain the duty of wifely obedience even when a woman is unjustly treated by her husband. Consider the extent to which Othello and Desdemona and Iago and Emilia accept and represent these ideals, and what consequences follow when they do or do not comply.

FROM EDMUND TILNEY, *A BRIEF AND PLEASANT DISCOURSE OF DUTIES IN MARRIAGE, CALLED THE FLOWER OF FRIENDSHIP*
(London: 1568. STC 24076)

[1] [T]he Lady *Julia* desireth to hear of our friendly *Flower*, whereto now I return, and say, that equality is principally to be considered in this

matrimonial amity, as well of years, as of the gifts of nature, and fortune.
For equalness herein, maketh friendliness. . . .

[2] The office of the husband is, to go abroad in matters for profit, of
the wife, to tarry at home, and see all be well there. The office of the
husband is, to provide money, of the wife, not wastefully to spend it.
The office of the husband is, to deal, and bargain with all men, of the
wife, to make or meddle with no man. The office of the husband is, to
give, of the wife, to keep. The office of the husband is to apparel him as
he can, of the wife, to go as she ought. The office of the husband is, to
be Lord of all, of the wife, to give account of all, and finally I say, that
the office of the husband is, to maintain well his livelihood, and the office
of the woman is, to govern well the household. And as the man may not
deny his wife things, that must be granted of necessity: so he ought not
grant her things of prodigality, and superfluous. For as great disorder is
it to grant the one, as to deny the other. . . .

[3] The eighth [virtue] is to be circumspect in matters that concern his
honesty, and not to be jealous of his wife. The Stoic philosophers say,
that jealousy is a certain care of man's mind, least another should possess
the thing, which he alone would enjoy. There is no greater torment, than
the vexation of a jealous mind, which, even as the moth fretteth the cloth,
doth consume the heart, that is vexed therewith. Two kind of persons
are commonly sore sick in this disease, either those that are evil themselves, or they, that in their youth have gone astray, supposing that as
other men's wives have done towards them, so will theirs do towards
others, which is vanity to think, more folly to suspect, and greatest foolishness to speak of. For as some lewd women be dissolute: so likewise
women there be, honest, and very circumspect. If the wife be to be suspected, let the man work as secretly, and closely, as he can to reprehend
her, yet all will not peradventure avail. For, trust me, no wisdom, no
craft, no science, no strength, no subtlety, yea, no patience suffiseth to
enforce a woman, to be true to her husband, if she otherwise determine.
Therefore to conclude to be jealous, either needeth not, or booteth
not. . . .

[4] Ye say well, Madam, quoth M. *Erasmus*. For indeed both divine, and
human laws, in our religion giveth the man absolute authority, over the
woman in all places. And, quoth the Lady *Julia*, as I said before, reason
doth confirm the same, the man being as he is, most apt for the sovereign
being in government, not only skill, and experience to be required, but
also capacity to comprehend, wisdom to understand, strength to execute,
solicitude to prosecute, patience to suffer, means to sustain, and above
all a great courage to accomplish, all which are commonly in a man, but

in a woman very rare: Then what blame deserve those men, that do permit their wives to rule all, and suffer themselves to be commanded for company. . . .

[5] For this married woman, whom I have taken upon me to describe, must of duty be unto her husband in all things obedient, and therefore if he, sometimes moved, do chance to chide her, she must forebear. In doing whereof he shall neither eat the more at his dinner, nor she have the less appetite to her supper. This wise woman must consider, that her husband chideth, either without reason, or hath good cause. If reason move him, then of duty she is bound to obey, if otherwise, it is her part to dissemble the matter. For in nothing can a wife show a greater wisdom, than in dissembling with an importunate husband. Her honesty, her good nature, and her praise is showed in nothing more, than in tolerating of an undiscreet man, and to conclude, as the woman ought not to command the man, but to be always obedient: so ought he not to suffer himself to be commanded of his wife.

QUESTIONS FOR WRITTEN AND ORAL DISCUSSION

1. Shakespeare's Sonnet 116 uses a series of images to describe what love is and what it is not. Identify the metaphors in the first twelve lines and explain how they help to construct the poem's definition of love. Then paraphrase the negative and positive aspects of love. What is the relationship between love and time?

   Having reflected on the poem, consider whether or not the love between Othello and Desdemona is a "marriage of true minds." What evidence in the play supports your position? If there appears to be contradictory evidence, how can you explain the inconsistencies?

2. In Sonnet 138, what connections does the speaker make between the opposites of truth and false-speaking and of youth and age in a relationship of love? If there is some value in "seeming trust," what is it? Do vanity and flattery have a place in love, and, if so, how or why? Does this poem reflect a realistic or idealistic expression of love and relationships? Explain.

   Consider how this sonnet illuminates Othello and Desdemona's relationship. What parallels exist between their love and the love described in the poem? What is the importance of age? Does Othello or Desdemona ever speak falsely to the other for love's sake? If so, is the result positive or negative? Does the sonnet invite you to make any connections with Iago and Emilia's relationship? Is "false-speaking" different in their relationship than in Othello and Desdemona's? Explain why or why not.

3. Pretend you are the speaker in either Sonnet 116 *or* 138, and write a letter of advice, encouragement, warning, or disapproval to Othello *or* Desdemona at a specific point in the play where you have observed the couple's behavior to each other and feel the need to respond. Are you concerned about their love or impressed by it?

4. Review the information about the courtly tradition and the debate about women included in this chapter. The first idealizes love and the second occasionally voices the faults and abuses of love. Draw on these conventions to discuss the degree of idealism or realism in Desdemona and Othello's relationship. Is their love romantic or practical or both? Does one partner have more idealistic or realistic expectations than the other? What is the difference between a fault and an abuse in their relationship? Provide examples. Discuss what you think it means to "love not wisely, but too well" and how this phrase might characterize either Othello or Desdemona or both.

5. In an essay, compare Othello and Desdemona's marriage with Iago and Emilia's, drawing on information about conventions and traditions included in this chapter.

6. Describe the tone of Jane Anger's *Protection for Women*. Do her arguments seem fair or biased? Explain why. Do you find her views of men and women surprising and unusual for the sixteenth century? In your answer, refer to evidence in this chapter and in *Othello*.

7. How does Jane Anger define a fair man as opposed to a foul man? Perhaps try paraphrasing her position in your own words. Comments about "fairness" also appear frequently in *Othello*, in contrast to blackness, ugliness, or meanness. Using evidence from the play, draw conclusions about how its characters define fairness. Is it more often associated with women than men, or not? Do the qualities that constitute a fair man differ from those that define a fair woman? For Jane Anger, "wealth," "wit," and "beauty" do not necessarily make a foul man fair. Can you think of men in *Othello* who share these attributes? Are they fair or foul according to Anger's definition?

    Write an essay exploring the topic of "fairness" in *Othello* from one of the following angles:

    a) relate it to views expressed in the formal debate about woman or the courtly love tradition;

    b) compare it to "foulness" in the play;

    c) consider whether it sets up differences between men and women in the play;

    d) examine how expectations about it contribute to the play's tragedy.

8. Compose and optionally perform a dialogue about women between Jane Anger and Iago. Refer to specific passages in Anger's essay and in *Othello* as you prepare your exchange, but also use your imagination to develop the dynamics of the relationship between the two "characters." How, for example, will the dialogue differ from or compare to the exchange between Desdemona and Iago in 2.1.108–162?

9. According to John Dod and Robert Cleaver's *A Godly Form of Household Government*, what are the main conditions that make a marriage contract legal and binding? Under what circumstances might a promise of marriage not be binding? And if it were not binding, what actions could the parents take to end or overturn it? How are the main conditions and expectations that Dod and Cleaver describe in a marriage contract enacted or challenged in Othello and Desdemona's marriage and responses to it?

10. Consider Dod and Cleaver's warning against a hasty or secret marriage and the dangers of such a match. How does this position invite you to view the marriage between Desdemona and Othello? Are you more sympathetic to Shakespeare's couple as lovers or to Dod and Cleaver's role as a marriage advisors? Dramatize a meeting between

Dod, Cleaver, and Brabantio after Othello and Desdemona have left for Cyprus. Recalling Gratiano's comment in 5.2 about the grief that leads to Brabantio's death, determine how the three men will discuss the distresses of children who marry against their parents' wishes. Is Brabantio sympathetic? Are the other two men moralistic or compassionate in their responses?

11. According to Edmund Tilney, what are the qualities that create "friendliness" or equality in a marriage? Are these qualities part of Othello and Desdemona's marriage? If so, provide evidence. If not, does their marriage suggest a different definition of equality, or is it entirely unbalanced? Explain your position.

12. Consider how Tilney's list of the duties of husbands and wives reflects the patriarchal system in Renaissance England. Does his balance between male and female roles suggest equality and companionship or a hierarchy based on male dominance and female submission or aspects of both? Explain your position.

13. What reasons does Tilney's Lady Julia offer for a man's authority over a woman? Although her argument may seem offensive from a modern perspective, consider how it compares to the contemporary dramatization of male and female relationships in *Othello*. Do the qualities of courage, patience, strength, or wisdom appear more obvious in Shakespeare's men or women, or are the virtues simply not gender-specific? What happens in the play when men exercise authority over women or when women assert independence? Write a formal paper addressing some of these issues by answering the following question: "Is Shakespeare's portrayal of relationships between men and women in *Othello* traditional or unconventional?"

14. The conversation between Emilia and Desdemona in 4.3 is one of the most intimate scenes in the play. Discuss what their opinions about men and women suggest about their own characters, as well as how their dialogue reflects the behavior of men and women throughout the play.

15. Discuss the three female perspectives that Desdemona, Emilia, and Bianca offer to the play's exploration of love and marriage. Why do you suppose Shakespeare includes Bianca at all? What do the women say about men in general or their mates in particular, and how do the women act in their own relationships? Are their words and actions consistent? If so, explain how. If not, consider how their inconsistencies affect your view of them as sympathetic characters.

16. Discuss the views of Othello, Iago, and Cassio about love and/or marriage, considering what they say and how they act. Do the attitudes of one character affect your sympathies towards another? Debate in

an essay or in small groups one of the following questions: Is Cassio a gentleman or a womanizer? Is Othello a victim or a victimizer? Is Iago a wife-abuser or (prior to murdering Emilia) merely a traditional patriarchal husband?

17. Tilney [3] warns against a husband's jealousy and [5] counsels in favor of a wife's obedience. In his view, why should a man not be jealous and a woman be obedient? Consider Othello's and Desdemona's behavior in light of Tilney's advice. Compose a dialogue between one of Tilney's characters and Othello *or* Desdemona. Choose an earlier or later section of the play as a basis for your conversation, or create a split dialogue that reflects Othello's *or* Desdemona's position near the beginning and end of the play. Will your portrayal of the quality of Othello's jealousy or the degree of Desdemona's obedience reflect their wisdom or their foolishness, their sympathy or their tragedy, their traditional attitudes or their strong individualism? Is tragedy inevitable because of their values and expectations?

SUGGESTED READINGS

Colie, Rosalie L. *Shakespeare's Living Art*. Princeton: Princeton University Press, 1974.

Dreher, Diane Elizabeth. *Domination and Defiance: Fathers and Daughters in Shakespeare*. Lexington: University of Kentucky Press, 1986. See especially Chapter 2, "The Renaissance Background."

Lewis, C. S. *The Allegory of Love: A Study in Medieval Tradition*. Oxford: Oxford University Press, 1936. See Chapter 1 on courtly love. (Out of print.)

Macfarlane, Alan. *Marriage and Love in England: Modes of Reproduction, 1300–1840*. Oxford: Basil Blackwell, 1986. See especially Part III.

Rose, Mary Beth. *The Expense of Spirit: Love and Sexuality in English Renaissance Drama*. Ithaca: Cornell University Press, 1988.

Stone, Lawrence. *The Family, Sex, and Marriage in England, 1500–1800*. New York: Harper and Row, 1977.

Valency, Maurice. *In Praise of Love: An Introduction to the Love-Poetry of the Renaissance*. New York: Octagon Books, 1975.

Wayne, Valerie, ed. Introduction. *The Flower of Friendship: A Renaissance Dialogue Contesting Marriage*, by Edmund Tilney. Ithaca: Cornell University Press, 1992. 1–94.

Woodbridge, Linda. *Women and the English Renaissance: Literature and the Nature of Womankind, 1540–1620*. Urbana: University of Illinois Press, 1984.

Wrightson, Keith. *English Society, 1580–1680*. London: Hutchinson, 1982. See especially Chapters 3 and 4.

4

Historical Context: War and the Military

War appears to be a less prominent topic than love in *Othello*. Although the threat of war with the Turks provides an atmosphere of anxiety and unrest and Cyprus is identified as "this warlike isle" (2.3.55), the plot gradually moves inward to Othello's tortured mind where jealousy turns order into chaos and love's harmony into the discord of violence and murder. It would be an oversight, however, not to recognize how the warlike setting and accompanying military values and expectations contribute to the central discord in the play. While the backdrop of war provides an ominous setting for romantic passion, Othello's public life based on military codes of conduct imposes an obvious source of tension with the private intimacy of his new marriage. Not only does the public mood of impending crisis affect personal bonds of love and friendship, but the soldier's world also emphasizes masculine behavior and relationships in a way that threatens to undervalue women and create divisions along gender lines. Furthermore, the military hierarchy of officers influences Iago's, Cassio's, and Othello's perceptions of themselves, their motives for action, their attitudes toward each other, and their reasons for trust or distrust. Warfare consequently serves as much more than an unsettling backdrop for love. It becomes integrated into the many conflicts and sacrifices that turn Othello and Desdemona's marriage into an overwhelming tragedy.

"What is your occupation?"—a question raised by this chapter's topic of war and the military in *Othello*—is closely related to questions addressed in the two previous chapters, "Who are you?" and "How do you love?" A sense of "place" in the play comes not only from physical setting and ethnic or racial origin, but also from one's occupation, from the function and status of military office. At the beginning of the first scene, Iago expresses the competition built into this military society as he complains about Cassio's appointment as Othello's lieutenant, saying, "I know my price; I am worth no worse a place" (1.1.11). Who gets what place and why, who keeps and who loses his occupation forms an important thread in the play's unfolding plot. The impact of shifting occupations says much about the relationship between characters' public and private selves, the difficulty of connecting the two, and the dire consequences of confusing them. When Othello begins to believe Iago's lies about Desdemona's infidelity, he concludes with a somewhat surprising lament: "Farewell! Othello's occupation's gone!" (3.3.354). Identifying his military occupation with his marriage seems undeniable and indisputable to Othello because his success as a soldier and as a husband both affect his male image and perception of his own authority. For Othello, the answer to the question "How to you love?" is, therefore, strongly influenced by the parallel question, "What is your occupation?"

The role of occupation, the importance of public responsibility and image, and the dynamics especially between male characters in *Othello* take on greater significance in light of relevant aspects of sixteenth-century military history. Exploring Shakespeare's attention to contemporary military codes and concerns can help us understand more clearly how the rank and status of office and the virtues and values of soldierly conduct are incorporated into a tragedy not simply about love but about the volatile interaction between love and war.

MERCENARIES AND "ARMCHAIR" SOLDIERS

In the sixteenth century, methods of warfare and military organization were in a state of transition. The development of gunpowder in the previous century changed how wars were fought.

Cannons and guns gradually began to replace long bows and swords, foot soldiers became more important than cavalry, and sieges became more common than battlefield combat. The size of armies grew and the rank and titles of soldiers underwent a period of instability as offices evolved with the size and improved organization of the military. These changes were happening all across Europe. Although England, as an isolated island, sometimes fell behind or drew apart from cultural or political influences on the Continent, it was actively involved in the European military revolution. England sent soldiers to fight in Continental wars and engaged in an ongoing written debate about military concerns that crossed national borders. Two issues arising during this time of change that bear relevance to *Othello*'s military context are the increased used of mercenary soldiers and the conflict between soldiers with battlefront experience and those with "armchair" theory or "bookish" knowledge.

Although armies grew as warfare evolved, permanent or "standing" armies had not yet become widely accepted or well-developed. England had no standing army during Elizabeth I's reign in the late sixteenth century and while some European nations began to recruit permanent soldiers and officers, none had an army large enough to wage war without further recruitment. It became common to increase troop strength by hiring mercenary soldiers for service from a foreign country. These soldiers were professionals paid for their skill rather than conscripted for their patriotism or national duty. The wealthier a nation or state, the more qualified mercenaries it could hire. As an unusually wealthy city-state, Venice could afford good mercenaries and had a reputation for doing so. (See the section on Venice in Chapter 2, especially excerpts from Gasper Contareno's *The Commonwealth and Government of Venice*.)

In *Othello*, the Moor and Cassio are foreign mercenaries, while Iago is a Venetian soldier. Much is made of Othello's military skill, his past experience, and his superior qualities as a leader: he is the obvious choice as general of the Venetian army and governor of Cyprus. His status as a professional soldier is important because it indicates that warfare and command indeed define his sole "occupation." The same is true for Cassio, although his rank and stature are not as great. That either of them should behave in ways that would threaten their livelihood or damage their public identity is devastating to them. Such behavior not only undermines their professionalism but suggests to those who have hired them for their skills that if they are not worth their place, they have little other merit or value. For Othello, this public measure of his worth is especially apparent because it appears that only his military title and usefulness excuse his otherwise undesirable marriage within the Venetian community.

Cassio's military position becomes for Iago the source of another common sixteenth-century subject, the debate about the authority of "armchair" or "bookish" soldiers. As artillery and siege warfare grew more complicated, tactics and strategies of war required much more theory. Scholars with knowledge of mathematics and geometry began writing manuals and treatises as guidebooks for battle, describing the best way to build fortifications, to break through them, and to arrange the most effective formations of armed foot soldiers. Sometimes these scholars also had battlefront experience; sometimes they did not. Iago's complaint against Cassio as "a great arithmetician . . . / That never set a squadron in the field, / Nor the division of a battle knows" (1.1.16–20) reflects part of this debate. Soldiers with years of field experience resented the advice of men who offered "Mere prattle without practice" (1.1.23), who knew little or nothing about the realities of war.

Historically, however, "bookish" soldiers provided necessary and valuable tactical information as warfare changed and there is little indication that their theory was less useful because they lacked experience as foot soldiers. Even within *Othello*, Iago's initial opinions appear to stand alone in attempting to discredit Cassio's qualifications. But as an introduction to the play, Iago's criticisms can hardly be dismissed as insignificant. They do perhaps suggest more about Iago's character than Cassio's, offering a motive or reason for resenting Cassio. Whether valid or not, such intense militant resentment would have caught the attention of Shakespeare's audience—an audience familiar with debates surrounding popular military conduct books, their authors, students, and critics but also sensitive to the hazards of emotional extremes.

RANK AND STATUS

The relationships between Othello, Cassio, and Iago draw attention to the rank and status of military officers and the effect their titles as soldiers has on their attitudes toward one another. Modern scholars have debated the extent of Shakespeare's military knowledge, pointing out apparent discrepancies in his use of titles and the division of martial duties in *Othello*. Othello, for example, is referred to as a soldier, a captain, a general, and a governor. While military titles were still not entirely stable at the beginning of the seventeenth century, the association between captain and general in *Othello* has raised a number of questions because these titles represent different levels of command. A captain was typically responsible for a company of soldiers; a general was in charge of the whole army. Sometimes one officer shared several titles, however, and any apparent discrepancies in *Othello* do not interfere with the overall sense of "place" or position that characterizes the male hierarchy within the play. In fact, the military chain of command in *Othello* focuses on three major roles: Othello as captain but chiefly as general, Cassio as lieutenant, and Iago as ensign or ancient.

The general was the army's superior officer with the greatest status and responsibilities. He made crucial decisions about strategies and tactics of war, as well as disciplining soldiers over whom he held supreme authority. He was accountable only to the government itself, which either appointed or hired him as their military leader, and retained him as long as he was needed or performed with appropriate influence and skill. In *Othello*, because the Moor's military duties take him to the garrison outpost of Cyprus, he also becomes the temporary governor or political ruler of that island. When the Turks are drowned at sea, his function shifts from fighting war to maintaining order within an unstable, warlike environment of social and moral chaos.

The lieutenant was second in command to the general or captain. This was a prestigious but also ambiguous position. The lieutenant was expected to take commands from the general and assist him in overseeing control and discipline among the ranks, but he was also considered general-in-waiting, ready to assume the general's position if or when the general was unavailable or removed from office. Thus, while trust was essential between the two officers, possible tension existed if the general had any reason to believe that his lieutenant had premature aspirations to take his place. This competitive element might add to Othello's outrage when he believes Desdemona has been unfaithful to him, not with anyone, but specifically with his own lieutenant. "Cuckold me!" Othello says of his wife, "With mine officer!" (4.1.202, 204). When public and private worlds merge, the military rank and place of Othello and Cassio affect their friendship, as well. Throughout the play, the words "office," "occupation," and "place" carry a potential double meaning, referring to both the military world and the private relationship of intimacy, privilege, or possession that a husband assumed with his wife.

The third officer, the ensign, whom the English often also referred to as the "ancient," was the army's sign bearer or standard-bearer. He was expected to carry the flag or standard into war as a sign of the army's identity as well as its honor. His rank clearly fell below the lieutenant, for the ensign was a common soldier elevated to a special position, while the lieutenant was a commissioned officer with the status of a gentleman. The ensign's role was significant, however, because he was perceived to be an important military representative, personally reflecting the reputation of the army as a whole. This was especially true of the general's personal ensign or standard-bearer because, while each company or band of soldiers within the army also had its own ensign, the general's ensign assumed a higher profile and more responsibility than did the others. As Othello's ancient or ensign, chosen for his "honesty" and courage, Iago is in a position of double influence because he has the trust of the army's leader and the respect of fellow soldiers. What he does not have is the prestige that belongs to the lieutenant which is one of his main grievances when the play begins. He sees himself as a soldier with added responsibility and even recognition but without the status he feels he deserves. Cassio simply reinforces this military hierarchy of place and privilege when he reminds Iago of their respective titles, saying—perhaps even in a mocking tone of superiority—"The lieutenant is to be saved before the ancient" (2.3.106–107).

In fact, Shakespeare appears to make the lieutenant's office the center of controversy in *Othello*'s military setting. Iago wants the title and complains first that Cassio—as an inexperienced "bookish" soldier—is ill-suited to the task and second that Othello has played favorites in appointing a good friend rather than a worthy candidate. Favoritism was a common military abuse addressed in conduct books and discussed on the streets in Shakespeare's time and so Iago is again touching on historical issues, raising a concern that might generate sympathy in the audience. Othello initially trusts his lieutenant but trusts his ensign more, perhaps not only because Iago has a reputation for plain-speaking and honesty but also because the Moor has more to fear from the power granted to his lieutenant as second in command. Cassio is accused from both above and below. Furthermore, he forsakes the main peace-keeping responsibilities of his office when provoked, thus turning his own military authority against himself. He is summarily dismissed or "cashiered." When Iago encourages him to regain his position and shows him how, Cassio's friendship with Othello and Desdemona ultimately heightens rather than decreases the uncertainty of his public "place" or office. The rank and status of all three male characters—as general, lieutenant, and ensign—play a significant part in the way they react to genuine and false accusations, in their resentment or assumption of superiority, and in their tendency to trust or distrust one another.

MILITARY VALUES AND VIRTUES

Military values and virtues represent a code of conduct different from civilian laws and customs, and these differences also influence the tragic direction of *Othello*'s plot. Again, changes in military standards and practices in the sixteenth century are reflected in the play. As a holdover from earlier medieval knighthood and warfare, the values of chivalry were still recognized and affirmed, including a strong code of honor, a belief in the glory and nobility of war, and the gentlemanly courtesy of warriors or soldiers towards women. Consequently, "reputation"—the value of a good name and the public image of honor and respect—were vital to military society. So, too, was pride in the courage and mastery of war. Idealized love for women also emerged from this chivalric tradition. (For more on this discussion of men and women, see the section on "Courtly Love" in Chapter 3.)

By contrast, sixteenth-century realities of military organization included, alongside mercenaries paid for service, a motley crew of recruits, many of them untrained, undisciplined, ill-paid men, often including vagabonds and thieves open to bribery, willing to defect, and suffering from poverty. In this context, one of the virtues most commonly stressed and addressed was not reputation, but discipline because no army could survive without order and many armies lacked appropriate discipline. Writers of Elizabethan and European conduct books returned to classical Roman and Greek history for examples of military discipline as models to correct deficiencies of training and order which they saw in undisciplined contemporary armies.

One virtue that brought together the value of reputation connected with medieval chivalry and the need for discipline emphasized in the Renaissance military was justice which, properly administered, rewarded honorable soldiers and punished, dismissed, or "cashiered" offenders. Military justice differed from civilian justice because the crisis mode of war stood in contrast to the more relaxed atmosphere of a well-governed society. On the one hand, military justice allowed for murder as necessary and even valiant on the battlefield, while the same violence would result in serious consequences in normal public life. On the other hand, military justice relied on a rigid chain of command and required absolute obedience to orders. Any quarreling between soldiers was subject to severe punishment because—unlike civilian life—the slightest unrest might disturb the entire chain of command, incite mutiny, and destroy the organization and purpose of the army itself.

These values or virtues—reputation, discipline, and justice—strongly influence the male characters' behavior in *Othello*. However, because public military lives in the play keep conflicting with private relationships of love or friendship, and because an old code of chivalry and honor runs contrary to the hard realities of disloyalty, deception, and personal gain, *Othello* does not simply dramatize the desirability of these military ideals. Instead, it exposes the dangers that can arise when ideals are misguided, misplaced, or misunderstood. The play explores what happens when "reputation" is based on mistaken "honesty" or lost because of false accusation. It considers what happens when the swift and inflexible "discipline" needed to maintain military order amongst soldiers is imposed on a personal relationship of love and based on unfounded jealousy. And it asks what happens when "justice" becomes an excuse for cruel revenge against innocent victims. Although *Othello* is most commonly recognized as a tragedy of love, the military context contributes much to the play's setting, characterization, and plot by emphasizing the rank and status of a male hierarchy and a war-oriented code of conduct. Together these two influences shape dramatic relationships and increase the level of suspicion or distrust between characters and between genders until it reaches disastrous proportions.

The remainder of this chapter includes excerpts from two military conduct books that outline general guidelines for Elizabethan soldiers and describe specific duties and expectations for the titled officers that also appear as characters in *Othello*. Spelling has been regularized and modernized throughout.

SOLDIERS, ENSIGNS, AND LIEUTENANTS

William Garrard's *The Art of War* was one of more than two hundred military tracts, pamphlets, and conduct books published in
England during Queen Elizabeth's reign (1558–1603). These books
addressed tactics and weaponry of war, as well as appropriate soldierly conduct. The excerpts below focus on three topics. The first
holds up as an example for Christian soldiers the Turkish army's
reputation for discipline and uses that illustration to introduce the
six common principles expected in the military. These principles
include hardiness and "secretness" along with the four cited below:
silence, obedience, sobriety, and truth and loyalty. Secondly, Garrard describes the character and responsibilities of a good ensign
(referred to also as the Alfierus), and thirdly, he records the duties
and qualities of a lieutenant. As you read each section, keep both
Iago and Cassio in mind, considering how they measure up to
Garrard's standards. You might also envision Othello as the captain
identified as the superior officer. What evidence is there to suggest
that armies did not always follow the ideal expectations set before
them? Look for specific references to disorder or corruption.

FROM WILLIAM GARRARD, *THE ART OF WAR*
(London: 1591. STC 11625)

[1] It is written in the history of Pietro Bizari, touching the incredible
and marvelous obedience of the Turkish soldiers, that a certain Gentleman at his return from Constantinople did declare unto the Earl of Salma,
that he had [seen] four miracles in the Turkish dominions: which was,
first an infinite army almost without number, consisting of more than
four hundred thousand men. Secondly, that amongst so many men, he
saw not one woman. Thirdly, that there was no mention made of wine.
And last, at night when they had cried with a high voice *Alla*, which is
God: there continued so great a silence through the whole camp, that
even in the Pavilions they did not speak but with a low soft voice, a thing
worthy to be admired, to the great shame of the confusion of Christians:
therefore if the infidels observe such strict discipline, why should not we
that be Christians endeavor ourselves to surpass them therein[?] . . . But
together with silence to set down certain other virtues, take them here
as I find them written.

• • •

OBEDIENCE.

Such obedience must be used, that none regard the persons but the office to them appointed, diligently observing the same: any offending to the contrary, runneth into the danger of the law, for longer than obedience is used and maintained, there is no hope of good success.

• • •

SOBRIETY.

In Sobriety consisteth great praise to the soldiers, who using the same are ever in state of preferment, such regard their duties, and reprove the rash busybodies. Drunkards, etc. are ever in danger of punishment.

• • •

TRUTH AND LOYALTY.

The virtue of loyalty and truth is far exceeding my capacity to write, the practices of the contrary, are not worthy of life, but to be soon adjudged. Subtle enemies approve to corrupt soldiers with gifts, and the devil to entrap them with the sweet enticing baits of lewd liberty. But since the reward of truth is everlasting life, & the untrue and dissembler looseth the same in continual darkness, I trust none of our countrymen will learn the one for the other, will be false to his sovereign. . . . (29–31)

[2] THE OFFICE OF AN ALFIERUS OR ENSIGN BEARER.

• • •

Having solemnly received the Ensign of his Captain, like a noble and expert Soldier, he ought carefully to keep the same, and bear a certain reverent respect to it, as to a holy thing, yea and be jealous over the safety thereof, no less than an amorous person over his loving mistress: Since that only with the sacred shade of the ensign, being well guided, the general reputation of all the band and company is conserved.

Therefore the Alfierus ought to be endowed with such custom, and use himself with such courtesy and civility, that he may not only procure the love of his confederates, and friends, but of all the entire company. (62–63)

The Alfierus must be a man of good account, of a good race, honest and virtuous, brave in apparel, thereby to honor his office. . . .

Finally he must be a man skilful, hardy, and courageous, of able courage to advance and bear up the Ensign in all extremities, secret, silent, and zealous, able often to comfort, animate and encourage the company to take in hand, and maintain such extremities, enterprises, as they are appointed unto, and never to refuse, but when of noble policy the higher officers command the same. (67–68)

[3] THE OFFICE OF THE LIEUTENANT OF A COMPANY.

• • •

Therefore that a soldier may deservedly mount up to this degree of worthy honor and martial dignity, he must use all circumspect care to perform his office like an expert Lieutenant, that the company be well governed, which he must accomplish with a forward and willing mind . . . as well to content the mind of his captain, as to augment his own honor and reputation. He must never appropriate unto himself any one point of authority, but diligently decipher and understand all things, and make relation thereof to his captain, of whom it is necessary he take all his commissions and directions. His part is to give willingly and readily counsel and advice to his captain, as often as he is demanded, and otherwise never, unless he see that the same may do manifest good, or in case of present peril.

The Lieutenant ought to carry with him a diligent care of concord, for that particularly the pacification of discords & difference amongst the soldiers of his company, appertains unto him, which must be done without choler or passion, and must still handle them very indifferently and courteously. For his indifference, besides the gaining of him trusty credit, both make easy the deciding of any difference or disagreement, and is one point which of necessity is most convenient to an honorable peacemaker, although it be a very difficult thing to procure peace in points of honor, especially amongst soldiers . . . and for that respect is it very hard to use a just balance: therefore in such causes it is most requisite that everyone . . . show at the full his entire cause, the which is a thing not vulgar, neither of small importance. And although the pacifier ought never to hang more upon the one side than the other, yet it is convenient he have some small respect to him that is wronged against reason, rather than to him that is the unlawful worker of the injury. But if he find any difficulty in resolving these differences, let him confer with the Captain, to the end that he, who is known to be the occasion and will not agree to an honest end, may be immediately discharged . . . to shun a great scandal: for to enter into unquiet quarreling and discord, one equal with another . . . is not the part and quality of a subject soldier, but of a free careless cutter, and band buckler, and of an insolent and importunate person, whose nature doth argue in him that his doings tend to another end, than to become excellent in the honorable exercise of arms. . . . So that quarreling and killing one the other, as often it falls out in resolute persons or putting him to a dishonor or open foil: such a one doth not only deprive the Captain of a soldier, but also of himself likewise: for the law of reason doth bind the Captain not to maintain an importunate person, a malefactor, and an homicide, in one band no less than a well-ordered city. (68–70)

He must observe great affability and fraternity with the Alfierus, and friendly consult with him . . . let the Lieutenant be very careful (as that he is the chief) to avoid all stomaching and strife that might arise betwixt him & the Alfierus, for thereby oftentimes great scandals have fallen out, and the division of the company, a thing above all other to be carefully foreseen and shunned. (70–71)

The Captain being absent, the Lieutenant possesseth the principal and chief place, and ought to be obeyed as captain. Nevertheless in his presence, it is requisite he use certain brotherly friendship and familiarity towards all, yet that notwithstanding, he must proceed in all things with such modesty and gravity, as he may retain such authority and reputation, as the office he doth hold, doth most worthily invest him withall. (71)

THE OFFICE OF THE GENERAL AND CERTAIN LAWS OF THE FIELD

Thomas Styward's conduct book *The Pathway to Martial Discipline* (1581) anticipates topics in Garrard's later study, *The Art of War* (1591), suggesting the influence military writers may have had on each other. Of the two excerpts included below, the first addresses the office of the general and the second cites several of more than eighty laws or guidelines for soldiers, including possible consequences for disobedience. As you read consider Othello's reputation as a general and to what extent he meets Styward's ideals. How do the selected laws of the field mentioned below appear relevant to *Othello*'s plot?

FROM THOMAS STYWARD, *THE PATHWAY TO MARTIAL DISCIPLINE*
(London: 1581. STC 23413)

[1]   A General ought to be temperate, continent, and not excessive in eating and drinking: Patient in travail, of wit prompt, whereby in the night time by quietness of mind the counsels of Captains examined, may more perfectly be confirmed . . . it doth appertain to a General that he in the time of turmoils of the war, may be the last that is weary. He must be quick witted . . . that with his thought he may most quickly discuss everything, and with his mind make judgment, and as it were divine afar off and foresee that which is to come: lest when there happen chances neither foreseen nor looked for, the General be constrained suddenly and unprovided for to take counsel, and the safeguard of things to commit most fearfully to fortune. It behooveth him to be liberal, and not to be covetous and desirous of gain. . . . He ought to be a fair speaker. . . . Likewise, the General being confirmed in his degree, should be pleasant, gentle, and cheerful to them that will come to him, gladly and willing to recompense the valiant and good, both with the liberality of the purse, and dignity of office, and with sharp punishment to punish the slothful, malefactors, and offenders. Also he ought not in every place and to every man show himself so benign and gentle, lest he happen to be despised, neither so proud and stout that he move other to bear him hatred. And that he do this to the intent that with too much license and benignity he cause not the army to be dissolute, or with sharpness and severity make

them alienate their minds and become enemies. . . . It is necessary that the General with his warlike counsel do deliberate upon every matter, & they being partakers of the counsels are sworn in time and place to tell their judgments, the which together with him of everything ought to debate, for so much as all those things not any man hath of himself found: he may alone by study with himself examine, but he ought not straightways to approve and confirm it, for that our thoughts and counsels . . . easily . . . may beguile us, and many times it is found full of errors, contrariwise those things that by judgment and opinion of others be approved, do assure the mind and keep things stable and sure. Notwithstanding no man ought so little to trust to himself that always he be of opinion weak & doubtful, nor of himself so much to presume that he think other cannot find counsel better than his. (2–5)

[2] THE LAWS AND CONSTITUTIONS OF THE FIELD
• • •

14   Item, that no soldier shall be suffered to be of a ruffian-like behavior, either to provoke or to give any blow or thrust, or otherwise willfully strike with his dagger, to injure any his fellow soldiers with any weapon, whereby mutinies many times ensueth, upon pain of the loss of his life. (51)

17   Item that no soldier or soldiers draw his or their sword or swords, or use any other kind of weapon with violence to do hurt within or without the camp during the time of the wars, upon pain of death. It hath lately been used with more favor of life, as such an offender, to lose his hand, but it is the discretion of the Lord chief General, in whose hands lieth both life and death of offenders, after their arraignment & just condemnation.

18   Item, the like law is against the officer and officers of any band in the camp, if he strike any soldier, without such occasion as is permitted him in the articles to do. (52)

35   Item, that no man of what degree so ever he be of, shall commit adultery with married wives, nor enforce widows maids or virgins: & by violence defile them, shall without mercy be punished with death. (57)

QUESTIONS FOR WRITTEN AND ORAL DISCUSSION

1. What, according to William Garrard, made the Turkish army an admirable model? Why might this example of discipline seem particularly offensive or shameful to the English or other Europeans? (See, in addition, the section on "The Turk" in Chapter 2.)

2. Imagine you are a citizen in Cyprus and have just read Garrard's report about the Turkish military. Having witnessed the behavior of Venetian soldiers on your island, write a "letter to the editor" or a personal letter to Othello, the general himself, comparing the Turkish reputation with what you have observed amongst Venetian soldiers. What is the tone of your letter? What compelled you to express your opinions publicly? It may be useful to refer to the well-known principles of military behavior Garrard also mentions.

3. After reading Garrard's description of an ensign (or Alfierus), make a list of words that identify a good ensign, indicate whether Iago seems to exemplify each quality, and provide evidence, including act, scene, and line numbers, that demonstrate how he does or does not meet the standard. Compare your analysis with another student's analysis and then discuss how this exercise affects your understanding of Iago as a soldier and a villain in the play.

4. Summarize the qualities and duties Garrard attributes to the lieutenant. In a paragraph or two, describe how Cassio fulfills these expectations. In what ways does he succeed? In what ways does he fail?

5. Garrard emphasizes the importance of good relations between the ensign and lieutenant. What sort of "scandal" arises between these two officers in *Othello*, and does the fault lie solely with Iago or is Cassio partly to blame? Explain.

6. On first reading the play, did you find Othello's dismissal of Cassio harsh and extreme? Why or why not? Does reading Styward's or Garrard's military advice to officers change your initial reaction. Why or why not? Write a response in which you defend or condemn Cassio's behavior and draw conclusions about whether or not you find him a sympathetic character.

   Alternatively, hold a mock judicial inquiry investigating Cassio's dismissal. Call characters from the play to testify on behalf of his integrity and reputation or to provide evidence as witnesses of the quarrel that "cashiered" him. You may also want to refer to the "laws of the field" quoted from Thomas Styward. Will your inquiry support or overturn Othello's decision? When Othello steps in to assume Cassio's peacekeeping duty, does he do so fairly or rashly?

7. Summarize the qualities Styward describes in a good general. Explain in your own words the difficult balance a general ought to maintain between being gentle and being severe. Why is this balance important to the army as a whole?

8. Styward stresses that a general should consult and deliberate about military decisions but not lack confidence in his own opinions. Use this passage as a commentary on Othello's judgment and method of decision making. Does he achieve the balance Styward advises? If so, where? If not, does he rely too much on the advice of others or demonstrate too much confidence in his own judgment? Does he make decisions differently according to the public or private nature of the concern? In considering these questions, draw some conclusions about how Othello's skills as a general affect his personal life. Do your conclusions help you to justify and understand Othello's behavior toward Desdemona and Cassio or make you more critical of his actions?

9. In theory and largely in practice, sixteenth- and seventeenth-century military society was male-oriented and male-dominated. In *Othello*, however, Cassio refers to Desdemona as "our great captain's captain" (2.1.74), Othello calls her "my fair warrior" (2.1.179), and Iago says, "Our general's wife is now the general" (2.3.314–315). Discuss what role Desdemona plays in the military world of *Othello*. Does her behavior seem improper, inappropriate, or at all influential? Does it suggest Othello's weakness as a general or his devotion as a husband? How do public and private spheres connect or conflict?

10. Hold an open discussion or write a formal paper on one of the following military virtues represented in *Othello*: reputation, honor, discipline, or justice. Address the way one of these qualities or issues is dramatized in the play, considering both its potential virtue and the problems raised when characters abuse or confuse its meaning or purpose.

11. Referring to Othello's "Farewell" speech (3.3.342–354), as well as his initial speeches about the former "dangers [he] had passed" (1.3.166) and his final speeches in 5.2, describe Othello's view of war. Is it idealistic or realistic? Is he an honorable, valiant warrior or a vain, boastful soldier? Defend your position.

12. What is the relationship between love and war in *Othello*? How does one contribute to or affect the other? Does the main love story demonstrate any warlike qualities? Do the emotions of love interfere with the standards and expectations of the warlike setting in this play? Why or how?

Refer also to questions 6–8 in the section on Venice in Chapter 2, which address Othello's status and role as a mercenary soldier and governor of Cyprus.

SUGGESTED READINGS

Genster, Julia. "Lieutenancy, Standing In, and *Othello*." *Critical Essays on Shakespeare's "Othello*." Anthony Gerard Barthelemy, ed. New York: G. K. Hall & Co., 1994. 216–237.

Hale, John R. *The Art of War and Renaissance England*. Washington DC: The Folger Shakespeare Library, 1961.

Hale, John Rigby. *War and Society in Renaissance Europe, 1450–1620*. Leicester: Leicester University Press, 1985.

Jorgensen, Paul A. *Shakespeare's Military World*. Berkeley: University of California Press, 1956. (Out of print.)

Vaughan, Virginia Mason. *Othello: A Contextual History*. Cambridge: Cambridge University Press, 1994.

Webb, Henry J. *Elizabethan Military Science: The Books and the Practice*. Madison: The University of Wisconsin Press, 1965.

5

Performance and Interpretation

This chapter traces four centuries of *Othello*'s performance history and interpretation. Arranged chronologically, each section reflects the appeal of Shakespeare's art in general and of this tragedy in particular. There has rarely been a time when *Othello* has not been popular on stage, although the play has also sparked considerable debate and controversy among generations of critics, actors, and audiences. Cultural, social, and political conditions have necessarily influenced these responses. Racial attitudes during years of slavery in England and the United States and subsequent prejudice have shaped perceptions about Othello's blackness and his tragic sympathy. To a lesser extent, changing views of women, the military, and heroism have also played their part.

From an artistic standpoint, the development of different acting styles and technologies constantly remake and renew the play. Large open-air playhouses give way to small intimate theaters, while cameras eventually lead to movie versions of *Othello*, and creative innovators adapt Shakespeare's text by adding music or radically rewriting the plot. All these revivals, revisions, and adaptations remind us that drama necessarily requires the skills and insight of directors and actors to bring the text to life, and that each age receives, interprets, and understands *Othello* according to its own expectations, values, and assumptions. The main sections of this chapter conclude with questions that provide opportunities for reflection and discussion. They include acting exercises that encourage an appreciation of stage skills and creativity, as well as group debates or trial scenes that foster an awareness of some of the arguments and counter-arguments that *Othello* continues to generate among its viewers and readers.

THE JACOBEAN STAGE

Shakespeare is referred to as a Renaissance dramatist because he worked and wrote during the period of humanist rebirth or "renaissance" which began on the European continent in the fourteenth century and occurred in England in the sixteenth and seventeenth centuries during his lifetime (1564–1616). He is also known as both an Elizabethan and a Jacobean playwright because his dramatic career from 1590 to 1613 spanned the years of two reigning monarchs, Elizabeth I (1558–1603) and James I (1603–1625). *Othello* is likely the first tragedy Shakespeare composed after James ascended to the throne, for there is a record of its performance on November 1, 1604. Shakespeare's previous tragedy, *Hamlet*, was written in 1600–1601 during Elizabeth's reign. Changes in the monarchy had a noticeable effect on the world of English playwrights and playhouses. But the dramatic tradition in which Shakespeare began his career and his own artistic development and exploration also continued to be reflected in his work. Records of Renaissance stage history are sketchy at best, and only a few specific references to *Othello* exist. These details, however, suggest the play's relative popularity, indicating that it was probably performed quite regularly until the Civil War closed theaters in 1642. Piecing together factual accounts and historical knowledge about acting companies, playhouses, and audiences at the turn of the seventeenth century can help us understand how *Othello* may have been performed and received in its early years.

ACTORS

Actors in Shakespeare's time belonged to professional acting companies whose right to perform publicly depended on the patronage or support of English aristocrats. During Elizabeth's reign, several such companies evolved gradually out of a long tradition of traveling players and wandering minstrels. The development of these companies and the construction of theater buildings helped to legitimize drama as a form of entertainment and increase its popularity. Initially Shakespeare wrote for a troupe supported by the Lord Chamberlain and known as the Chamberlain's Men. The company played in London and also traveled to the countryside, particularly when the plague threatened the city, inciting a ban on public performances to prevent the spread of disease. When James became England's king, he gave actors preferential status by assuming the patronage of the Chamberlain's Men which, then renamed the King's Men, became the leading company in London. As members of the royal household, the King's Men not only continued to perform regularly in public theaters but also were commissioned to entertain at court numerous times throughout the year. In fact, the first recorded performance of *Othello* in 1604 was at a banqueting house at Whitehall Palace as entertainment for the king and his guests. Years later, in 1612–1613, *Othello* was again performed at Court during the marriage celebrations of Princess Elizabeth, King James's daughter.

Acting companies in Shakespeare's time were relatively small, consisting of nine to twelve men, with extras occasionally hired as needed. Because women were not allowed to perform on stage, boy actors played women's parts. Richard Burbage, considered to be one of the greatest performers of the Elizabethan and Jacobean periods, was the leading actor in the Chamberlain's Men and the King's Men. He played the major tragic roles in Shakespeare's plays, and we know that Othello was one of his parts because of an elegy written at his death in 1619. One manuscript of the elegy includes comments on Burbage's Othello:

> 'But let me not forget one chiefest part
> 'Wherein, beyond the rest, he mov'd the heart,
> 'The grieved Moor, made jealous by a slave,
> 'Who sent his wife to fill a timeless grave,
> 'Then slew himself upon the bloody bed.
> 'All these and many more with him are dead.'[1]

Reference to the "grieved Moor" in this verse not only indicates who played Othello in Shakespeare's time but how the character may have been acted and received—as a man tragic and sympathetic in his suffering and his loss.

Another account of a performance of *Othello* draws attention to the boy actor who played Desdemona. A member of an Oxford college praises the part in response to a production of the play he saw in 1610. An excerpt of his letter, originally in Latin, is translated as follows:

Sept. 1610

—In the last few days the King's players have been here. They acted with enormous applause to full houses. . . . They had tragedies (too) which they acted with skill and decorum and in which some things, both speech and action, brought forth tears.—

Moreover, that famous Desdemona killed before us by her husband, although she always acted her whole part supremely, yet when she was killed she was even more moving, for when she fell back upon the bed she implored the pity of the spectators by her very face.[2]

The account of this Oxford performance suggests the emotional impact the play had on its audience, the overwhelming sympathy for Desdemona, and the importance of action and expression as well as speech in evoking a public response to the character. These rare specific reports of *Othello* offer small glimpses into its success in Shakespeare's time.

PLAYHOUSES

While the King's Men acted at Court and on tour to places such as Oxford, their main public performance space was a playhouse called the Globe, located on the south side of the Thames River in a theater district of London known as Bankside. The Globe was built in 1599 by two men, Richard Burbage—the great actor—and his brother Cuthbert Burbage. The enterprise also involved the participation of five other actors as shareholders, one of whom was Shakespeare. His position is unique among the theatrical men of his time because he was not only a playwright but also an actor and a businessman. As the Globe became the main venue for his plays, he became a reasonably wealthy man. After 1609 Shakespeare expanded his financial interests to the Blackfriar's Theater, another playhouse where the King's Men also began performing.

The Globe was a large, three-story, polygonal building with an unroofed center or yard that was open to the air and provided standing room for spectators to crowd around the stage. This yard was surrounded by three levels of roofed galleries with benches for wealthier spectators, who paid a higher price to sit and watch the performance. Some gallants may even have sat on the stage itself or in balcony seats above it, where they could be seen as well as see. The yard, galleries, and stage provided room for between 2,000 and 3,000 people, but with much more cramped seating and standing arrangements than exist at theaters and concert halls today.

The stage platform in the Globe was a thrust or apron stage, extending out into the yard and providing relatively intimate interaction with the audience surrounding three sides. Two doorways at each side of the back wall allowed for entrances and exits while a third larger curtained opening between them could also be used as an entrance or discovery space for secret or interior action. The trap door in the stage floor supplied another opportunity for unexpected appearances or disappearances. The canopy extended over the stage, and behind the back wall was a tiring room or dressing room, roofed as the galleries were and including a second story that could be used not only for spectators but also for performers in two-tiered action.

The balcony was likely used several times in *Othello*. Brabantio appears from "above" when Iago and Roderigo rouse him from his bed in the first scene. The two levels of action help to distinguish Brabantio's home—a bedroom window, perhaps—from the public street below. Later, at the beginning of Act 2, the nameless gentleman from Cyprus probably also appears on the balcony, the lookout point from which he reports to Montano below about the stormy conditions at sea.

STAGING

In addition to knowledge about the performance space used by Shakespearean actors, other information about staging allows us to imagine early productions of *Othello*. The apron stage surrounded by spectators on three sides meant that no curtain distinguished one scene from another. Instead, the characters' exits, entrances, and words provided crucial details about scene changes, setting, and atmosphere. The dialogue beginning Act 2, for example, vividly describes the coastal storm, announcing the important shift from Venice to Cyprus and establishing an atmosphere of apprehension and uncertainty about the safety of the travelers at sea:

MONTANO: What from the cape can you discern at sea?
FIRST GENTLEMAN: Nothing at all, it is a high-wrought flood.

> I cannot 'twixt the heaven and the main
> Descry a sail.

MONTANO: Methinks the wind has spoke aloud at land;
> A fuller blast ne'er shook our battlements.
> If it hath ruffianed so upon the sea,
> What ribs of oak, when mountains melt on them,
> Can hold the mortise? What shall we hear of this? (2.1.1–9)

These lines paint a dramatic scene of violent weather, encouraging the audience to imagine what would otherwise be invisible on the bare stage.

Simple props also contributed to the visual experience. A table and a few chairs might mark a public setting like the late-night Senate meeting in *Othello*; a single bed could be rolled in on wheels to indicate an intimate domestic scene such as the last one in the play. One of the most important props in *Othello*—the handkerchief—is simple indeed, yet crucial to the unfolding of the plot. Its appearance and reappearance as it changes hands—from Desdemona to Othello to Emilia to Iago to Bianca to Cassio—increases the dramatic tension by drawing visual or "ocular" attention to the lie that gradually entangles and destroys the main characters.

Costuming was much more elaborate than props or sets, especially for public figures such as kings or dukes. Records indicate that acting companies owned valuable collections of costumes, including garments that originally belonged to aristocratic families. *Othello*, a play with few ceremonial scenes or royal figures, does not offer the same opportunity for elaborate, showy attire as other Shakespearean plays about kings and courts but costumes certainly would have indicated characters' class or stature. The Duke would have been impressively dressed and the difference between a military captain such as Othello and plain soldiers would likely have been apparent in their dress. Costuming reflected contemporary English styles with little attention paid to historical or cultural accuracy. The most striking feature of appearance in *Othello* would most likely have been the black makeup used to distinguish the Moor from all the other characters.

Lighting was another aspect of staging that added to the dramatic experience. Plays performed at the Globe Theater had to be staged in the afternoon during daylight. This circumstance meant that members of the audience were as visible to each other as the performers were to them. Consequently, off-stage distractions and disruptions could draw attention away from on-stage activity. In this respect, the atmosphere then more closely approximated a modern sporting event than an excursion to today's theater. In the context of the play itself, *Othello*'s numerous night scenes depended—as much of the staging did—on a combination of characters' speeches, costumes, and simple props such as candles or torches. When Brabantio enters after his rude awakening in Act 1, he likely appears in a nightshirt as he calls for a light:

> Strike on the tinder, ho!
> Give me a taper! Call up all my people!
> This accident is not unlike my dream.
> Belief of it oppresses me already.
> Light, I say! Light! (1.1.137–141)

Much later in the play, a candle is again an important prop as Othello begins the murder scene with a soliloquy that compares the effect of extinguishing the "flaming minister" in his hand to the light of Desdemona's life. Here, staging and metaphor combine to contribute to the climax of the play.

When the King's Men also began to perform at the Blackfriar's Theater after 1609, the effect of lighting was altered. As a small, indoor theater, the Blackfriar's relied on candles and torches to light the building and all scenes. The darkness of night scenes required less imagination than the brightness of daytime scenes. On the whole, however, Elizabethan and Jacobean performances demanded that audiences adapt to and engage in a dramatic illusion that relied on the spoken word much more than on realistic and elaborate staging.

Court performances for the king also required that actors be creative and adaptable. When the King's Men presented *Othello* as royal entertainment, they did so in one hall or another, relying on a temporary stage platform at the end of the room or acting in the center, surrounded by audience members on all sides. With no balcony or convenient backstage dressing room and a much smaller acting space, players improvised as necessary without radically revising the script. The king occupied the best seat at a Court play and actors performed directly to him.

AUDIENCE

Shakespeare's plays drew their audiences from many classes in English society. Those attending Court performances would have been an exclusive group of royalty and nobility but performances in public playhouses attracted spectators from working classes as well as the aristocracy. Evidence indicates that the cost of attending a theater such as the Globe ranged from one penny to sixpence (six pennies). For the cheapest price viewers stood in the yard in front of the stage and for the most expensive admission an audience member could sit in a balcony room over the stage (Gurr and Orrell 54–55). Consequently, people with a variety of incomes could be present at the same play. Some modern scholars contend that poor citizens in England would have been unable to attend performances in London's playhouses because even one penny for "standing-room only" would have been extremely costly for workers such as laborers, servants, and apprentices. Furthermore, afternoon performances would have conflicted with their employment obligations. However, records suggest that audiences at London's playhouses did represent a broad spectrum of classes, and so today's discussions about the composition of Shakespeare's audiences continue.

CONCLUSION

Although little specific information about *Othello*'s early stage history exists, the few accounts and references suggest the play's wide appeal and popularity. As well as Court performances, Globe performances, and the Oxford production already mentioned, later records confirm that the King's Men were still performing *Othello* in the 1620s and the early 1630s, almost thirty years after it was written and more than fifteen years after Shakespeare's death. Clearly, this tragedy endured on the Renaissance stage without falling prey to political controversy or public boredom. Its later stage history, after the revival of theaters following the English Civil War, offers much more detailed records about acting styles and public responses. What we can know and understand about *Othello*'s first decades, however, requires the skills of a detective, closely reading the text and drawing connections between it and recognized research about stage history in Shakespeare's time.

NOTES

1. *The New Variorum Shakespeare. Othello*, Ed. Horace Howard Furness, Vol. 6 (Philadelphia: J. B. Lippincott Co., 1886), 396.

2. From a letter in Corpus Christi College Library. *Eyewitnesses of Shakespeare: First Hand Accounts of Performances, 1590–1890*, Gamini Salgado, ed. (Sussex University Press, 1975), 30.

QUESTIONS FOR WRITTEN AND ORAL DISCUSSION

1. The Globe Theater is central to understanding early performances of Shakespeare's plays. Construct a model of the Globe using the discussion in this chapter as well as more detailed research and diagrams found in other sources in libraries or on the Internet. Documentation of the excavation and reconstruction of the Globe in London in 1996 may provide recent information about the theater's history. Choose whatever materials seem appropriate: cardboard, paper, wood, or plaster. This may make a good group project, possibly including a presentation to the class about how the architecture and design of the building affected the way plays were acted and received.

2. Write a synopsis of *Othello*'s plot that might serve as an act-by-act summary for an actor of the play preparing to accept a role. What is the main action in each act? What connects one act to the next?

3. Draw a comic-book version of *Othello*, deciding which scenes or actions are most important to the plot and how many frames are necessary to portray the main story line. Your drawings may be as detailed or as simple as you choose. Decide what captions to include, whether specific quotations from the play or modern paraphrases. Also determine before you start whether your illustrated version will reflect the tragedy of the original play or turn it into a comic parody—perhaps a melodramatic soap opera about love and jealousy.

4. Richard Burbage was noted not only as one of the greatest tragic actors in Shakespeare's time but as one who changed standard acting styles by emphasizing the private, personal experience of characters rather than their public positions. Referring to the quotation from Burbage's elegy in this chapter, use your imagination to write one of the following:

   a) an interview with Burbage that addresses his interpretation of Othello's character as "The grieved Moor, made jealous by a slave";

   b) an excerpt from Burbage's diary before or after his first successful performance of *Othello*;

    c) a response from a spectator that describes how Burbage made Othello appear sympathetic.

5. Imagine you are watching the first performance of *Othello* at the Globe. Assume the position of either a lower class citizen with standing room in front of the stage or a wealthier patron with a more expensive balcony seat. Write a personal response to the play that reflects your social class and your physical location in the audience. What strikes you about the play? Refer, for example, to the reaction of the audience member at Oxford quoted in this chapter.

    Furthermore, what is happening in the audience around you which either adds to or detracts from the drama on the stage? Did you go to the play partly to be seen in public dressed in your fine attire, or did you have to sneak away from your employment as a servant or apprentice for an afternoon's entertainment? How do these conditions affect your response to the event?

6. Imagine you are a publicist for the King's Men trying to attract attention to a new tragedy called *Othello, the Moor of Venice*. Design a poster that will be copied and displayed prominently in public places.

7. Knowing that sets were simple in Shakespeare's time and stage directions rare and brief, select a scene from *Othello* and study the lines carefully, looking for words and phrases that provide information about atmosphere, setting, and specific actions. Write a summary of your findings, indicating what the text suggests about characters' movements, emotions, and gestures, as well as details of place and mood.

8. Imagine that you are directing *Othello* at the Globe in 1604. Choose one act or several scenes and determine how they should be performed. Write notes and possibly include stage diagrams or explanations to indicate what props are necessary, where characters will enter and exit, and where they will stand in relation to one another and the audience as they deliver their lines. The positioning or "blocking" of characters might be especially interesting in scenes where the audience hears lines from one character that other characters are obviously not intended to hear. If groups of characters appear, who should have center stage at what time and why?

SUGGESTED READINGS

Aliki. *William Shakespeare and the Globe*. New York: HarperCollins Publishers, 1999.

Cook, Ann Jennalie. *The Privileged Playgoers of Shakespeare's England:*

1576–1642. Princeton, NJ: Princeton University Press, 1981. Argues that only wealthy, privileged people went to the theater.

Gurr, Andrew. *Playgoing in Shakespeare's London*. Cambridge: Cambridge University Press, 1987; 2nd ed., 1996. Provides details about playhouse buildings, audiences, and performances.

Gurr, Andrew, and John Orrell. *Rebuilding Shakespeare's Globe*. New York: Routledge, 1989. Describes the project of reconstructing a new Globe Theater based on research about the original building.

Harbage, Alfred. *Shakespeare's Audience*. New York: Columbia University Press, 1941. (Out of print.)

Hattaway, Michael. *Elizabethan Popular Theatre: Plays in Performance*. London: Routledge, 1982. Argues that theaters attracted people from all social groups in Shakespearean times.

Hodges, C. Walter. *Shakespeare's Theatre*. London: Oxford University Press, 1964. An illustrated guide to the Globe Theater and plays performed in Shakespeare's time.

THEATER FROM THE RESTORATION TO THE NINETEENTH CENTURY

When the English Civil War began in 1642, theaters were closed as a war measures act and their buildings eventually destroyed. Under the Puritan government of Oliver Cromwell, acting was forbidden as an idle, frivolous, suspicious pastime. When the monarchy was restored in 1660 and Charles II returned to the throne, the stage became an acceptable place for entertainment once again. Theaters were rebuilt, but these structures were much different from the large open-air Globe of the early seventeenth century. New theaters were small, indoor buildings designed for hundreds rather than thousands of spectators. The stage, like modern stages, had a curtained arch serving as an invisible fourth wall rather than an apron performance space extending out into the audience. Stage sets became much more elaborate, acting styles changed, and play-going became the entertainment of middle and upper classes.

New plays began to be written, but initially many old plays were revived, including some of Shakespeare's. *Othello* was one of the first to be performed and continued to be one of Shakespeare's most successful revivals into the eighteenth century. It was also one of the earliest plays to include women. Social and cultural attitudes had changed since before the revolution and King Charles legislated that acting companies must include women actors because men in female roles no longer seemed believable or morally respectable. A prologue to a production of *Othello* announces this significant change while mocking the out-dated effect of men as female characters:

> But to the point:—In this reforming age
> 'We have intents to civilize the stage.
> 'Our women are defective, and so siz'd
> 'You'd think they were some of the guard disguis'd:
> For to speak truth, men act, that are between
> 'Forty and fifty, wenches of fifteen;
> 'With bones so large, and nerve so incompliant,
> 'When you call Desdemona, enter Giant.—

'We shall purge everything that is unclean,
'Lascivious, scurrilous, impious, or obscene;
'And when we've put all things in this fair way,
'Barebones himself may come to see a play.'[1]

"Barebones," referred to in the last line of the prologue, was a strong advocate of Oliver Cromwell's Puritan government and presented a petition in the last Commonwealth Parliament that absolutely opposed the restoration of the monarchy. Hence, he represented antagonism not only to Charles II but also to the revival of theatrical entertainment.

In retrospect, *Othello*'s persistent popularity in the eighteenth and nineteenth centuries seems somewhat surprising given the moral, sexual, and racial concerns it dramatized at a time when these were potentially controversial issues. In fact, while some of Shakespeare's plays—such as *Macbeth* and *King Lear*—were radically adapted and virtually rewritten in the Restoration, the original Jacobean texts of *Othello* remained the main sources for stage productions. Nevertheless, artistic, social, and political changes affected both the interpretation and presentation of the play. The following account of *Othello*'s reception indicates how the play was revised to reflect surrounding cultural and historical issues and events.

THE FIRST CRITIC

With the revival of theatrical activity after 1660 came renewed interest in the art of acting as well as formal criticism of performances and the plays themselves. While few records exist from Shakespeare's time, a wealth of written material has survived since the late seventeenth century in the form of diaries, essays, and public reviews. Consequently, the first thorough response we have to *Othello* comes almost ninety years after the play was written. In 1692 Thomas Rymer published a treatise entitled *A Short View of Tragedy* which includes a full account of *Othello*'s plot and an extremely negative, sarcastic criticism of the play. Rymer's reaction is both literary and moral. Not only does he find fault with the construction of the plot and its credibility, but he also takes exception to the lack of moral teaching value in the play's conclusion where virtue is destroyed rather than affirmed. He is best known for calling *Othello* not a tragedy, but "a bloody farce."

Given the obvious popularity of *Othello* on stage, it seems unlikely that Rymer's opinions represented the general audience's
response any more than a single movie critic's taste today determines or reflects box office success. Rymer's treatise clearly had an
impact, however, for literary and theatrical critics that followed him
often referred to his scathing attack, if only to challenge it with a
more positive evaluation. Furthermore, although Rymer's views
were extreme, his concerns about the stage as a place for instruction rather than for mere entertainment continued to be a part of
eighteenth- and nineteenth-century culture, and his reasons for
questioning the tragic impact of *Othello* resurfaced again in the
twentieth century.

TEXTUAL CHANGES

Although *Othello* was not radically rewritten as were other
Shakespearean plays in the Restoration, performance copies of the
play typically cut parts of the original text. Some cuts were necessary because of time restrictions. From Shakespeare's day until
the present, few of his plays have ever been acted in their entirety
because the acting time of three hours or more seems uncomfort-
ably long for performers and audiences. What directors and producers choose to cut, however, often reflects both their creative
bias and public expectations.

The creative bias that influenced post-Restoration performances
of *Othello* favored tragic nobility and heroism. Consequently, stage
versions of the play eliminated words and scenes that portrayed
the main character in a potentially undignified light. For example,
one section that did not appear in theaters for nearly 150 years
was the portion of 4.1 where Othello falls into a trance or seizure
from his jealousy and later eavesdrops on a dialogue between Iago
and Cassio about the handkerchief. According to the sensibilities
of the time, this scene revealed characteristics of Othello which
were unpleasant and inconsistent with his greatness as a tragic
figure.

In a similar vein, domestic scenes were omitted because they
interfered with a desired overall impression of grandeur. Desdemona's Willow Song and Emilia's criticism of men in 4.3 fall into
this category. The habitual removal of these intimate moments between the women also reflected concerns about decency, morality,

and social values. Emilia's opinions about men and marriage were undoubtedly offensive and a bedroom preparation scene seemed indecent on a public stage. Bianca, the courtesan or prostitute, was removed from the cast, and all explicitly sexual language was deleted. *Othello* may not have been completely rewritten for eighteenth- and nineteenth-century audiences, but the text was reduced by up to a third of the total lines, with omissions suggesting both what was important and what was unacceptable to several generations of performers and audiences.

COSTUMES AND SETTINGS

Compared to the bare stage and simple props of early seventeenth-century public playhouses, stage sets in post-Restoration theaters became a much more detailed and important part of performances. Elaborate painted scenes were mounted on grooves so that they could slide into place and be exchanged easily as the play action progressed. While these sets were beautifully designed, they did not necessarily reflect the geography or the time period of the play itself. Often *Othello*'s backdrop did not specifically represent Venice or Cyprus. The appeal was artistic rather than historical.

The same was true of costumes which, as in Shakespeare's era, tended to be contemporary or "modern" rather than period dress. Othello, for example, might typically appear in a British military uniform. Iago's villainy was often noted by a black wig and black eyebrows. In the two hundred years prior to the twentieth century, however, occasional exceptions challenged this standard approach. One eighteenth-century actor added a turban to the traditional English costume, sparking more mockery than respect for his innovation. Another actor later received a more positive response by playing Othello in the loose-fitting garment of a Moor rather than a British soldier. Towards the late nineteenth century, one performer chose Oriental robes and jewels to emphasize Othello's exotic character rather than his military position.

More than the garments themselves, the makeup used to indicate Othello's race became a crucial and controversial aspect of costuming as the slavery movement radically changed English and North American perceptions of black people and interracial marriages. Immediately following the Restoration and into the eighteenth century, a black-faced Othello was still generally considered acceptable on stage. Gradually, however, English audiences found the marriage between a black man and white woman offensive or simply unconvincing and unrealistic as a tragic plot. Even after slavery had been abolished in Britain and its colonies, many considered their stereotypical view of African fierceness to be unsuited to Othello's noble character. These attitudes became especially pronounced in the nineteenth century, and actors began playing Othello in lighter make-up, more tawny than black, a choice that suggested the Arabic rather than African heritage of Moors.

Amidst this controversy, one black American actor, Ira Aldridge, attempted the part of Othello in 1852 but did so on the European continent where racism was less prominent. In countries such as Russia, France, and Germany he was well-received while audiences and actors in England and, even more so, in the United States continued to deliberate over an acceptable shade of makeup for the title character. One American woman is renowned for her blatant prejudice in insisting that "Othello *was a white* man!" In the social and historical context of racism against blacks, the question of Othello's African heritage and its impact on stage became an increasingly sensitive issue that continued into the twentieth century, influencing costumes, casting, and makeup.

THE MAIN CHARACTERS

A primary challenge in producing *Othello* on stage is interpreting the main characters in a manner that is balanced and convincing to an audience influenced by its own cultural and social issues. While Othello is the central tragic figure, the significance of Desdemona in the love plot and the crucial, if not dominant, role of Iago in orchestrating events requires choices about the focus on stage and about the relationships between these three characters. In the post-Restoration period Desdemona's role was downplayed and simplified. With many of her best lines deleted, she appeared as an innocent, weak, and virtuous young woman, a stereotypical victim overshadowed by those plotting against her. Not until the end of the nineteenth century did she begin to be recognized as a potentially interesting individual with sufficient complexity and vitality to draw Othello away from the freedom and adventure of a single life and stir him to the pitch of jealousy. Given Desdemona's diminished role, attention turned to the balance and tension between Iago and Othello. The interpretation of these parts in the eighteenth and nineteenth centuries reflected shifting dramatic styles, as well as actors' abilities and theatrical expectations.

Initially, the theatrical community expected a clear tragic hero and Othello dominated the plot. His nobility and sympathy starkly contrasted Iago's obvious villainy. The style of acting in the eighteenth century was formal, deliberate, and artificial. Thus, an actor playing Othello followed a series of conventional gestures and movements, reciting his lines with exaggerated expression and tone. This approach reinforced Othello's dignity and decreased the passionate intensity that is equally apparent in Shakespeare's text. When one actor in that period tried to present Othello with more emotion and less formality, audiences and actors perceived his interpretation as a failure rather than an innovation. They were not ready for a change in dramatic style or for a fresh view of Othello's character.

In the nineteenth century, however, a more natural style of acting began to alter the interpretation of Othello's part, while, simultaneously, Iago became a much more prominent presence on stage. He began to be played with more wit and subtle manipulation that made Othello's turn toward jealousy more convincing. The temptation scene in 3.3 came to be recognized and portrayed as the pivotal moment in the play, and by the end of the nineteenth century, actors began to see Iago as an enviable role to play, at least as inviting as Othello, if not more so. Some actors alternated between the two parts in the same theatrical season or over a period of years.

While Iago's stature increased, Othello's character became less formal, his dignity less central to the plot, and his energy, violence, and emotion more pronounced. His private personal struggle began to overshadow his public authority and nobility. Tommaso Salvini, an Italian actor playing Othello in the 1870s and 1880s, gave the century one of its fiercest and most passionate interpretations of the part, speaking in Italian while the rest of the cast used Shakespeare's English. In the temptation scene, Salvini threw Iago onto the floor and raised a foot over him as if to kill him in a rage. He was also the first "Othello" to strike Desdemona physically. Even in its time, Salvini's performance was considered bold and daring— albeit very successful. A century earlier such a performance would have horrified the sensibilities of an audience expecting a grand and "noble Moor."

This brief history of how *Othello*'s main characters were understood and portrayed prior to the twentieth century indicates the range of possibilities available to actors and directors and suggests some of the challenges in producing a successful performance. If Othello is noble and sympathetic, can he also be fierce and passionate? If Iago is villainy personified, can he be convincing to other characters as an "honest" man? If Desdemona is passive, can Othello's love for her and her disobedience to her father be believable? Just as generations of actors after the Restoration found their own answers, each age continues to address these questions anew, seeking to be true to the text and to tradition but also daring to stretch the boundaries of innovation.

OPERATIC ADAPTATIONS

The nineteenth century produced two operatic versions of *Othello*, the first by Gioacchino Rossini in 1816 and the second by Giuseppe Verdi in 1887. Rossini's *Otello*, virtually forgotten in the twentieth century, is considered neither a remarkable reinterpretation of Shakespeare's drama nor a great musical work of art. It radically alters the original plot, making Desdemona the central character and focusing the tragedy as much on her conflict with her father as on the jealousy of her lover.

Verdi's later *Otello* is much truer to Shakespeare's play and is considered one of the composer's finest works, as well as an operatic masterpiece. It captures the psychological and emotional intensity of the original drama by relying predominantly on the music and spectacle of the operatic medium. Othello's love of Desdemona is dominant, although Iago's overt evil propels the tragedy forward. Verdi had even considered calling the opera *Iago* because the character's villainy fascinated him. Curiously enough, both Verdi's and Rossini's adaptations of *Othello* departed from theatrical tradition by increasing Desdemona's significance at a time when stage producers were habitually cutting her lines and diminishing her role. Perhaps the music and spectacle of opera made romance more attractive, allowing Desdemona a more balanced position beside the title character. The two operas offer further evidence of *Othello*'s appeal in the Victorian age, a time when racial prejudices and sexual decorum could have made the play's content too explicit for public entertainment. Instead, such "artful" treatment of sexual jealousy may have enhanced its popularity within a relatively repressive society and culture.

THE STAGING OF *OTHELLO*

The following excerpts from critics and actors in the post-Restoration period prior to the twentieth century reflect past attitudes and expectations about theater, tragedy, and *Othello*'s main characters, as well as personal responses to specific players' interpretations of their parts. These reviews and observations not only provide insight into *Othello*'s stage history but also reveal general questions and concerns that the play raises in its transition from text to dramatic performance. Spelling in the excerpted documents has been regularized and modernized where necessary.

THOMAS RYMER'S CRITICISM OF *OTHELLO*

Englishman Thomas Rymer, the first recorded critic of *Othello*, has gained a long-standing reputation for his strong opinions and vigorous attack of the play. The following excerpts capture his sarcastic tone as well as some specific objections to this tragedy. Morality is clearly one of his main concerns, indicated by his comments on the lack of "instruction" or "edification" available to the audience. Plot, referred to as the "Fable," is his second concern. Notice these two key parts of Rymer's argument and try to identify his reasons for finding the morality inexcusable and the plot unbelievable.

FROM THOMAS RYMER, *A SHORT VIEW OF TRAGEDY*
(London: 1693)

From all the Tragedies acted on our English Stage, *Othello* is said to bear the Bell away. The *Subject* is more of a piece, and there is indeed something like, there is, as it were, some phantom of a *Fable*. . . . (86)

Whatever rubs or difficulty may stick on the Bark, the Moral, sure, of this Fable is very instructive.

1. First, This may be a caution to all Maidens of Quality how, without their Parents' consent, they run away with Blackamoors. . . .

Secondly, This may be a warning to all good Wives, that they look well to their Linen.

Thirdly, This may be a lesson to Husbands, that before their Jealousy be Tragical, the proofs may be Mathematical. (89)

The Character of that State [Venice] is to employ strangers in their Wars; But shall a Poet thence fancy that they will set a Negro to be their General; or trust a *Moor* to defend them against the *Turk*? With us a Blackamoor might rise to be a Trumpeter; but *Shakespeare* would not have him less than a Lieutenant-General. With us a *Moor* might marry some little drab, or Small-coal Wench: *Shakespeare*, would provide him the Daughter and Heir of some great Lord, or Privy-Counselor: And all the Town should reckon it a very suitable match: Yet the English are not bred up with that hatred and aversion to the *Moors*, as are the Venetians, who suffer by a perpetual Hostility from them. . . . (91–92)

So much ado, so much stress, so much passion and repetition about an Handkerchief! Why was not this called the *Tragedy of the Handkerchief*? What can be more absurd . . . [than] . . . for this Handkerchief . . . to raise everywhere all this clutter and turmoil[?] Had it been *Desdemona*'s Garter, the Sagacious Moor might have smelt a Rat: but the Handkerchief is so remote a trifle, no Booby, on this side [*sic*] *Mauritania*, could make any consequence from it. . . .

Rather may we ask here what unnatural crime *Desdemona*, or her Parents had committed, to bring this Judgment down upon her; to Wed a Blackamoor, and innocent to be thus cruelly murdered by him. What instruction can we make out of this Catastrophe? Or whither must our reflection lead us? Is not this to envenom and sour our spirits, to make us repine and grumble at Providence; and the government of the World? If this be our end, what boots it to be Virtuous? ([139–142] pagination errors)

What can remain with the Audience to carry home with them from this sort of Poetry, for their use and edification? how can it work, unless (instead of settling the mind, and purging our passions) to delude our senses, disorder our thoughts, addle our brain, pervert our affections, hair [i.e. terrify] our imaginations, corrupt our appetite, and fill our head with vanity, confusion . . . and Jingle-jangle . . . ? Our only hopes, for the good of their Souls, can be, that these people go to the Playhouse, as they do to Church, to sit still, look on one another, make no reflection, nor mind the Play, more than they would a Sermon.

There is in this Play, some burlesk, some humour, and ramble of Comical Wit, some show, and some *Mimickry* to divert the spectators: but the tragical part is, plainly none other, than a Bloody Farce, without salt or savour. (146)

EDMUND KEAN'S OTHELLO

Edmund Kean was considered not only one of the best nineteenth-century presenters of Othello, but, in some opinions, greater than any actor of the part until Laurence Olivier's performance over a century later in 1964. William Hazlitt, theatrical and literary critic, responds to one of Kean's earlier performances in the actor's long history as Othello from 1814 to 1833. Like many modern movie and stage reviewers, Hazlitt qualifies overall high praise with specific criticisms. In considering the complexity of Othello's character, Hazlitt identifies some of the key conflicts to be embodied and expressed on stage and suggests when and how Kean made a poor choice of interpretation. As you read the following review, consider the importance of both speech and action or gesture in an effective performance and notice how Hazlitt addresses both aspects of Kean's Othello.

FROM WILLIAM HAZLITT, "MR. KEAN'S OTHELLO" (1816)
(*Dramatic Essays*, Ed. William Archer and Robert W. Lowe, London:
Walter Scott, 1895)

Examiner, January 7, 1816.
MR. KEAN'S Othello is his best character, and the highest effort of genius on the stage. We say this without any exception or reserve. Yet we wish it was better than it is. In parts, we think he rises as high as human genius can go: at other times, though powerful, the whole effort is thrown away in a wrong direction, and disturbs our idea of the character. There are some technical objections. Othello was tall; but that is nothing: he was black, but that is nothing. But he was not fierce, and that is everything. It is only in the last agony of human suffering that he gives way to his rage and his despair, and it is in working his noble nature up to that extremity, that Shakespeare has shown his genius and his vast power over the human heart. It was in raising passion to its height, from the lowest beginnings and in spite of all obstacles, in showing the conflict of the soul, the tug and war between love and hatred, rage, tenderness, jealousy, remorse, in laying open the strength and the weaknesses of human nature, in uniting sublimity of thought with the anguish of the keenest woe, in putting in motion all the springs and impulses which make up this our mortal being, and at last blending them in that noble tide of deep and sustained passion, impetuous, but majestic, "that flows on to the Propontic and knows no ebb," that the great excellence of Shake-

speare lay. Mr. Kean is in general all passion, all energy, all relentless will. He wants imagination, that faculty which contemplates events, and broods over feelings with a certain calmness and grandeur; his feelings almost always hurry on to action, and hardly ever repose upon themselves. He is too often in the highest key of passion, too uniformly on the verge of extravagance, too constantly on the rack. This does very well in certain characters, as Zanga or Bajazet, where there is merely a physical passion, a boiling of the blood, to be expressed; but it is not so in the lofty-minded and generous Moor.

We make these remarks the more freely, because there were parts of the character in which Mr. Kean showed the greatest sublimity and pathos, by laying aside all violence of action. For instance, the tone of voice in which he delivered the beautiful apostrophe, "Then, oh, farewell!" struck on the heart like the swelling notes of some divine music, like the sound of years of departed happiness. Why not all so, or all that is like it? why not speak the affecting passage—"I found not Cassio's kisses on her lips"—why not speak the last speech, in the same manner? They are both of them, we do most strenuously contend, speeches of pure pathos, of thought, and feeling, and not of passion, venting itself in violence of action or gesture. Again, the look, the action, the expression of voice, with which he accompanied the exclamation, "Not a jot, not a jot," was perfectly heart-rending. His vow of revenge against Cassio, and his abandonment of his love for Desdemona, were as fine as possible. The whole of the third act had an irresistible effect upon the house, and indeed is only to be paralleled by the murder-scene in *Macbeth*. (76–78)

EDWIN BOOTH'S IAGO

Edwin Booth helped transform public perception of Iago as he played the role from 1860 to 1891. Most actors in the two hundred years before Booth had cast Iago as a straightforward villain, as Evil personified. Booth fashioned a much smoother, more attractive character with humor and energy to engage the audience. At the same time, after Kean's earlier success as Othello, few actors managed to convey the grandeur of the central tragic hero, and consequently interest began to turn to Iago. William Winter's observations below describe Booth's success and raise a question of interpretation which became even more pronounced in the twentieth century: What makes Iago an appealing character and can he or should he be—as Winter concludes—"the most interesting figure" in the play?

FROM WILLIAM WINTER, *SHAKESPEARE ON THE STAGE*
(New York: Moffat, Yard and Company, 1911)

Booth gave incomparably the best performance of *Iago* that has been seen on our stage within the last fifty years. His *Iago*, when in company, was entirely frank and not only plausible but winning. The gay, light-hearted, good-humored soldier whom he thus presented would have deceived anybody, and did easily deceive *Othello*, who, as Kemble truly and shrewdly remarked, is "a slow man,"—meaning a man slow to those passions which shatter the judgment. Nothing could be more absolutely specious and convincingly sympathetic then Booth's voice, manner, and whole personality were when he said, "There's matter in 't *indeed*, if *he* be *angry*!" The duplicity of the character, when visible in association with others, was made evident to the audience by the subtle use of gesture and facial play, by perfect employment of the indefinable but instantly perceptible expedient of *transparency*,—and it was only when alone that his *Iago* revealed his frightful wickedness and his fiendish joy in it, and there was, in that revealment, an icy malignity of exultation that caused a strange effect of mingled admiration and fear. Although we must test *Iago* even while we admire and shudder at him, he not only supplies the motive and inspires the action of the tragedy, but also he is the most interesting figure in it, even if the interest be akin to the fascinated loathing inspired by a deadly reptile. (271–272)

HELENA FAUCIT'S DESDEMONA

Although Desdemona's part was simplified and diminished throughout most of the eighteenth and nineteenth centuries, Helena Faucit revived interest in the character with her interpretation in the first half of the nineteenth century. Consider why her interpretation might have seemed original and what effect her livelier Desdemona apparently had on her acting partner, William Charles Macready, playing Othello.

FROM LADY HELENA SAVILLE MARTIN (FAUCIT), *ON SOME OF
SHAKESPEARE'S FEMALE CHARACTERS* (1893)
(New York: AMS Press, 1970)

September 10, 1880
. . . In the gallery of heroes and heroines which my young imagination had fitted up for my daily and nightly reveries, Desdemona filled a prom-

inent place. How could it be otherwise? A being so bright, so pure, so unselfish, generous, courageous—so devoted in her love, so unconquerable in her allegiance to her "kind lord," even while dying by his hand. . . .

Of course I did not know in those days that Desdemona is usually considered a merely amiable, simple, yielding creature, and that she is generally so represented on the stage. This is the last idea that would have entered my mind. . . .

[M]y Desdemona was peculiarly welcomed as rescuing the character, as I was told, out of the commonplace, and lifting her into her true position in the tragedy. . . . Mr. Macready, my Othello . . . told me my brightness and gaiety in the early happy scenes at Cyprus helped him greatly . . . and, above all, that I added intensity to the last act by "being so difficult to kill." Indeed I felt in that last scene as if it were a very struggle for my own life. I would not die with my honour tarnished, without the chance of disabusing my husband's mind of the vile thoughts that clouded it. I felt for *him* as well as for myself—for I knew what remorse and misery would overwhelm him when he came to know how cruelly he had wronged me; and therefore I threw into my remonstrances all the power of passionate appeal I could command. (47–50)

NOTE

1. *The New Variorum Shakespeare. Othello*, Ed. Horace Howard Furness, Vol. 6 (Philadelphia: J. B. Lippincott Co., 1886), 397.

QUESTIONS FOR WRITTEN AND ORAL DISCUSSION

1. *Othello* made history as one of the first plays to include female actors instead of young men or boys in women's roles. Write an imaginary diary entry of the original woman playing Desdemona or Emilia, including personal reflections about how you felt on stage and how other actors and audience members responded to you. Alternatively, pretend to be an audience member writing a letter to a friend about seeing Desdemona acted by a woman for the first time. Did you find the innovation effective and appropriate or not?

2. Thomas Rymer depends on sarcasm to express his objections to *Othello* by using two techniques: verbal irony that says the opposite of what he means and rhetorical questions that include an implied but unspoken answer. Find examples of verbal irony in Rymer's criticism and discuss why you believe Rymer does not expect his readers to take these words seriously. Secondly, make a list of the questions he asks. If you feel he assumes specific answers, what are they? How do these two techniques strengthen his argument?

3. In small groups, discuss Rymer's criticism of *Othello*'s "Fable" or plot. How many examples can you find of his reasons for dismissing the plot as unbelievable? Do you agree with any of them? Can you suggest how his views may be influenced by his culture and history? Also discuss a related topic, Rymer's complaints against the immorality of the play. What are his specific criticisms? Again, do you agree? Why or why not? How do your culture, history, and view of entertainment affect your response?

4. Choose one of the following three exercises:

   a) With a partner, compose and perform a dialogue between Rymer and someone from the same time period who found *Othello* a delightful and entertaining play. Debate your positions, being as formal and polite or as a sarcastic and disagreeable as seems appropriate.

   b) Imagine an opportunity to travel through time and meet Rymer after having seen a modern stage or film production of *Othello*. Act out a discussion of your views, considering how your differing historical contexts influence your opinions. Should the theater, for example, be a place of moral education or entertainment or both?

   c) Write a strong disagreement to Rymer's criticism in the form of a "Letter to the Editor" for a newspaper where presumably his views have been quoted or personally expressed. Can you use irony and rhetorical questions as effectively as he does or is a different tone better to express your opinion?

5. Rymer considers *Othello* a "bloody Farce" rather than a tragedy. As a small group, choose a portion of *Othello* or construct a mini-version of the entire play and perform it for the class as a farce with intended humor. Perhaps even use Rymer's suggested title, *The Tragedy of the Handkerchief*, as a start.

6. Explain how you would stage a production of *Othello* in "modern dress," deciding on appropriate costumes to indicate the main characters' public stature and private lives. Include sketches, magazine pictures, or computer-generated drawings to present your choices. Alternatively, after researching the history of Venice and Africa in the sixteenth century, describe and illustrate costumes for a "period dress" *Othello* that reflects Shakespeare's original setting.

7. Edmund Kean was considered the best Othello in the nineteenth century, yet William Hazlitt qualifies his review with criticism. What is the main weakness of Kean's interpretation as far as Hazlitt is concerned? What does Hazlitt identify as Kean's main success?

8. Kean's performance was more natural and lively than the formal, re-served styles used by many previous "Othello" actors. In pairs or small groups, recite one of Othello's speeches in different acting styles, considering the distinctions Hazlitt makes between "energy" and "calmness," "grandeur" and "passion." This exercise will work best for speeches from 3.3 to the end of the play. Follow the per-formances with a discussion about the strengths and weaknesses of each interpretation. Which style appears truest to Othello's character and why?

9. Why does William Winter believe Booth's Iago to be the best inter-pretation on stage for fifty years? What seems to be the most impor-tant element? Familiarize yourself with several key words—duplicity, transparency, and malignity—and discuss how they suit Iago's char-acter, giving specific examples.

10. Act out a portion of one of Iago's main scenes in two different styles, the first demonstrating typical, obvious villainy and the second em-phasizing a more subtle combination of wickedness, wit, and good humor. Discuss which seems a more appropriate interpretation and why. How does the interpretation of Iago affect Othello's credibility and sympathy?

11. Divide into three groups and hold a class debate about Winter's view that Iago "is the most interesting figure" in *Othello*. The first group will defend Winter's statement, the second will oppose it, and the third will hear both arguments and meet to choose the most con-vincing position, providing specific reasons for its decision.

12. Referring to the excerpt from Helena Faucit's reflections, *On Some of Shakespeare's Female Characters*, discuss what constitutes a her-oine and whether Desdemona fulfills the criteria.

13. Act out contrasting versions of Desdemona's dying scene, playing her as a "simple, yielding creature" and as someone who is "difficult to kill." Discuss which interpretation seems more valid and why.

14. Write a diary entry for Mr. Macready, Helena Faucit's Othello, in which he privately responds to the effect of acting beside an unusu-ally lively Desdemona. Why does the experience seem so refreshing and how does it change your interpretation of your own part?

15. Gestures and vocal expression are both important in conveying a dramatic role. Perform a portion of *Othello* such as 4.1, 5.1, or 5.2 in two ways. Produce it as a "radio play," recording voices and sounds on tape. Then act it as a mime without words. Discuss how the two versions—voice with no action, and action with no voice—affect your appreciation of both elements of performance. Does either version

allow you to understand the play or the characters in a new way? If so, how?

16. Watch a video or listen to a recording of Verdi's opera *Otello*. Write a review, focusing especially on the music and how you feel it interprets or reflects feelings and actions in Shakespeare's play. You might want to consider the effect of including choruses and duets—musical options that did not exist in the original play.

17. Choose musical selections—modern, classical, or both—that you feel would enhance a production of *Othello*. Limiting this exercise to a portion of the play, such as several scenes or acts, write a short report explaining where, why, and how your selections contribute to the *Othello*'s atmosphere and action.

Suggested readings for this section appear at the end of the next section, "Twentieth-Century Performances."

TWENTIETH-CENTURY PERFORMANCES

Twentieth-century productions of *Othello* shared with previous centuries some similar reasons for appeal and similar challenges. The passionate intensity and emotional devastation of the tragedy continued to make for compelling drama, while racial concerns remained influential in casting choices. Likewise, difficulties in balancing the roles of Othello, Iago, and Desdemona still raised questions of interpretation for directors, actors, and audiences. Changes in the political, social, and cultural landscape over the decades affected decisions about acting styles and settings for the play. Technological advances also added an important new dimension to performance with the rise of television and film industries that allowed for expanded audiences as well as innovative opportunities for producing and interpreting Shakespeare's text. The camera did not simply make possible more diverse and realistic settings but also offered the potential for wide-angle and close-up shots that could create visual symbolism and deliberately draw attention to specific characters.

This century produced a number of film and stage versions of *Othello*, some recognized as landmarks in the play's performance history for their innovation, controversial perspective, or achievement in capturing the richness and complexity of human experience expressed in Shakespeare's text. The following brief survey of some noteworthy productions demonstrates the scope of interpretive possibilities and the ways in which art and reality continue to interact to make Shakespeare's plays current and valid in each new age.

PAUL ROBESON, LONDON (1930) AND BROADWAY (1943)

Although a black actor played Othello successfully in Europe in the late nineteenth century, Paul Robeson was the first African American to break racial barriers in England and United States by gaining broad-sweeping public support for his stage performance of the title role. Trained and known internationally as a concert singer with a rich baritone voice, Robeson was recognized for

Paul Robeson as Othello and Jose Ferrer as Iago on Broadway, 1943. Vandamm Studio, Billy Rose Theatre Collection, The New York Public Library for the Performing Arts, Astor, Lenox and Tilden Foundations.

dramatizing Othello's dignity, majesty, and nobility. In 1930 London reviewers found his voice and his physical stage presence powerful and effective in portraying Shakespeare's character. In spite of this enthusiasm, however, Robeson did not appear on an American stage until a dozen years later because the theater community still felt that an African Othello was too controversial for a country steeped in racial prejudice. When one director, Margaret Webster, finally had the courage to cast Robeson in an American performance of the play, she began with a tour of several less risky academic stages before mounting the production on Broadway in 1943.

Robeson's popularity in New York was unprecedented. He received a twenty-minute ovation on his first night and broke the record for the longest continuous Broadway run of a Shakespeare play. The previous record for *Othello* in New York was fifty-seven performances and for any Shakespearean play in America was 157; Robeson played Othello in New York for 296 continuous performances (Hill, 128). His achievement was as much a social and political statement as it was a cultural and artistic event. He called the play "a tragedy of racial conflict . . . rather than of jealousy," and his acceptance in a mixed-cast production of *Othello* radically changed public perceptions of the play and its main character. Whereas prior to his success many critics and audiences considered a black man as Othello unthinkable, after Robeson's Broadway run some people began to suggest that *only* a black man could play the part effectively. Thus, although Robeson did not remove racial attitudes towards the play, he significantly transformed them.

Margaret Webster, who risked her reputation as director to cast Robeson as Othello on Broadway, later published the memoirs of her career. In the excerpt below, she captures the audience's enthusiasm for Robeson, while suggesting that in spite of his powerful stage presence the trained singer might have been a "good" rather than a "great" Othello. Some reviewers, in fact, felt that Robeson was too stiff as an actor in such an emotionally demanding role. Nevertheless, his popularity and achievement remained without question.

FROM MARGARET WEBSTER, *DON'T PUT YOUR DAUGHTER
ON THE STAGE*
(New York: Alfred A. Knopf, 1972)

From the moment he walked onto the stage and said, very quietly, " 'Tis better as it is," he endowed the play with a stature and perspective which I have not seen before or since. I wrote to May: "Is it possible to be a great Othello without being a good Othello?" No. But the moment lent it greatness. The Robeson *Othello* became more than just a successful revival; it was a declaration and its success an event in which the performance itself was of less importance than the public response. (107)

The audience tribute that I valued most of all came to me by letter from a boy in the U.S. Army who was stationed some distance from New York and came up with four buddies on a weekend leave. He wrote:

Last Saturday night I saw *Othello*. It took a lot of coaxing to get four soldiers to spend a Saturday night of the first weekend leave in a month, in a theatre, watching something by Will Shakespeare. . . . Well, what followed is only natural. We all of us, for those few brief hours, went into a trance; we were living every emotion of the play. . . . Incidentally, going back on the troop train . . . for the first time in my army career I saw five soldiers sprawled over the seats, feet in the air, sleeves rolled up, shirts open, talking not about the babe they met at Broadway Brewery, but of all things, a thing called *Othello*. (115)

LAURENCE OLIVIER, LONDON (1964, FILM 1965)

Laurence Olivier's performance of Othello at the National Theatre in London in 1964 is often regarded as equally significant as Paul Robeson's achievement, if not more so, and stands in stark contrast to Robeson's interpretation of the part. Olivier's Othello has been recognized as both a masterpiece of artistic skill and a highly controversial rendering of Shakespeare's character. Under the direction of John Dexter, Olivier presented a "realistic" or "modern" Othello by deliberately challenging traditional views of the character's nobility. Olivier's Othello appeared self-centered and egotistical, as a man who, contrary to his own words, is "easily jealous" and whose initial veneer of civility quickly turns to savage behavior. In the temptation scene where the shift occurs, Othello symbolically tears the crucifix off his neck as a sign that he has abandoned the pretense of social values.

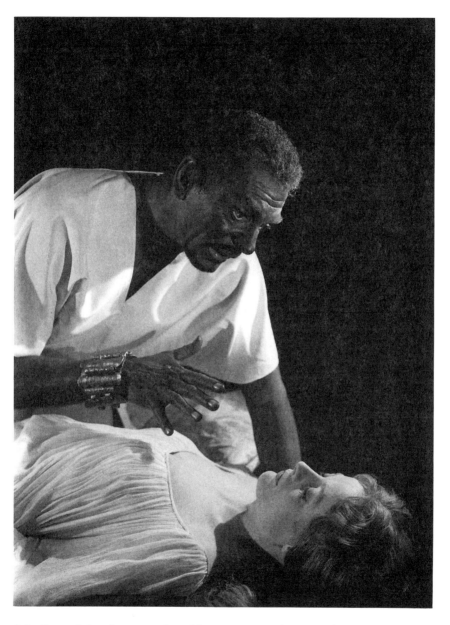

Othello and Desdemona played by Laurence Olivier and Maggie Smith at the National Theatre of Great Britain, 1964. Angus McBean Photograph. The Harvard Theatre Collection, The Houghton Library.

Race played an important part in Olivier's interpretation. As a white man, he transformed himself into a black African using almost full-body makeup, costuming himself in a simple belted tunic, bare feet, anklets and bracelets, and developing a particular walk and quality of voice that gave him the appearance and presence of a tribal African leader rather than a noble Venetian general. His Othello was a black man superior in the knowledge of his racial difference. Much of the praise for his performance came from this technical achievement of becoming convincingly "black" as well as from the artistry with which he mastered attention to both small gestures and a broad range of emotions. Iago was overshadowed by this Othello and while Desdemona, played by Maggie Smith, offered a convincingly passionate counterpart to the central character, the performance clearly belonged to Olivier. Although some felt that his interpretation inappropriately diminished the tragic, heroic dimensions of Shakespeare's character, most recognized Olivier's impressive talent as an actor, and many saw his portrayal of Othello as the most successful and innovative attempt in the twentieth century.

The following excerpt by Kenneth Tynan, literary manager of Olivier's 1964 *Othello*, quotes the director John Dexter's impressions of Othello and gives Tynan's own reaction to Olivier's first rehearsal or "reading" of the part.

FROM KENNETH TYNAN, ED. *OTHELLO: THE NATIONAL THEATRE PRODUCTION*
(London: Rupert Hart-Davis Ltd., 1966)

[Dexter:] "Othello . . . is a pompous, word-spinning, arrogant black general. At any rate, that's how you ought to see him. He isn't just a righteous man who's been wronged. He's a man too proud to think he could ever be capable of anything as base as jealousy. . . ."

[Tynan:] This was not a noble, "civilised" Othello but a triumphant black despot, aflame with unadmitted self-regard. . . . There are moral flaws in every other Shakespearean hero, but Othello is traditionally held to be exempt. Olivier's reading made us realise that tradition might be wrong; that Othello was flawed indeed with the sin of pride. (4–5)

ORSON WELLES FILM (1952, RE-RELEASE 1992)

Orson Welles produced a film version of *Othello* in 1952, the decade before Olivier's stage performance, which was also subsequently filmed in 1965. But while the Olivier/Dexter film closely recreated the stage experience, Welles deliberately used camera technology to provide viewers with an interpretation of Shakespeare very different from what theaters could offer. He was making a movie rather than a play. He used authentic settings in Venice and in Morocco. His film relied on self-conscious cinematography with close attention to light and shadows and to downward and upward camera angles that conveyed a sense of epic grandeur in some scenes and a dizzying sense of chaos in others. Welles's *Othello* was charged with the symbolism of images and sound: vast landscapes of towers, cliffs, and crashing waves; confined spaces created by narrow corridors, pillars, beams, grates, and bars; and sounds of cannon blasts, drums, bells, and haunting choirs.

The text itself was of secondary importance. Welles turned a three-hour drama into a ninety-minute film, cutting about half the play and replacing emotional intensity and intimacy with a highly visual experience. For some critics, this approach diminished the tragedy of Shakespeare's original text because the characters were not developed enough to be sympathetic. For others, the production is a testament to the camera's creative potential in presenting new interpretations and impressions of a classic work. The re-release of the movie in 1992 gives audiences today an opportunity to judge Welles's artistry for themselves, to see it not only as another twentieth-century version of Shakespeare's play but also as an early innovation in modern filmmaking.

Welles's *Othello* has a fascinating four-year production history with numerous delays and complications because of ongoing financial needs. The first scene filmed in Morocco, the killing of Roderigo in 5.1, had to be completely adapted because only Iago's costume had arrived. Welles chose to shoot the scene in a public bath setting with most of the characters wrapped and turbaned in towels borrowed from hotel rooms where they were staying. The following excerpt from the diary of Michael MacLiammoir, the actor playing Iago, describes this modification, the results of which were ultimately dramatic and effective.

FROM MICHAEL MACLIAMMOIR, *PUT MONEY IN THY PURSE:*
THE FILMING OF ORSON WELLES' "OTHELLO"
(London: Eyre Methuen, 1976)

[Welles] has decided to open fire with the camera on the attempt on
Cassio's life and on the subsequent murder of Roderigo by Iago, and as
the incidents usually take place . . . in a street, and as this would neces-
sitate clothes for Cassio and Roderigo . . . he has emerged from a sleep-
less night with the idea of making the murder happen in a *steam-bath*,
with M. and B., God help them, stripped and draped and turbaned in
towels. This, as well as dealing with the clothes question until it can be
settled, effective and sinister twist of the bloody business of Act Five
Scene One with which he is opening.

Roderigo, draped in towels, discovered lying on small straw divan in a
rest room after the bath and playing with ears of lapdog . . . as he says to
Iago (fully clothed and peering playfully round doorway) 'Every day thou
doffest me with some device, Iago.' Action then proceeds through comedy scene of Iago's instructions about the murder of Cassio to series of
shots in crooked stone passages and wash-rooms hung with dripping
towels and full of vague shapes of bathers. . . . Bob . . . and me . . . plotting and peering through ominous gratings and barred windows at Cassio
being massaged while I hiss 'It makes us or it mars us, think of that'; and
we come right down to Roderigo, having made his abortive attempt on
Cassio and been himself imprisoned under slatted floor, crying 'O
damned Iago! O inhuman dog!' During this Iago stabs him through the
slats with his sword in the manner of fish-catching in tropical waters, the
vapour growing denser as he does it. (92–93)

THE LAURENCE FISHBURNE AND KENNETH
BRANAGH FILM (1995)

While Paul Robeson was the first African American to play Othello on stage, Laurence Fishburne was the first to appear in the
role on film—in 1995. This movie, directed by Oliver Parker, is a
Hollywood version of *Othello* that makes Shakespeare readily ac-
cessible to the general public. It takes full advantage of the camera's creative potential by filming realistic settings, using close-ups
for intimate scenes, allowing for flashbacks and dream sequences,
as well as symbolic shots, such as a recurring chess board identified
with Iago's manipulation of the other characters. As director, Parker attempted to focus on the relationship between Othello and
Desdemona, saying,

Iago is totally fascinating—a Machiavellian mind manipulating everyone . . . and he's riveting to watch. But for me, at the centre of the play is the all-consuming love between Othello and Desdemona. . . . I wanted to reinvest the tragedy with passion and romance, because without romance there is no real tragedy.[1]

This intention is achieved partly through Fishburne's erotic, passionate portrayal of Othello which emphasizes the hero's private rather than his public role. Bedroom scenes are prominent, and Irene Jacob's Desdemona is a convincing romantic partner. At the same time, Kenneth Branagh's Iago is a conspicuous schemer from beginning to end, as the camera consistently draws attention to his part in the unfolding of a love story gone tragically wrong.

ADAPTATIONS

Some renditions of *Othello* deliberately depart from Shakespeare's original words and plot by altering the story or experimenting with the performance medium for specific political or artistic purposes. These productions adapt rather than simply reinterpret the play. For example, a 1972 play called *An Othello* significantly revised *Othello*'s basic plot by redesigning scenes, combining modern slang with Shakespeare's language, making Iago a black character, too, and having Othello murdered at the end of the play. Political views guided this adaptation as the relationship between Iago and Othello clearly alluded to the history of African American conflict represented by figures such as Malcolm X; questions about Othello's racial loyalty and integrity became more important than his role as a tragic lover.

An early 1970s rock musical called *Catch My Soul* again used the outlines of *Othello* to explore social and historical issues, setting the performance in America's Deep South, incorporating voodoo elements and the interplay of magic and ritual. Years later, in 1997, music again became the main artistic element as The American Ballet Theatre presented a dance version of *Othello* at the Metropolitan Opera House. As an historical event, this performance recalls the racial significance of Paul Robeson's 1943 Broadway *Othello*, because The American Ballet's *Othello* drew a larger African American audience than any of its previous productions. These examples of *Othello* adaptations suggest a range of creative possibilities and experiments that reflect both the continued appeal of Shakespeare's play and the impact of new artistic visions and technologies within cultural contexts that continually evolve and change.

NOTE

1. *Jet*, 89.9 (January 15, 1996), 32.

QUESTIONS FOR WRITTEN AND ORAL DISCUSSION

In addressing modern film versions of *Othello*, the following topics include general questions that could apply to any production of *Othello*, as well as specific discussion questions designed for several more readily available movies.

1. Watch any film production of *Othello* and write a review, evaluating its effectiveness in realizing the themes and characters of Shakespeare's play, and offering your opinion as to its success or failure as a movie. What do you feel the movie was attempting to achieve? What kind of rating would you give it in a movie guide?

2. Watch two movie versions of *Othello* and write an essay comparing and contrasting them. Consider, for example, their use of camera techniques and settings, their ability to create sympathetic characters and engage you as an audience, and their effectiveness in portraying tragedy to modern viewers. Or hold a class discussion about which production you preferred and why.

3. Referring to Margaret Webster's account of the response to Paul Robeson on Broadway in 1943, imagine you are one of the five soldiers who just saw the performance and are discussing it on the train afterwards. Compose a conversation with your friends. What impressed you about the play? Are you embarrassed or surprised by your own and each other's reactions?

4. Choose a partner and hold an imaginary interview with Paul Robeson after his first night on Broadway. What is his reaction? What do you suppose he meant in calling *Othello* "a tragedy of racial conflict . . . rather than of jealousy"? As an option, research Robeson's history as a performer and social activist to give yourselves a better understanding of his perspective in his time.

5. Olivier intended his interpretation of Othello to be "realistic" and "modern" rather than traditional, and his character was meant to be "arrogant" and "proud." Why do you suppose these flaws are consid-

ered modern? Do you think Othello is a flawed or flawless hero? Is
he arrogant or not? Write a short paper or hold a class debate that
addresses these issues. Alternatively, watch the movie and decide
whether or not you agree that Olivier's performance matches Kenneth Tynan's description included in this chapter. Does Olivier appear as arrogant and proud as Dexter and Tynan say he is? Is he
sympathetic and convincing? Does his rendition seem controversial
to you? Why or why not?

6. Discuss the question of race in performing or watching *Othello*. In
your community and social environment is this a relevant issue?
Should it matter whether Othello is played by a black man or a white
man in black makeup? Why or why not? Does race seem to be an
important part of the play to you?

7. Orson Welles is considered one of the early gifted filmmakers of the
twentieth century. Respond to his use of lighting, imagery, and/or
symbolism in *Othello*. What effect do they have? Consider, for example, the frequent appearance of grills, grates, bars, and beams,
and/or the shots of wide-open spaces and the sky. Why do you
suppose Welles uses stairways and angled shots so often? What is the
impact of filming part of the temptation scene between Othello and
Iago up on a cliff? How does Welles's decision to begin at the end
with Othello and Desdemona's funeral procession and film the rest
as a flashback affect your response? Address any of these questions
or respond to other aspects of the film that either appeal to you or
do not and explain why.

8. Referring to MacLiammoir's diary account of the "bath scene" modification in Welles's *Othello*, discuss how effective it is in the movie
itself. Considering this example, offer your own adaptation of a scene
or section of *Othello*, attempting to remain true to the play's atmosphere and action while portraying it in a new way.

9. Watch Oliver Parker's 1995 movie of *Othello*. Is he successful in his
intent to make the love between Othello and Desdemona central to
the film? If so, how? Do you agree with Parker that "without romance
there is no real tragedy"? Why or why not? Does Branagh's Iago appear to take second place to this main focus? Explain why or why
not. Consider any aspects of interpretation that surprised you, appealed to you, or disappointed you. Explain your reaction. For example, how does the chess board symbolism work? What is the effect
of close-up shots? What do you think of the decision to have Cassio
slip Othello the suicide weapon in the final scene? Why do you suppose Parker added that? Do you like or dislike the decision to have
Iago accompany the three dead people, Desdemona, Emilia, and Oth-

ello, on their "death bed"? Why or why not? Address some or all of these questions in a group discussion or include one or two in a written response to the movie.

10. Discuss the relationship between Othello and Desdemona in one of the available films. What do you think the director and actors hoped to achieve? What effect might the time period in which the movie was filmed have on the approach? Is the love convincing? Are the roles balanced? Explain why you do or do not agree with the interpretation. You could also address these questions by comparing several movie versions.

11. Use a video camera to film a portion of *Othello*—possibly one or two scenes—paying attention to the use of lighting and camera angles, and including a written explanation of your choices and the effect you intended to achieve.

12. Create a collage of *Othello*, using visually symbolic images and materials that reflect your understanding of the play.

SUGGESTED READINGS

Carlisle, Carol Jones. *Shakespeare from the Greenroom: Actors' Criticisms of Four Major Tragedies*. Chapel Hill: University of North Carolina Press, 1969.

Hankey, Julie, ed. *Othello, William Shakespeare: Plays in Performance*. Bristol: Bristol Classical Press, 1987.

Hill, Errol. *Shakespeare in Sable: A History of Black Shakespearean Actors*. Amherst: University of Massachusetts Press, 1984.

Jorgens, Jack. *Shakespeare on Film*. Bloomington: Indiana University Press, 1977.

Matteo, Gino J. *Shakespeare's Othello: The Study and the Stage, 1604–1904*. Salzburg: Institut Fur Englische Sprache Und Literatur, 1974.

Rosenberg, Marvin. *The Masks of Othello*. Berkeley: University of California Press, 1961.

Sprague, Arthur C. *Shakespeare and the Actors: The Stage Business of His Plays (1660–1905)*. Cambridge: Harvard University Press, 1944.

Vaughan, Virginia Mason. *Othello: A Contextual History*. Cambridge: Cambridge University Press, 1994.

Wine, Martin L. *Othello: Text and Performance*. London: Macmillan, 1984.

CURRENTS OF CRITICISM: THE TWENTIETH CENTURY AND BEYOND

As a play, *Othello* is recreated or "reinvented" each time it is dramatized on stage or film. But *Othello* is more than a script. It is also a text rich with poetry and themes that encourage multiple inquiries into aspects of human interaction, the nature of love, the history of race and gender, and other topics. As such, Shakespeare's play is the subject of literary debate and cultural exploration. While performance requires single, specific choices about how each line will be delivered and each character portrayed, reading allows for many perspectives to coexist in tension or in balance with one another. *Othello*'s issues and characters are sufficiently complex to allow for more than one point of view; response and counter-response are important in recognizing and appreciating these complexities. The following survey of critical approaches in the twentieth century reveals a diversity of interpretations and suggests that these perspectives are shaped not only by Shakespeare's text, but also by the cultural expectations of readers and scholars, as well as by critical trends and new discoveries in research. The three categories included below are not all-encompassing or mutually exclusive; many observations and approaches cross over the boundaries or go beyond them. These headings, however, offer some clarity and direction as you begin to engage in the critical debate, agreeing or disagreeing with what others have said, and, by so doing, broadening your understanding of the play.

STRUCTURE AND CHARACTER

Studies that specifically address *Othello* as a tragedy often focus on structure and character, reflecting two key elements of Aristotle's definition of tragedy: its unity of plot and its ability to engender fear and pity in audiences and readers (see Chapter 1). Many scholars have noted that *Othello* conforms to Aristotle's definition more closely than other Shakespearean tragedies because of its relative unity of time and place and its lack of plot digressions that might diminish the intensity and impact of the main story line. Another common topic of discussion concerns the way *Othello*'s

beginning seems to adopt the structure and assumptions of comedy until tragedy moves forward in Act 2. Love and jealousy, for
example, are typical comic subjects; an unsuccessful, intervening
father like Brabantio is a familiar comic character type; and marriage is the usual goal and resolution of the comic form. That
Shakespeare turns these conventions to a tragic end in *Othello*
invites interest in what the play suggests about the darker side of
comedy and about the tragic potential of a domestic love plot, so
unlike most of Shakespeare's other tragedies that depict public
lives of kings and princes.

By far the most prominent critical exchange about *Othello* has
revolved around character analysis, again with several underlying
assumptions: a) Aristotle's view that tragedy deals with heroes, and
b) a traditional understanding that heroes manifest some form and
degree of nobility. Iago's prominent and essential role in the plot
has sparked an ongoing debate about whether his motives and
dramatic function diminish Othello's dignity and nobility. Two extreme positions exist. One sees Othello as a truly tragic hero with
noble stature that parallels or surpasses other Shakespearean figures such as Hamlet or Macbeth. From this perspective, Othello is
sympathetic throughout, and Iago is a devilish manipulator incar-
nating evil as he leads the hero to his downfall. The other position
sees Othello as a proud, self-deluded man who hardly needs Iago
to lure him to his crimes of passion and who is almost anti-heroic
and certainly incapable of measuring up to conventional tragic proportions. Exemplifying the two extremes, A. C. Bradley's influential
early twentieth-century study, *Shakespearean Tragedy*, depicts
Othello as romantic, noble, and sympathetic, while F. R. Leavis's
response three decades later argues strongly against Othello's heroism. Most critics would say that Leavis takes his position too far,
but the popular Laurence Olivier *Othello* in 1964 used his argument as its main interpretive guideline. The following excerpts
from Bradley and Leavis set out the conflicting viewpoints that
have defined the boundaries of *Othello*'s character discussion for
over a century.

FROM A. C. BRADLEY, *SHAKESPEAREAN TRAGEDY* (1904)
(London: Macmillan, 1905)

Othello is, in one sense of the word, by far the most romantic figure among Shakespeare's heroes; and he is so partly from the strange life of war and adventure which he has lived from childhood. He does not belong to our world, and he seems to enter it we know not whence—almost as if from wonderland. . . . (187)

And he is not merely a romantic figure; his own nature is romantic. . . . (188)

The sources of danger in this character are revealed but too clearly by the story. In the first place, Othello's mind, for all its poetry, is very simple. He is not observant. His nature tends outward. He is quite free from introspection, and is not given to reflection. Emotion excites his imagination, but it confuses and dulls his intellect. . . . (189)

This character is so noble, Othello's feelings and actions follow so inevitably from it and from the forces brought to bear on it, and his sufferings are so heart-rending, that he stirs, I believe, in most readers a passion of mingled love and pity which they feel for no other hero in Shakespeare. (191)

Evil has nowhere else been portrayed with such mastery as in the character of Iago. (207)

Iago stands supreme among Shakespeare's evil characters because the greatest intensity and subtlety of imagination have gone to his making, and because he illustrates in the most perfect combination the two facts concerning evil which seemed to have impressed Shakespeare most. The first of these is the fact that perfectly sane people exist in whom fellow-feeling of any kind is so weak that an almost absolute egoism becomes possible to them, and with it those *hard* vices—such as ingratitude and cruelty—which to Shakespeare were far the worst. The second is that such evil is compatible, and even appears to ally itself easily, with exceptional powers of will and intellect. (232–233)

. . . [Iago] was destroyed by the power that he attacked, the power of love; and he was destroyed by it because he could not understand it; and he could not understand it because it was not in him. Iago never meant his plot to be so dangerous to himself. . . . The foulness of his own soul made him so ignorant that he built into the marvellous structure of his plot a piece of crass stupidity. (236–237)

FROM F. R. LEAVIS, "DIABOLIC INTELLECT AND THE NOBLE
HERO; OR, THE SENTIMENTALIST'S OTHELLO," *THE COMMON
PURSUIT* (1937)
(London: Chatto & Windus, 1952; Rpt. from *Scrutiny* 6 [1937])

Othello is . . . the chief personage in such a sense that the tragedy may
fairly be said to be Othello's character in action. Iago . . . is not much
more than a necessary piece of dramatic mechanism. . . . (138)

[Othello's] self-idealization is shown as blindness and the nobility as
here no longer something real, but the disguise of an obtuse and brutal
egotism. Self-pride becomes . . . ferocious stupidity, an insane and self-
deceiving passion. . . . Othello's noble lack of self-knowledge is shown as
humiliating and disastrous. . . . (146–147)

. . . there is no tragic self-discovery . . . the tragedy doesn't involve the
idea of the hero's learning through suffering. (150–151)

Between the two extremes which Bradley and Leavis represent,
a more moderate debate considers how Othello's nobility and
weaknesses can coexist and whether Iago's stated motives—revenge, resentment, personal insult—are believable and under-
standable reasons for his desire to destroy other people. For some,
this character analysis is defined as a battle between Good and Evil
in which Othello is torn between the goodness of Desdemona and
the evil of Iago. For others, especially with the rise of psychoana-
lytic theory in the second half of the twentieth century, character
is identified in more psychological terms. Iago often draws the
greatest interest, being identified with words like "neuroses," "aggression," "self-contempt," and "sadomasochism," while "narcis-
sism" has occasionally been used to describe Othello.

Desdemona is noticeably absent in this overview of "Structure
and Character" partly because she has been ignored, simplified, or
dismissed in many discussions of the play. However, critical debate
about her receives due attention under the third heading "Politics,
Race, and Gender."

IMAGE AND THEME

In contrast to detailed psychological analysis of character and
partly in reaction against it, some scholarship has focused more
on poetry and language patterns that reflect the thematic signifi-

cance and appeal of *Othello*. New Criticism, an approach that became popular in the mid-twentieth century, emphasized close
reading of the text for images and metaphors that demonstrated
artistic unity and addressed the play more as a dramatic poem than
as a script for performance or a study of character. From this perspective, meaning in *Othello* derives from clusters of words and
images such as animals and monsters, devils and hell, webs and
weaving, wit and witchcraft, food and drink, money and property,
blackness and whiteness, and stars and heaven. The repetition and
recurrence of these image patterns lead to views about *Othello*'s
main themes, addressing subjects such as love, jealousy, power,
race, temptation, justice, misunderstanding, intrigue, and deception.

For literary critic G. Wilson Knight, the exotic, extravagant quality of Othello's poetry is more important than any specific set of
images, and his language becomes a form of "music" that sets him
apart from others, especially Iago. This analysis, excerpted below,
tends to ignore psychology or human complexity, instead seeing
characters as dramatic symbols of qualities such as honor, beauty,
or cynicism.

FROM G. WILSON KNIGHT, *THE WHEEL OF FIRE*
(London: Methuen, 1930)

When Othello is represented as enduring loss of control he is . . . ugly,
idiotic; but when he has full control he attains an architectural stateliness
of quarried speech, a silver rhetoric of a kind unique in Shakespeare. . . .
This is the noble *Othello* music: highly-coloured, rich in sound and
phrase, stately. (103–104)

. . . Iago is pure cynicism. That Iago should scheme . . . to undermine
Othello's faith in himself, his wife, and his 'occupation', is inevitable. . . .
As ugly and idiot ravings, disjointed and with no passionate dignity even,
succeed Othello's swell and flood of poetry, Iago's triumph seems complete. The honoured warrior, rich in strength and experience, noble in
act and repute, lies in a trance, nerveless, paralysed by the Iago-
conception. . . . But Iago's victory is not absolute. During the last scene,
Othello is a nobly tragic figure. His ravings are not final: he rises beyond
them. He slays Desdemona finally not so much in rage. . . . He slays her
in love. (117–118)

. . . [Iago's] failure lies in this: . . . at the moment of his complete triumph . . . the *Othello* music itself sounds with a nobler cadence, a richer flood of harmonies, a more selfless and universalized flight of the imagination than before. The beauties of the *Othello* world are not finally disintegrated: they make 'a swan-like end, fading in music'. (119)

Some studies of image and theme have connected language patterns more closely to character development than G. Wilson Knight does. Many critics have noted that conflicting modes of speech reflect *Othello*'s central tension and devastation. Othello's and Iago's language patterns are separate and distinct until Othello begins to see the world through Iago's eyes, at which point he also begins to imitate Iago's speech. In the latter part of the twentieth century, this shift in the play has been the focus of an approach called Deconstruction that contrasts New Criticism by emphasizing the instability and unreliability of words rather than their unity and coherence. Because recurring words like "honest" do not mean what they say in *Othello* and because Iago's lies can deceive and mislead almost everyone, it becomes impossible to distinguish appearance from reality, innocence from guilt, truth from falsehood. And this confusion, according to some scholars, is caused by language itself which has the power to create unreality, to destroy innocence and truth.

As in critical approaches to character, studies of *Othello*'s language produce a variety of conflicting perspectives arguing that words and images can demonstrate themes about unity, diversity, or utter chaos in the play.

POLITICS, RACE, AND GENDER

Social and historical issues in *Othello* have attracted interest for most of the twentieth century as scholars have attempted to place the play in its time and appreciate how Shakespeare's portrayal of Venetian society, racial attitudes, military roles, and marital status reflects or conforms to commonly held Renaissance views. These topics receive much fuller exploration in the three previous chapters about historical context. As the twentieth century turns into the twenty-first, however, critical focus has responded to increased political awareness about prejudice, rights, and equality with respect to race and gender. Discussion often combines modern values and expectations with historical knowledge to offer new readings of *Othello*. The words "power," "difference," and "possession" can help to clarify the direction of these recent perspectives.

Politics is about power, which is manifest in *Othello* not only by the use of language to create self-image and destroy others but also by social expectations and assumptions that define and confine characters. Public roles and distinctions are important especially against the play's military backdrop, but also in terms of class relations as they influence attitudes about a young gentlewoman's behavior and views about appropriate suitors for her. *Othello's* relationships are about the dynamics of love and hate; they are also about social and political status based, in part, on race and gender.

Race, for example, is a matter of difference. Critics in the past have denied its importance, avoided its controversial impact, or examined it carefully in light of documented views of Africans in Shakespeare's time. Recently, however, many readers have emphasized its centrality in the play's tragic development. While some suggest that blackness itself is not as important as the fact that Othello is culturally and socially a foreigner, others say blackness matters most. Either perspective recognizes Othello as a "stranger," a figure of interest to scholars examining the influence of colonialism, imperialism, and "otherness" on racial identity throughout history. These readers suggest that Othello's difference creates an inherent insecurity in his relation to Venetians who willingly accept him as a military leader but disapprove of his marriage into their community. Iago can easily awaken this insecurity because society has already established it. Othello and Desdemona's mutual devastation consequently results from Othello's crisis of identity grounded in his social difference which others treat as inferiority. This interpretation leads to conflicting conclusions that racism manifested in the play either reveals Shakespeare as a racist or indicates his willingness to question the accepted political views and prejudices around him.

Gender in the play has become an issue of possession and property in the wake of feminist perspectives and voices expressing views about *Othello's* dramatization of marriage and patriarchy. In the past, Desdemona has either been idealized as a helpless, passive, innocent victim or degraded as an unconventional woman whose boldness and independence explain or even justify her violent end. Many recent discussions have focused more on the tension between Desdemona's assertiveness and the limitations placed on her by a father and husband with legitimate male rights of possession. For some, Desdemona is the central tragic figure in a society that denies women natural freedoms and rights as people. For others, both Desdemona and Emilia demonstrate the courage of women who attempt to challenge the confining expectations of marriage and gender. Again, Shakespeare himself gets mixed reviews. The articulated misogyny or hatred of women in the play leads to accusations of Shakespeare's misogyny or, contrarily, to suggestions that he dared to challenge restrictive patriarchal views by making his female characters more attractive, thoughtful, and sympathetic than his male characters. The following paragraph from Irene Dash's exploration of Shakespeare's women characters raises some valuable questions about the tragic stature of Desdemona and Emilia in a play that most often focuses on the tragedy of Othello.

FROM IRENE G. DASH, *WOOING, WEDDING AND POWER: WOMEN IN SHAKESPEARE'S PLAYS*
(New York: Columbia University Press, 1981)

Although the play examines marriage, it is not a domestic tragedy. . . . Domestic tragedy usually presents characters of limited power in imagination and background. The magnificence of Othello, the range in Desdemona as a woman, including her intelligence, originality, and defiance of convention, belie this designation of the work. But it is the tragedy of a woman, of women, pummeled into shape by the conventions that bind. For Shakespeare takes not one, but two marriages—one new and fresh, one old and worn—to give us a double vision of the experience. Some critics tend to prefer Emilia, the wife of Iago, to Desdemona because Emilia's story ends defiantly on a positive note, offering hope for women. But the extremity of the force that breaks her submission to her husband hardly argues for her independence. Desdemona's tragedy is the more usual—a slow wearing away of resistance, a slow imposition of patterns—a slow loss of confidence in the strength of the self, always with the aim of adjusting to marriage. Coleridge believed that she was just the woman every man "wishes . . . for a wife." How sad that this should be a man's dream. (104)

CONCLUSION

Critical trends and approaches to *Othello* are vast and varied. Sometimes two positions stand in stark opposition to each other; sometimes one perspective replaces another as historical knowledge advances or as social values and cultural attitudes evolve and change. The overview included here touches on several main threads of discussion with a view to encouraging your own critical thinking about the play. Some enduring questions about Shakespearean criticism have no easy answers. When we read and interpret Shakespeare's plays, how necessary is it to consider his historical context, how valuable is it to impose our modern thinking on a centuries' old text, and how possible is it to avoid or ignore either one of these two opposing perspectives? What is the best balance between the two? These questions underlie the currents of debate and reflection about *Othello* as it falls in and out of favor with different people yet continues to engage them, touch them, and disturb them.

QUESTIONS FOR WRITTEN AND ORAL DISCUSSION

1. Love and marriage are typical subjects of comedy rather than tragedy. Discuss how Act 1 of *Othello* reflects comic ideals and expectations. What seems potentially good or celebratory in this act? What foreshadows the development of tragedy? Find specific examples.

   As a group project, perform a version of Act 1 as if it were a mini-comedy about love and romance complete with conflict and resolution. Remember that Shakespeare's comedy depends less on humor than on the fulfillment of harmony and community in spite of obstacles, although a character like Brabantio could be made to appear humorously foolish and old-fashioned. Discuss how this exercise makes you see *Othello*'s tragedy from a different perspective. If Act 1 can almost stand alone, could the rest of the play exist without it? Why or why not?

2. A. C. Bradley describes Othello as a romantic figure, a man from "wonderland." What might Bradley mean by "romantic" and what evidence in the play supports this viewpoint? What weaknesses does Bradley identify in Othello and do you agree? Offering examples, explain why or why not.

3. What are the two facts about evil that Bradley sees in Iago? Do you agree with Bradley's depiction of Iago? Why or why not?

4. Choose one of the following ideas:

a) Write an essay in which you choose between Bradley's and Leavis's views of the play and argue your position.

b) Hold a class debate in which one group defends Bradley's position about Othello's nobility, while a second group supports Leavis's argument about Othello's pride and egotism. According to your defense, what function does Iago play and to what extent is *Othello* a tragedy? Designate a moderator or judge to guide the debate (perhaps the teacher or someone from outside the class) and allow for organized argument and counter-argument.

c)   Hold a trial against *either* Othello or Iago, designating judge and jury, and calling witnesses (friends or foes in the play) to testify for or against one of the two. This may require certain liberties with the play. You could, for example, assume that the murders and suicide were attempted and unsuccessful, you could hold the trial in the absence of the guilty party, or you could imagine ghosts of the dead returning and other characters appearing to answer questions about the motives and crimes of the accused. Do, however, use evidence from the text in your defense or prosecution.

5. After watching the Laurence Olivier movie of *Othello*, write a response that indicates whether or not you feel it reflects Leavis's comments about *Othello*, used by the director as a guideline for his interpretation.

6. Discuss heroism in *Othello*, developing your own definition or using information provided in this chapter. Is Othello a tragic hero? Why or why not?

7. Pretend to be Iago's psychiatrist and write a summary analysis or series of observations based on sessions you have had with him or on his own testimony in monologues at the end of Act 1, 2.1, and near the end of 2.3. How would you diagnose this character and explain his behavior? How do his motives and actions correspond?

8. G. Wilson Knight uses the metaphor of "music" to describe Othello's speech and observes a change in his language from beauty to "idiotic ravings" and back to beauty. Does Othello's language seem more musical than the language of other characters? Explain and give examples. Trace the pattern of change in his speech, selecting examples from his early, middle, and late appearances in the play. What do these changes reveal to you about Othello's character? Do you agree with Knight's view that Othello slays Desdemona in love rather than rage? Why or why not? Do you agree or disagree that the play ends in beauty? How and why?

9. Write an essay explaining how specific image patterns contribute to the characterization, action, and resolution in *Othello*. Choose from the following: animals and monsters, webs and weaving, wit and witchcraft, food and drink, money and property, blackness and whiteness, devils and hell, or stars and heaven.

10. Write an essay about one of the play's themes. You might begin with the sentence "*Othello* is a tragedy about ____" and fill in the blank with one of the following words: love, jealousy, marriage, power, race, insecurity, temptation, justice, injustice, misunderstanding, intrigue, or deception. Use evidence from the play to argue your position.

11. Write a paragraph or two about the importance of the word "honest" or "reputation" in *Othello*, considering how either one reflects the contrast between appearance and reality in the play.

12. How important do you think Othello's racial and cultural difference is to the tragic outcome of the play? Does it matter that he is black or simply that he is a foreigner? Does his difference contribute to his insecurity? If so, explain how and why.

13. The fact that some characters express racial prejudice does not necessarily mean that Shakespeare shares the same prejudices. Debate in small groups or argue in an essay whether you think Shakespeare is a racist or not. Consider your historical context and his as you reflect on this issue, and try to explain how those different perspectives affect your position. (See Chapter 2.)

14. As in the previous question, similarly the misogynist comments of some characters do not necessarily make Shakespeare a misogynist. Because Iago seems to hate women, does Shakespeare? Discuss Shakespeare's portrayal of women in *Othello* and draw some conclusions, providing evidence from within the play to support your view. (See Chapter 4.)

15. Respond to Irene Dash's position that *Othello* is a tragedy about women. Do you prefer Emilia or Desdemona? Explain why. Is Desdemona passive, self-assertive, or both? Can you argue, as some critics have, that Desdemona's behavior in any way contributes to Othello's suspicions about her? If not, is she simply a victim of circumstance? Does either perspective make her more or less sympathetic in your eyes? Would you say that the play is Desdemona's tragedy as much as Othello's? Why or why not?

16. Write a monologue in the voice of Desdemona or Emilia, expressing your private thoughts and concerns at some point near the end of the play. How does Desdemona understand her love for Othello and

his behavior towards her? Or how might Emilia feel about Iago and herself after the truth has been revealed, her mistress is dead, and Iago is taken away to be tortured?

17. Imagine Desdemona or Emilia discussing love and marriage with a modern feminist who has either radical or moderate views. Compose or improvise a dialogue. Do the women agree or disagree with one another and on what grounds? As another possibility, you could give Bianca a voice. What does she have to say for herself and about Cassio? Would a modern feminist find her sympathetic? Do you?

SUGGESTED READINGS

Adamson, Jane. *Othello as Tragedy: Some Problems of Judgment and Feeling*. Cambridge: Cambridge University Press, 1980.

Barthelemy, Anthony Gerard, ed. *Critical Essays on Shakespeare's "Othello."* New York: G. K. Hall & Co., 1994.

Bloom, Harold, ed. *Major Literary Characters: Iago*. New York: Chelsea House Publishers, 1992.

Bradley, A. C. *Shakespearean Tragedy*. London: Macmillan, 1904.

Dash, Irene. *Wooing, Wedding and Power: Women in Shakespeare's Play*. New York: Columbia University Press, 1981.

Dean, Leonard F., ed. *A Casebook on "Othello."* New York: Thomas Y. Crowell Co., 1961.

Elliott, G. R. *Flaming Minister: A Study of "Othello" as a Tragedy of Love and Hate*. New York: AMS Press, 1965.

Hyman, Stanley Edgar. *Iago: Some Approaches to the Illusion of His Motivation*. New York: Atheneum, 1970.

Kaul, Mythili, ed. *Othello: New Essays by Black Writers*. Washington: Howard University Press, 1997.

Knight, G. Wilson. *The Wheel of Fire*. London: Methuen, 1930.

Leavis, F. R. *The Common Pursuit*. London: Chatto & Windus, 1952.

Muir, Kenneth, and Philip Edwards, eds. *Aspects of "Othello": Articles Reprinted from "Shakespeare Survey."* Cambridge: Cambridge University Press, 1977.

Snyder, Susan, ed. *Othello: Critical Essays*. New York: Garland, 1988.

Vaughan, Virginia Mason, and Kent Cartwright, eds. *Othello: New Perspectives*. London: Associated University Presses, 1991.

Wain, John, ed. *Shakespeare; Othello: A Casebook*. London: Macmillan, 1971.

Wine, Martin L. *Othello: Text and Performance*. London: Macmillan, 1984.

6

Contemporary Applications

The previous chapters have addressed ways of understanding and appreciating *Othello* by considering the literary elements and techniques that contribute to its dramatic form, the historical context in which the play was written, and the interpretations and responses appearing on stage and in print over the centuries. This final chapter begins with the assumption that we can also expand our vision and perceptions of the play by discovering that some of the reasons for its continuing popularity and controversy can be found in contemporary events happening around us or in experiences that affect or touch us personally. Allowing *Othello* and our modern world to interact and illuminate each other can generate insights about truths that fact and fiction share.

The first part of this chapter, "From the Headlines," examines the connection between themes or issues presented or raised in *Othello* and similar topics of concern at the center of relatively recent events that have received significant coverage on television, in newspapers, and in magazines. Three stories are included. The first, O. J. Simpson's murder trial, investigates the impact of domestic violence and its potentially tragic consequences. The second, the Unabomber's mail-bombing terrorism, explores the nature of psychopathic behavior, what motivates it and how society responds to it. The third, President Bill Clinton's scandalous relationship with Monica Lewinsky and its political impact, considers how private lives and public office affect each other. Headlines and tabloids have sensationalized some of these events and personalities, triggering responses of disgust, impatience, or even boredom. This chapter, however, attempts to recover relevant and genuine concerns that made these news stories so public and controversial to begin with, and to suggest comparisons and contrasts with conflicts dramatized in *Othello*.

The second part, "From the Storylines," opens up the definition of "contemporary" to include fiction that is not necessarily recent but that draws us into imaginary worlds where time becomes almost irrelevant as characters engage us in stories that remain current even when settings and cultural contexts change. The discord between love and hate and between good and evil that gives *Othello* its powerful emotional and dramatic appeal also shapes the narratives of other poems, short stories, and novels. The selections included in this chapter challenge us to recognize fiction's capacity to expand the boundaries of our experience and to teach us new ways of understanding our own struggles to know and be ourselves.

FROM THE HEADLINES

DOMESTIC VIOLENCE: O. J. SIMPSON

The arrest of O. J. Simpson on June 17, 1994, for the murders of his former wife, Nicole Brown Simpson, and her friend, Ronald Goldman, launched one of the most public criminal trials in American history and captured the interest, imagination, and passions of people around the world. The case against Simpson became known as the "Trial of the Century," and yet ironically, the national and international attention it attracted focused on an all-too-common private tragedy: the pain, suffering, and devastation arising from marital discord and abuse. Like Shakespeare's *Othello*, the account of O. J. Simpson's arrest and subsequent criminal and civil trials revolved around the issue of domestic violence and its extreme consequences. For some of the same reasons that Othello's personal tragedy becomes a public concern in Shakespeare's play, Simpson's story, too, became high-profile news appearing in daily headlines. Shakespeare's tragic character and O. J. Simpson share very public personalities in their own worlds, one as a fictional army general and the other as an historical sports and entertainment figure. Both achieved success and recognition in spite of racial prejudice and both defied social conventions as black men choosing to marry white women. Their stories of domestic violence, therefore, become inextricably connected with their images as public heroes and with their society's judgments and expectations.

It might be tempting to dismiss these parallels between Othello and Simpson, to suggest that the similarities are too superficial to merit attention, or that fiction and history have little in common. Some might say that Shakespeare's tragedy represents true high drama while the theatrical displays in Simpson's case reveal little more than media manipulation, a sensationalized scandal, and a courtroom circus. Others might argue that there is far more relevant tragedy in the murders of Nicole Brown Simpson and Ronald Goldman than in the "dead" bodies of characters lying on a bed in the final scene of a play. Because the two stories are not identical, however, does not mean that their parallels cannot illuminate the personal concerns and social issues involved in both. Differences can be as enlightening as similarities, and there is much room for discussion. As stories of domestic violence, *Othello* and the events surrounding O. J. Simpson's court cases invite consideration and debate about the causes and consequences of marital abuse, about the relationship between love and jealousy, about passion and reason, about justice and judgment, about the social impact of seemingly private matters, and about the strong emotional reactions evoked in public spectators or theater audiences.

On October 3, 1995, the verdict of "not guilty" in Simpson's criminal trial was a dramatic moment. It concluded a nine-month court case that saw a number of jurors dismissed and replaced; heard the damaging testimony of a racist detective, accompanied by accusations of police corruption and judicial incompetence; witnessed the flawed use of material evidence including a bloody glove, footprints, and DNA testing; and caused deep divisions in public opinion about Simpson's guilt or innocence based on attitudes towards race and wealth. In the end, the jury ruled according to the criminal trial standard—"beyond reasonable doubt"—and found sufficient doubt for acquittal.

The criminal trial was followed, however, by a civil "wrongful death" suit launched by Ronald Goldman's family and Nicole Brown Simpson's estate. A year after being acquitted on murder charges, Simpson found himself in court again on September 17, 1996, accused of being responsible for the same two deaths, but facing possible financial punishment rather than imprisonment or the death sentence. In February 1997 the jury in this second, much less publicized, court case entered a verdict of "liability" for Simpson based on the civil trial standard—"preponderance of the evidence"—meaning that the twelve jurors accepted as a greater likelihood that Simpson committed the murders than that he did not. The court ordered Simpson to pay over $33 million in damages, a high figure for any civil case and much more than legal experts or the public expected.

In short, O. J. Simpson was found both guilty and not guilty in the brutal slayings of his former wife and her friend. The contradictory sentences leave room for questions about his guilt or innocence in their deaths. However, any doubts about the history of violence in his relationship with Nicole were dispelled by evidence and testimony emerging in the court proceedings. The public furor around his trials raised national and international awareness of many social ills and injustices, and evoked widespread expression of the passion and suffering accompanying those tragedies and inequities. If *Othello* is one of Shakespeare's most emotionally compelling plays, O. J. Simpson's story is one of America's most emotionally charged events in recent history. The drama that it unfolds challenges each one of us to examine the passions and judgments in our own responses, to see beyond the tabloid headlines to human faces and voices not only publicized in Simpson's courtroom scenes but hidden in our neighborhoods and communities, marked with their own stories of abuse, violence, and injustice.

The following brief chronology identifies some key dates and events in O. J.'s relationship with Nicole and the trials following her murder. The remainder of this section includes a series of excerpted newspaper articles, editorials, and published perspectives that provide facts and opinions about the two trials, their outcomes, and the larger social issues they represent.

Brief Chronology of O. J. Simpson's Criminal and Civil Law Suits

Feb. 2, 1985	O. J. Simpson marries Nicole Brown.
Jan. 1, 1989	New York City Police called to a domestic dispute between the Simpsons. Nicole is bruised and beaten; O. J. is charged.
March 1992	Nicole leaves O. J.
May 1994	Nicole ends relationship after attempted reconciliation.
June 12, 1994	Nicole Brown Simpson and Ronald Goldman found murdered.
June 17, 1994	O. J. arrested on murder charges after a televised police chase through Los Angeles.
June 30, 1994	Preliminary hearing begins in criminal trial.
Sept. 26, 1994	Jury selection for trial begins.
Jan. 23, 1995	Criminal trial commences.
Oct. 3, 1995	Jury announces "not guilty" verdict.
Sept. 17, 1996	Civil trial begins in "wrongful death" suit against O. J.

Oct. 23, 1996	Courtroom statements begin.
Nov. 22, 1996	O. J. admits previous violence against Nicole but denies murder charges.
Feb. 4, 1997	Jury finds O. J. "liable" in civil trial and awards the Goldman family $8.5 million in compensatory damages.
Feb. 10, 1997	Jury orders O. J. to pay $25 million in punitive damages, $12 million each to the Goldman family and Nicole Brown Simpson's estate.

THE PUBLIC DRAMA BEGINS

Five days after the murders of Nicole Brown Simpson and Ronald Goldman, police attempted to arrest O. J. Simpson, but the encounter led to a highway chase captured on national television. The excerpted account below records the details of that event, including a letter from Simpson hinting at suicide, and references to the history of domestic violence in O. J.'s relationship with Nicole. Pay attention to the way police and spectators respond to Simpson and to the way Simpson's words and actions represent himself. Think about whether these various perspectives stimulate any suspicion or sympathy for O. J. Note the reporter's reference to Simpson's past domestic violence and consider how that information affects the overall portrayal of O. J. Try to set aside your knowledge of events following Simpson's arrest and ask yourself whether, having read this newspaper report, you would have been sufficiently unbiased to be chosen as a juror in his criminal trial.

FROM DAN MEYERS, "SIMPSON ARRESTED IN DRIVEWAY AFTER
LEADING POLICE ON HIGHWAY CHASE"
(Knight-Ridder/Tribune News Service, June 18, 1994)

LOS ANGELES—After a bizarre chase along the freeways of Los Angeles that ended with an hourlong standoff in the drive of his Brentwood estate, O. J. Simpson was arrested Friday night on charges that he murdered his ex-wife and a male friend.

In an extraordinary drama played out before a national television audience, Simpson was taken into custody just before 9 p.m. local time after tense negotiations with police who had surrounded the white Ford Bronco containing the armed former football star.

His arrest followed a 60-mile chase that ended at about 10:50 EDT when the Bronco—driven by Al Cowlings, a former teammate of Simpson's—pulled into Simpson's driveway as police looked on.

For the next hour, Simpson sat unseen in the darkened interior of a Ford Bronco as Cowlings shuttled back and forth talking with detectives standing in the doorway.

As negotiations continued into the evening, crowds gathered around the estate. Bystanders chanted and carried signs, one saying, "Save the Juice."

Outside the estate's walls, members of Simpson's family hugged each other and cried after word of the arrest came out.

A cheer came up from the crowd of 300 spectators.

His arrest marked the climax of an extraordinary day that saw first the announcement that Simpson would be charged with murder, then word that he had fled arrest and finally the surreal televised image of dozens of police cars trailing a white Ford Bronco as it rolled slowly north along emptied freeways.

As much of the final act played out live on national television, Simpson, a gun pressed to his head, rode in the passenger seat of the Bronco driven by Cowlings.

"He demanded that he would not give himself up," said Carl Williams, who was monitoring police scanners for KCBS television. "He's in the back of the vehicle. He has a gun to his head and he will hurt himself. He is demanding to be taken to his mother."

Simpson had disappeared sometime before noon after police notified his lawyer they planned to arrest him for the murder of Nicole Brown Simpson, 35, and Ronald Lyle Goldman, 25.

Simpson left behind a letter suggesting he was considering suicide. In the letter, he contended he was innocent of murder, but declared: "I can't go on."

"Everyone understands I had nothing to do with Nicole's murder," Simpson wrote in the letter. "I loved her.

"I think of my life and feel I've done most of the right things. So why do I end up like this. I can't go on. No matter what the outcome, people will look and point. I can't take that. I can't subject my children to that."

The letter ends: "Don't feel sorry for me. I've had a great life, great friends. Please think of the real O. J. and not this lost person. Thanks for making my life special. I hope I helped yours. Peace and love. O. J." . . .

The Simpsons, who had dated since Nicole was 18, were married in 1985. Early in the morning of New Year's Day, 1989, a battered Nicole Simpson summoned police to her house and claimed her husband was trying to kill her. Simpson pleaded guilty to beating his wife.

Despite the recommendation of prosecutors that he serve 30 days in jail, and despite the fact that police had been called to the house eight times before, Simpson was let off with a fine, probation, and a requirement that he perform community service, and seek counseling.

In the letter he left Friday, Simpson sought to defend himself in that case also.

"Unlike what has been written in the press, Nicole and I had a great relationship for most of our lives together. Like all long-term relationships, we had a few downs and ups," he wrote.

"I took the heat New Year's 1989 because that's what I was supposed to do. I did not plead no contest for any other reason but to protect our privacy and was advised it would end the press hype.

"I don't want to belabor knocking the press, but I can't believe what is being said. Most of it is totally made up. I know you have a job to do, but as a last wish, please, please, please, leave my children in peace. Their lives will be tough enough."

IMAGE, MEDIA, AND PUBLIC OPINION

In a study of race and justice published after Simpson's criminal trial and before the civil suit against him, clinical psychologist and author Jewelle Taylor Gibbs reflects on the significance of O. J.'s public personality and image in relation to his race and his criminal charges. In the excerpt below she draws attention to the media's role in forming that image, and makes observations that invite her readers to question the appropriateness of the words "hero" and "villain" as labels for Simpson. Consider whether you find her direct style thought-provoking or offensive. Note, in particular, her reference to Othello, especially since she associates Shakespeare's tragic hero with Rodney King, an "ordinary" black man whose mistreatment by police and the judicial system caused riots in the streets of Los Angeles in 1992. Her connection between Othello and King invites an obvious comparison between Othello and Simpson, but her view of Othello seems to focus not on any tragic or sympathetic qualities but rather on his "pathological" or abnormal behavior, especially his violence. Her comment, therefore, raises questions not only about Simpson's image and character but also about her view of Othello's status as hero or villain.

FROM JEWELLE TAYLOR GIBBS, *RACE AND JUSTICE: RODNEY KING AND O. J. SIMPSON IN A HOUSE DIVIDED*
(San Francisco: Jossey-Bass Publishers, 1996)

In hindsight, O. J. was establishing a significant pattern in his adult life—the public persona of a respectable and responsible family man versus the private persona of a promiscuous and abusive Don Juan. The seeds were sown for what would later emerge as O. J.'s split personality—the Jekyll-and-Hyde of the all-American hero. (125)

During the seven months that elapsed between O. J. Simpson's arrest in mid June and the beginning of his trial in late January, O. J. has been subjected to his first trial by the media, in the court of public opinion. . . . The same reporters who had created and nurtured the myth of O. J. Simpson the superstar, excused his dissolute lifestyle, and covered up his spousal abuse were now competing to tarnish and destroy his dignity and his reputation. His positive image as a sports legend, a celebrity businessman, and an assimilated black role model was irreparably damaged, presumably beyond any possibility of future rehabilitation.

The American media machine, in all of its power and persuasiveness, had succeeded in transforming O. J. Simpson, all-American hero, into O. J. Simpson, African-American villain. The media, which had once merchandised O. J. Simpson as the quintessential Oreo, had now repackaged and relabeled him as the pathological Othello, a brutish black man, just another Rodney King. (148)

GENDER LINES AND DOMESTIC VIOLENCE

The following newspaper article addresses the relationship between gender and domestic violence that drew public attention especially during O. J. Simpson's first court case. In an article originating in the *Orange County Register*, journalist Bonnie Weston records the responses of abused women living in a "safe house" as they hear the jury's verdict of "not guilty" that concluded Simpson's criminal trial. As you read the report, notice how personal and emotionally-charged the reactions are. The article shows how the outcome of one well-publicized domestic violence case affected victims in other potentially similar experiences, and, in so doing, raises awareness of how the tragedy surrounding any circumstance of domestic abuse involves both individual suffering and social costs.

FROM BONNIE WESTON, "ABUSED WOMEN FEAR ABUSERS MAY BE EMBOLDENED BY SIMPSON VERDICT"
(Knight-Ridder/Tribune News Service, October 3, 1995)

SANTA ANA, Calif.—The women stared hard at the big screen TV. Some held hands, others held babies. Like the onscreen defendant, they sat frozen. And why not?

The small group belongs to the inaugural class of Laura's House, a new shelter for battered women and their children. It opened in September in Orange County, Calif., partly thanks to state grants established in response to Nicole Brown Simpson's murder.

Glued to the television Tuesday, the women said that they, too, were on trial:

A verdict for O. J. Simpson would be a verdict against all women bruised and battered by men who claim to love them. The brash claims common to all their tormentors would be validated: You can't do anything. No one will believe you.

So when the jury acquitted O. J. Simpson, they felt it had shrugged off his history of spousal abuse, along with the beatings they, too, had endured.

"All those 911 tapes?" cried Amy, 20, who came to the shelter last week with her infant daughter. "All the reports? It's [saying] it's okay to beat up your wife. You can do whatever you want. Nobody cares what happens to us. Nicole said they never do anything. She was right."

"All that evidence and none of it's substantial?" asked Betty, 48. "I could even accept second degree murder. But nothing?"

The women, many still hiding from spouses and boyfriends, asked to be identified only by their first names.

"O. J. looks so innocent," said Jeannie, 33. "I wish he didn't do it. He has a long record of being a good man, giving away money, doing good things. But then he went home and beat his wife."

Most of the women, five residents and several shelter staffers, said they are fearful that abusers may be emboldened by the verdict, and less likely to get to the help they need. Most are also concerned that women may be more hesitant to leave an abuser—especially if they think he will be free to pursue them again.

Chris, 48, disagreed: "When I came here, I wasn't thinking of justice. I was thinking of saving my life. Women will still leave. They do need somewhere to go."

Scott, a teen-ager who came to the 16-bed shelter with his mother, worries about his new housemates, but not ultimate justice.

"Women have scary lives," he said. "They worry about getting raped, about getting beat-up, about getting killed. I figure if [Simpson] did it he'll go to hell. Let God deal with it. He's good at it."

RACIAL PREJUDICE AND JUSTICE

In contrast to Weston's preceding article on women victims of domestic violence, Loretta Green's article below, first appearing in the *San Jose Mercury News*, offers observations about the impact of racial divisions and prejudices in the publicity surrounding O. J.'s court cases. Responding to the announcement of the "liable" verdict and award of damages concluding the civil suit, Weston addresses reactions toward issues of race in both the criminal and civil trials. Note how clearly she articulates the impact of racial divisions, not only by reporting the contrasting public responses after each trial, but also by speculating about how reactions might have been different if the victim had been O. J.'s first African-American wife, Marguerite, rather than his second wife, Nicole. Green raises concerns about the negative influence of racial prejudice on the administration of justice, and then issues a broad challenge to everyone to take the opportunity to heal wounds that the months and years of O. J.'s trials so painfully exposed. Like Weston's article on abused women, Green's report on racial tensions indicates that the tragedy at the center of O. J.'s story spread far beyond the court cases about two murdered people, and that any personal and social recovery from that pain will require both time and effort.

FROM LORETTA GREEN, "O. J. SIMPSON CASE WAS MORE
ABOUT BLACK AND WHITE THAN FINDING THE KILLER"
(Knight-Ridder/Tribune News Service, February 20, 1997)

In one way the O. J. Simpson trial is over.

In another, it may never be over.

How, we must ask ourselves, has it all been so black and white?

How has it been so "us" against "them," rich against poor, famous against the undistinguished?

The facts have been presented, distorted, cloaked, analyzed, explained, manipulated, believed and contested.

Through it all, one thing never changed. Two people were tragically murdered and the killer has not accounted for it.

As the trials progressed, perhaps we were all caught off guard—surprised that the proceedings induced the eruption of symptoms of our social ills.

In polite and toxic circles of our day-to-day acquaintances, we still try to find tactful and politically correct ways to acknowledge that the anger is largely about black people's and white people's unresolved lives together.

"What next, O. J.? Golf, young white women or your kids?" asked a sign a white man held outside the courthouse recently.

"People don't want to see a black man have anything," said a black man after the civil trial verdict.

How deep and how smoldering, the issue of race.

It is present in many people's opinions of guilt or innocence. Everyone professes to want "justice," but justice in each trial has been for some a robe, and for others a shroud.

If there is any agreement, it is in mutually detesting the murder of a young mother and a friend caught in the wrong place at the wrong time.

And surely, we all hate the thought of murderers going free.

But beyond that, there is the feeling that if Marguerite Simpson—the pretty woman with black skin and black hair who was O. J.'s first wife—had been founded savagely murdered on her doorstep, it would never have become the story it did.

The nation would have been appalled, but the event's media shelf life would have been that of a sack of tomatoes.

The image of the blond, fair, pretty Nicole—a fragile, flaxen and coveted societal icon—heightened the emotional impact of the murders.

All along, while the issue should have been finding and prosecuting the responsible, it also was so much about black and white AND the haves and have-nots.

Ultimately, we witnessed our division on the 6 o'clock news.

Jubilation and shouting by African-Americans in public gatherings after the criminal trial's "not guilty" verdict. Stunned, angry silence by most whites.

Jubilation and shouting by whites at the civil trial's "liable" verdict. Stunned, angry silence by most blacks.

Over the decades we have come a long way toward better understanding. Years ago, the somewhat flawed, self-acclaimed poverty fighter Patrick Moynihan noted that while we had made progress, too often a seminal event revealed the great divide.

We will all passionately deny personal racial or cultural prejudice. And though we know everyone has some degree of it, our intellectual integrity will not permit us to admit to harboring any significant amount.

If there is any good to come out of the enormous Simpson tragedy, it is perhaps the stripping away of our pretenses about how we really feel about each other.

Perhaps in our nakedness, we can take the time to examine the places in us that need work to heal.

QUESTIONS FOR WRITTEN AND ORAL DISCUSSION

A number of words invite attention in examining the events surrounding O. J. Simpson's trials for murder and in comparing those events with the plot of *Othello*. Some of those words include the following: tragedy, drama, victims, justice, jealousy, heroes, villains, race, guilt, and innocence. Choosing one or two of these words, begin by considering their relevance in O. J. Simpson's case, consulting the questions below or devising your own as possible topics to stimulate a group discussion or debate, or a personal written response. Refer to the documents in this section as you form opinions and draw conclusions.

1. If there is tragedy at the center of Simpson's story, how would you define it, and whose tragedy is it? Should blame necessarily be a part of tragic events or is suffering the main concern?

2. If there is drama in the events of Simpson's trials, what conflict and tension create the drama, who are the characters and audience, and what is their relationship to each other? How is the media involved?

3. By what criterion might Simpson be considered a hero or a villain and is it fair or reasonable to insist that he be either? Explain why or why not.

4. By what standards might Simpson be considered guilty or innocent of wrongdoing? Is your judgment based on legal decisions, factual evidence, personal feelings or experience, media coverage or opinion polls? Which of these influences seems most relevant or important?

5. How significant is the role of race in the court proceedings and public attention to the trials? Are reasons for its prominence valid or inappropriate? What is the relationship between race and justice in Simpson's trials and to what extent might injustice also be part of the story? Who suffers from injustice?

6. Consider how the word "tragedy" applies to Simpson's story when viewed from the perspective of Bonnie Weston's article about abused women or Loretta Green's article about racial prejudice and justice. Discuss to what extent the two murders and the two trials represent larger tragedies beyond the Simpson, Brown, and Goldman families. Are the tragedies primarily personal or social or both? Explain how and why.

7. Consider how Loretta Green concludes her article (February 20, 1997) by inviting us as a society and as individuals "to examine the places in us that need work to heal" following the passions and divisions sparked by the two court cases. What needs to be healed and what specific ways can you suggest the healing take place? Look for answers at a social and national level and also offer answers from your personal perspective.

Expand your discussion to include *Othello*, considering how one or two of the words listed above allow you to compare Shakespeare's play with O. J. Simpson's story. Again, generate your own questions or refer to the following suggestions as guidelines for your exploration.

8. Who are the victims in each story? Is it possible to argue that Othello and Simpson are not only abusers but also, to some degree, victims? If so, how, and, if not, do the other more obvious victims receive adequate attention? Why or why not?

9. Compare the details of domestic violence in both stories, and consider the significance of jealousy in each. How are your observations and conclusions affected by the fact that Shakespeare's characters speak for themselves while the problems in O. J. and Nicole's relationship are filtered through media reports, lawyers' arguments, and the families' emotional responses?

10. Discuss the relative significance of these common elements of Shakespearean tragedy in *Othello* and Simpson's story: suffering, the capacity for self-awareness, and the ability to engender sympathy. You may want to refer to Aristotle's definition of tragedy in Chapter 1.

11. Consider the relationship between justice and judgment in both stories. Is justice served in either story, and if so, how and by whom? What judgments are expressed in either story and are they just or unjust, biased or impartial?

12. How does Othello's suicide affect your view of justice and tragedy in Shakespeare's play? How does it affect your comparison of Othello and Simpson as heroes or villains? How does the murder-suicide in *Othello*, compared to the accusations of murder in Simpson's story, shape your view of the play and the historical event as stories of domestic violence?

13. Do you find Jewelle Taylor Gibbs's comparison between Othello and O. J. Simpson effective and convincing in the excerpt from her book, *Race and Justice*? Are her comments insightful or offensive? What role does Rodney King play in her observations? Explain whether you agree with her use of the words "hero" and "villain" and indicate whether her perspective on O. J. or Othello changes your opinion of either.

14. Compare Desdemona and Nicole. How are their situations alike or different? How does Emilia's role and murder add to your perception of domestic violence in the play, and, likewise, how does the newspaper article in this section about battered women in a shelter contribute to your view of domestic violence in Simpson's story?

SUGGESTED READINGS

Abramson, Jeffrey, ed. *Postmortem: The O. J. Simpson Case: Justice Confronts Race, Domestic Violence, Lawyers, Money, and the Media*. New York: BasicBooks, a division of HarperCollins Publishers, 1996.

Gibbs, Jewelle Taylor. *Race and Justice: Rodney King and O. J. Simpson in a House Divided*. San Francisco: Jossey-Bass Publishers, 1996.

Morrison, Toni, ed. *Birth of a Nation'hood: Gaze, Script, and Spectacle in the O. J. Simpson Case*. New York: Pantheon Books, 1997.

Schiller, Lawrence, and James Willwerth. *American Tragedy: The Uncensored Story of the Simpson Defense*. New York: Random House, 1996.

PSYCHOPATHIC BEHAVIOR: THE UNABOMBER

On April 3, 1996, FBI agents arrested Theodore Kaczynski in an isolated cabin in Montana after leads linked him to a series of mail bombings across the United States. Kaczynski's arrest marked the end of one of the longest and most expensive manhunts in FBI history. Criminal court proceedings that followed in the next two years exposed Kaczynski as the infamous Unabomber, responsible for three deaths and more than two dozen injuries in sixteen random bombings over an eighteen-year period. The Unabomber's profile as a terrorist and serial killer raises disturbing questions about the nature of evil, about the apparent lack of conscience at the root of psychopathic behavior, about the reasons or motives for one person's inhumane destruction of others, and about society's search for ways to protect itself from such unpredictable violence.

These and other issues at the center of the Unabomber's story draw attention to similar troubling concerns about the presence of evil in *Othello*. Iago's villainy and the power of his influence in the play have intrigued and unsettled audiences and critics for centuries. The impulse to rationalize, explain, and understand his behavior suggests a need to control and contain it—a natural response to such overwhelming malice, to the horror and sense of vulnerability it evokes. Such responses also emerged in the wake of the Unabomber's devastating crimes. Like Iago, the Unabomber succeeded in damaging or destroying other lives while evading suspicion. Like culminating accusations and disclosures at the end of *Othello*, final revelations about the Unabomber's deeds challenge us to reflect on the deep moral problems they represent. Characters in Shakespeare's play eventually see Iago as some form of human monster. Many audience members agree. We can ask whether a closer look at the details of the Unabomber's story will lead to a similar conclusion about him or present a more complex view of dysfunctional human behavior, its causes, costs, and consequences.

After more than seventeen years of unsolved terrorism, an unusual sequence of events resulted in the Unabomber's arrest. The serial bomber sent a 35,000-word manifesto to two national newspapers and promised to end the bombings if the papers printed his document, which expressed his extreme views against technology and its negative effects on society. After the manifesto appeared in *The Washington Post*, Kaczynski's brother David recognized similarities between the document and his brother's beliefs. Choosing to alert the FBI about his suspicions, David Kaczynski narrowed the investigation, ultimately leading to Theodore's arrest.

The two years between the arrest in April 1996 and Kaczynski's sentencing in May 1998 were filled with discoveries, questions, speculations, apprehensions, and anticipation. Investigators uncovered substantial evidence against Kaczynski, including his personal journals, bomb-making information and materials in his cabin. A media inquiry into his past revealed personal details about an introverted, disturbed, but brilliant former math professor with few social skills and a troubled childhood. Meanwhile, legal experts and doctors addressed questions about Kaczynski's psychological health and mental competence to stand trial. Kaczynski demonstrated his own erratic, unpredictable behavior, disputing with his lawyers about their intent to use mental illness as an argument in his defense and, at the last minute before trial, requesting the right to dismiss his lawyers and represent himself—a request the judge denied. On the eve of the trial, public debate about the likelihood of a life sentence or the death penalty raised emotional responses from bombing victims, their families, and Kaczynski's own brother and mother.

In the end, an anticipated lengthy criminal trial never took place. Having pleaded "not guilty" to the initial charges in 1996, Kaczynski opted for a "guilty" plea on January 22, 1998, in a deal that assured him imprisonment rather than the death penalty. Consequently, much material evidence remained sealed and speculations about Kaczynski's psychological health and personal history remained largely unexamined. Contradictions between medical evaluations suggesting the diagnosis of paranoid schizophrenia and an assessment that found Kaczynski mentally competent for trial never became an issue. The Unabomber received a sentence of four life terms in prison, ensuring public safety, and at least partially satisfying the need for justice.

However, many attempts to make sense of the Unabomber's terrorism ended abruptly when Kaczynski entered his guilty plea and refused an opportunity at the final hearing to comment on his crimes. His conviction left the public—and may leave us still—with a feeling of incomplete closure not unlike the lack of resolution following Iago's last words in *Othello*: "Demand me nothing. What you know, you know. / From this time forth I never will speak word" (5.2.299–300). What we know at the end of *Othello* and after the Unabomber's conviction is that two guilty men—one fictional and the other historical—are caught and face punishment. What we also know is that too many innocent victims suffered before the day of discovery. What we still do not know is how any explanation of motives or causes—such as revenge, personal gain, mental instability—can settle our need to contain or control random acts of violence or understand the obvious, unaccountable pleasure that some people receive from destroying other lives.

Following a brief chronology of the Unabomber's story, this section concludes with a newspaper report on the day of Kaczynski's sentencing and a profile of psychopathic behavior.

Brief Chronology of Unabomber's Criminal History and Trial

May 25, 1978	First bombing occurs at a university campus in Illinois.
Dec. 11, 1985	Hugh Scrutton of Sacramento is the first victim murdered in the serial bombings.
Dec. 10, 1994	Thomas Mosser of New Jersey is the Unabomber's second murder victim.
April 24, 1995	Gilbert Murray of Sacramento is the third victim killed in the bombings.
Sept. 19, 1995	*The Washington Post* publishes the Unabomber's 35,000-word manifesto in return for a promise to end the bombings; national publication alerts David Kaczynski that his brother, Theodore, may be the Unabomber.
April 3, 1996	Theodore Kaczynski arrested in his isolated Montana cabin.
June 18, 1996	Kaczynski charged in four bombings that killed two people and injured two others.
June 25, 1996	Kaczynski pleads not guilty to the charges.
Nov. 12, 1997	Criminal trial begins with jury selections.
Jan. 5, 1998	Courtroom statements scheduled to begin but delayed by Kaczynski's effort to fire his lawyers and by a psychiatric assessment that finds him mentally competent to stand trial.

| Jan. 22, 1998 | Kaczynski pleads guilty to bombing murder charges as part of a deal to avoid the death penalty. |
| May 4, 1998 | Kaczynski receives four life terms in prison. |

THE MOMENT OF JUSTICE AND THE MEMORIES OF TERROR

The newspaper article below provides a brief synopsis of the Unabomber's history and then includes a variety of responses on the day of Kaczynski's sentencing, May 4, 1998. Quotations from legal experts, the judge, victims, and victims' families, Kaczynski and his family help to capture the moment of reckoning twenty years after the bombing terrorism first began. Consider how all these voices contribute to your thoughts and feelings about the personal and social impact of the Unabomber's crimes.

FROM HALLYE JORDAN, "UNABOMBER WILL SPEND THE REST
OF HIS LIFE IN PRISON"
(Knight-Ridder/Tribune News Service, May 4, 1998)

SACRAMENTO, Calif.—Showing no remorse while a parade of victims spoke of the pain the Unabomber has caused, a "cold, dead-eyed" Theodore Kaczynski was formally sentenced Monday to life in prison, without possibility of release.

The sentencing brought to an end a criminal saga that began in 1978 with the explosion of a relatively weak bomb on the Chicago campus of the University of Illinois, gradually escalating to more powerful fatal bombs that tore apart three men, the last victim in 1995. The killing spree injured 29 others, brought the nation's air traffic to a standstill and culminated with the arrest in Montana in April 1996 of the mathematician-turned-hermit, bringing to a close the largest manhunt in FBI history.

"Lock him so far down so that when he does die, he'll be closer to hell. That's where the devil belongs," Susan Mosser, the widow of the Unabomber's second victim, carefully told U.S. District Judge Garland E. Burrell Jr.

Dressed casually in a sweater and slacks, Kaczynski remained stoic while the victims of his 18-year reign of terror told of the physical and emotional damage they suffered at the hands of the Harvard-trained mathematician, who holed up in a small, filthy shack in the Montana wilds to build bombs and plot his revenge on a high-tech society that had shunned him.

The one-hour and 22 minute hearing was a formality; Kaczynski avoided the death penalty by pleading guilty Jan. 22 to killing Sacramento timber lobbyist Gilbert Murray in 1995, and New Jersey advertising executive Thomas Mosser in 1994.

Because his guilty plea aborted what was expected to be a four-month-long trial, much of the mountain of evidence seized from Kaczynski's cabin remained sealed. The sentencing hearing provided Kaczynski with his last opportunity to provide insight into, or remorse for, his actions, but he declined.

Instead, in a soft, high-pitched voice, Kaczynski used the forum to denounce the U.S. government for filing court documents intended to prove he acted for the sake of personal revenge, rather than to publicize the anti-technology doctrine he laid out in a 35,000-word "manifesto," which ultimately led to his arrest.

"Two days ago, the government filed a sentencing memorandum that was clearly political," Kaczynski told the court. "By discrediting me personally, they hoped to discredit the ideas espoused by the Unabomber. . . . At a later period of time, I expect to respond to the government's false statements. Meanwhile, I only ask the people to reserve judgment about me and the Unabomber case until all the facts have been made known."

Later, Special Assistant Robert J. Cleary referred reporters to dozens of excerpts from Kaczynski's personal [journal] that the government released last week when filing its sentencing memorandum and 92 pages of exhibitions.

"You can judge for yourselves whether it's an accurate portrayal," Cleary said, adding the numerous excerpts were filed because "the public had a right to know the basis of this case."

In the journals, written in English, Spanish, and a numeric code, in which several numbers made up one letter, Kaczynski "adopted the pretense that he was killing for the greater good of society," prosecutors wrote in their sentencing memorandum. But, they said, he first formed a "desire to kill" while a graduate student in 1966—years before he expressed any serious concerns about technology.

In one entry, Kaczynski writes, "My motive for doing what I am going to do is simply personal." He noted that if his crime seizes the public's attention, "it may help to stimulate public interest in the technology questions, and thereby improve the chances of stopping technology before it is too late."

But, he wrote, "I certainly don't claim to be an altruist or to be acting for the 'good' (whatever that is) of the human race. I act merely from a desire for revenge."

Kaczynski's decision to address Judge Burrell prompted Connie Murray and her sons, Wil and Gib, to rush out the courtroom door. The family returned when Kaczynski was finished, but Connie Murray did not testify.

In a statement read by FBI chaplain Mark O'Sullivan after the court hearing, Connie Murray said she walked out [because] "there was nothing he could say that I was willing to hear," and that anything she said to him would fall on "deaf ears."

Although she supported the death penalty for Kaczynski, Murray said the life sentence should keep "a serial killer from continuing to manipulate the system. Our hope is that he will go to prison and be forgotten."

David Kaczynski, who alerted federal authorities to the similarity of his older brother's writings after reading the Unabomber's manifesto, was in court, but did not speak on behalf of the brother he had not seen for 12 years before the trial began.

But after the session, David Kaczynski, who was praised by many of the victims for his moral courage, faced a barrage of TV cameras and reporters. "There really are no words to express the sorrow of today," the younger brother said. "The Kaczynski family offers our deepest apologies. We are very, very sorry."

David Kaczynski's 80-year-old mother, Wanda, who sat at his side during earlier hearings, did not come to court Monday. As he has during past court appearances, Theodore Kaczynski ignored his brother, who sat on the front row, directly behind the defendant.

Still, the day belonged to the victims and their chilling stories.

Susan Mosser, spoke in a shaky voice of sitting in the kitchen with her husband early on a Saturday, planning a day of Christmas tree shopping. She said her husband, still in his bathrobe, was reaching for a knife to open a package that had arrived the day before, when their 15-month-old daughter darted to the living room.

Susan Mosser followed, and was about to play "tea party" with Kelly when an explosion ripped through the house.

She found her husband in the kitchen, "face up on the floor. His stomach slashed open, his face was partially blackened and distorted. Blood, horror."

As he moaned softly, she grabbed towels and the baby's blanket, but "I wasn't sure what or where I could touch."

Lois Epstein, the wife of the Unabomber victim Charles Epstein, a genetic engineer who was maimed by a 1993 bomb, was next.

"Let me remind you that the construction of the bomb you sent to my husband was described in your notebooks in experiment 225," said Epstein, looking directly at Kaczynski. "Let me remind you that in your callous, contemptuous, quasi-scientific manner you described the results of that experiment as 'adequate, but no more than adequate.' " Lois Epstein, herself a Harvard-educated physician scientist, denounced Kaczynski for targeting "a gentle and brilliant man, a man who has never done you a moment of harm but has done the world a lot of good" through cancer research and hours put in at a children's clinic.

Her husband was taunted by Kaczynski, who sent him a letter after the explosion, scolding him for not being smart enough to know better than to open a package from someone he didn't know. On the stand, Charles Epstein turned the tables, berating Kaczynski for his "distorted view" that "the use of science to improve the human condition is merely a deception aimed at ultimately enslaving and controlling society."

"What right, then, do you have—hiding in your shack in a forest—to try to prevent me and my kind from trying to relieve the suffering of those who are afflicted by attempting to kill me and intimidate others?" Epstein asked. "To the extent that you really were trying to make some sort of statement about the potential problems engendered by science and technology, your murderous approach doomed you to failure. And, fail you did."

Nicklaus Suino said he was "shocked" at Kaczynski's lack of remorse and his bouncy gait as he strode into the courtroom. Suino was a college research assistant in Ann Arbor, Mich. in 1985 when he was slightly injured by a bomb disguised as a manuscript.

Suino said he had waited 13 years to face Kaczynski. The defendant "made cold, dead-eyed contact every time I looked at him."

Suino acknowledged the other victims had suffered more horribly than he, but urged them to put aside their thirst for revenge.

"The time you lose chasing your own anger never will be recovered," said Suino, a recent law school graduate. "There is no time for us to go on hating Mr. Kaczynski. Don't join him in that cell. You and I have more important things to do." . . .

In pronouncing the sentence, Burrell said Kaczynski had "committed unspeakable and monstrous crimes," and that if given the chance, he "would resume his vicious acts of terrorism."

"Because of the callous nature of his crime, the defendant presents a grave danger to society and should be incarcerated in a facility where he can be monitored to prevent any future acts of violence and intimidation," Burrell said.

The judge waived a $650,000 fine after finding Kaczynski [guilty] but ordered the defendant to pay $15 million in restitution. Under his order, Kaczynski will forfeit any financial gains stemming from book or media contracts to the restitution fund.

Burrell made no recommendation in which maximum security facility Kaczynski should be housed, leaving that to the U.S. Bureau of Prisons.

THE NATURE OF PSYCHOPATHY

The following excerpt from Robert Hare's book-length study of psychopathic behavior offers a profile of a psychopath and acknowledges the response of doubt and bewilderment with which others often confront such disturbing individuals. Measuring the Unabomber's history against this definition, try to determine whether and how the Unabomber might be classified as a psychopath. Also keep in mind the connections this chapter suggests between the Unabomber's inhumane and criminal behavior and Iago's villainous activity in *Othello*. Although psychological analysis is a twentieth-century development and "psychopathy" and "psychopath" are relatively modern terms, consider whether the description below can offer insight into comparisons between the Unabomber and Iago, and whether modern terminology sheds any light on Iago's intentions and behavior or the other characters' responses to him in the play.

FROM ROBERT D. HARE, *WITHOUT CONSCIENCE: THE DISTURBING WORLD OF THE PSYCHOPATHS AMONG US*
(New York: Pocket Books, Simon and Schuster Inc., 1993)

The most obvious expressions of psychopathy . . . involve flagrant criminal violation of society's rules. Not surprisingly, many psychopaths are criminals, but many others remain out of prison, using their charm and chameleonlike abilities to cut a wide swath through society and leaving a wake of ruined lives behind them.

Together, these pieces of the puzzle form an image of a self-centered, callous, and remorseless person profoundly lacking in empathy and the ability to form warm emotional relationships with others, a person who functions without the restraints of conscience. If you think about it, you will realize that what is missing in this picture are the very qualities that allow human beings to live in social harmony.

It is not a pretty picture, and some express doubt that such people exist. To dispel this doubt you need only consider the more dramatic examples of psychopathy that have been increasing in our society in recent years. Dozens of books, movies, and television programs, and hundreds of newspaper articles and headlines, tell the story: Psychopaths make up a significant portion of the people the media describe—serial killers, rapists, thieves, swindlers, con men, wife beaters, white-collar criminals . . . terrorists, cult leaders, mercenaries, and unscrupulous businesspeople. (2–3)

Psychopathic killers, however, are not mad, according to accepted legal and psychiatric standards. Their acts result not from a deranged mind but from a cold, calculating rationality combined with a chilling inability to treat others as thinking, feeling human beings. Such morally incomprehensible behavior, exhibited by a seemingly normal person, leaves us feeling bewildered and helpless. (5)

QUESTIONS FOR WRITTEN AND ORAL DISCUSSION

1. Is it appropriate to describe the Unabomber as a psychopath? Using the definition provided in the excerpt from Robert Hare's book and evidence about the Unabomber's history, argue your position clearly and specifically. Although it may not be entirely suitable to impose twentieth-century psychological terms on a seventeenth-century dramatic character, can you find evidence in *Othello* to suggest that Iago also demonstrates the traits of a psychopath?

2. There is often an urgent need or desire to make sense of horrifying crimes against humanity. Does knowing or understanding the motives behind such crimes satisfy that need? How many motives can you discover for Kaczynski's terrorism? Are they consistent? Do they explain his actions? What do you suppose underlies his need for "personal revenge"? How do speculations and suggestions about mental illness enter into the picture? As excuse or explanation? As context or simply part of the puzzle?

3. Compare Kaczynski's motives with the reasons or explanations supplied for Iago's actions in *Othello*. What motives does Iago express to the audience, and are they confirmed by the words or actions of other characters? How credible are Iago and Kaczynski in justifying themselves? Does a logical connection exist between their motives and their crimes? If so, explain what, and if not, how do you "make sense" of their actions?

4. One of the most disturbing observations following Kaczynski's sentencing is that he showed no remorse for his deeds. Discuss what it means to feel remorse and suggest how Kaczynski's lack of regret affects your response to him. If, in confessing his crimes, he had shown some remorse, do you think your response would be different? In what ways? What is the relationship between remorse and conscience? Consider, as a comparison, the different ways Othello and Iago react to the exposure of their crimes. How do the differences influence your views of the two characters?

5. Compose a psychological profile of Kaczynski in preparation for his trial. Choosing a partner, decide which one of you will act as defense and which as prosecution. Then determine how you will use the profile to support your case, eventually sharing your "arguments" with your partner. Alternatively, perform the same exercise with Iago as your criminal. You may even want to involve the entire class and act out a trial as an additional scene attached to the end of *Othello*.

6. Imagining yourself as the lawyer defending Kaczynski or Iago, compose a private diary entry expressing your personal feelings about your client and your role in the justice system.

7. The Unabomber's victims were innocent strangers; Iago's victims were personal friends and family who trusted him. Does that difference affect your impression of the tragedy or suffering in either story? Why or why not?

8. Consider the horrifying revelations that come to Othello and Emilia when they realize the effect of their blindness to Iago's malicious deception. Consider also David Kaczynski's role in his brother's arrest, and the apologies David offered to victims and their families on behalf of himself and his mother. How do you respond to these characters and people who have ties of friendship or kinship with Iago or the Unabomber? How might you apply the words "sympathy," "courage," or "tragedy" to their situations and their responses to discoveries about someone they trusted or loved? Imagine being in a similar circumstance and write some reflections about your feelings. Do you feel angry, responsible, guilty, shocked, or torn by many mixed emotions?

9. The spouse of one of Kaczynski's murder victims described him as "diabolical and evil." Someone else wrote a letter of opinion to a newspaper with the headline, "Terrorists like Unabomber are evil, not crazy" (Knight-Ridder/Tribune Information Services, Jan. 22, 1998). Do you agree with these opinions? Discuss the appropriateness of "evil" as a word to describe the Unabomber's actions or his personality. What makes an action or person evil rather than simply criminal? What do your opinions and observations suggest about your own moral values?

10. On Kaczynski's sentencing day, the Attorney General said, "Justice has been done." Charles Epstein, one of Kaczynski's victims, questioned whether there could be true justice, saying, "And, for those who are dead and those whom we leave behind, no punishment can repair their losses. I am afraid, therefore, that we have to settle for imperfect justice—one that will put a stop to your reign of terror" (*Los Angeles Times*, May 5, 1998). Discuss whether you think justice

was finally reached in the Unabomber's case or whether, as Epstein suggests, no perfect justice could be possible. Explain reasons for your position.

11. Consider another perspective on justice, Nicklaus Suino's advice to fellow victims to avoid "chasing your own anger" (in the newspaper article included in this section). His words discourage a common impulse to associate justice with revenge—"an eye for an eye." Does his warning seem valuable to you? Why or why not? What relationship do you see between justice and revenge or between justice and tragedy in this story?

PRIVATE LIVES AND PUBLIC OFFICE: BILL CLINTON

On February 13, 1999, U.S. President Bill Clinton was acquitted in an impeachment trial that stemmed from a judicial investigation into his extra-marital affair with White House intern Monica Lewinsky and his public denial of that relationship in a courtroom deposition in January 1998. Clinton's "scandal" brought to national and international attention not only the minute and sordid details of his infidelity, but much larger questions about the relationship between private lives and public office. When Richard Nixon resigned from the presidency in 1974 before facing an inevitable impeachment trial about Watergate, charges against him involved very public crimes of sabotage, espionage, and political cover-ups designed to undercut the democratic process. By contrast, although Clinton also faced criminal charges, they revolved around statements about his personal relationships with women. Clinton's acquittal relieved him from facing possible resignation from office in mid-term. However, the allegations, investigation, and impeachment proceedings preoccupied the White House and distracted the public for over a year, interfering with other government responsibilities and national concerns. Furthermore, the scandal sensitized people to a debate that will not likely easily disappear from the political scene for some time. That debate focuses on concerns about the ways private lives and public office affect each other, about the relationship between "character" and leadership and between public opinion and political performance, about reputation, "due process," and political influence.

Clinton's troubled second term in office may seem to have little in common with the tragedy surrounding false accusations of infidelity in *Othello*, and even the suggestion of comparisons may strike some as distasteful. Yet insofar as the association between public and private lives is an issue in *Othello*, as well as in the charges against Clinton, the stories share some connections. Clinton's dual role as president of the United States and Commander in Chief of the American military is parallel to Othello's dual public function as governor of Cyprus and top general of the Venetian army. Both Clinton and Othello think they can keep their public duties and their private lives separate. In Shakespeare's play, however, Othello's public responsibilities significantly affect the approval rating of his marriage in Act 1. Moreover, in the unfolding plot, tension builds as Othello attempts to fulfill his duties as military leader in a warlike society while becoming more deeply disturbed by a growing conviction that Desdemona and his right-hand man, Cassio, are involved in an illicit relationship. Untangling official business from domestic concerns becomes increasingly impossible, and when personal tragedy erupts, the public necessarily feels the impact. Ironically, the final scene is a bedroom filled with dead bodies and government officials.

Clinton's private affair with Monica Lewinsky became a public issue largely because both he and Lewinsky denied it under oath in a sexual harassment case launched against Clinton by Paula Jones, a civil employee in Arkansas when Clinton was its state governor before becoming president. Eventually that case was dismissed, but not before the media revealed that tape-recorded personal conversations between Lewinsky and a co-worker Linda Tripp confirmed Lewinsky's relationship with Clinton. That evidence persuaded Independent Counsel Kenneth Starr to extend the mandate of an ongoing investigation of the President, leading ultimately to charges of perjury and obstructing justice. Technically, then, Clinton's false testimony in court rather than his infidelity launched the impeachment proceedings. Nevertheless, what he did or did not do with Monica Lewinsky became the focus of grand jury questions and pre-trial hearings for over a year. The public had never had such a close view of a president's private life and while the media and political opposition capitalized on "soap opera" details, many people were as embarrassed as Clinton to see the integrity of the highest political office in the country reduced to such unsavory matters. Questions about what should or should not be politically relevant, about what defines political responsibility and makes or breaks public credibility linger even if most of America and the world are eager to sweep all the scandal's headlines under the rug.

Following a chronology highlighting important dates in the Clinton-Lewinsky scandal, this section concludes with a national address by Clinton mid-way through the judicial inquiry, and two newspaper editorials expressing opinions and offering observations about the effect of the impeachment proceedings on Clinton's credibility and the state of American politics.

Brief Chronology of Clinton-Lewinsky Scandal

June 1995	Monica Lewinsky begins work as White House intern.
Jan. 7, 1998	Testifying at the Paula Jones sexual harassment case, Lewinsky denies a sexual relationship with Clinton.
Jan. 16, 1998	Independent Counsel Kenneth Starr seeks permission to begin investigating Clinton on charges of perjury and obstruction of justice in the Paula Jones case.
Jan. 17, 1998	In a deposition for the Paula Jones case, Clinton denies having a sexual relationship with Lewinsky.
Jan. 21, 1998	*The Washington Post* reveals Clinton's relationship with Monica Lewinsky.
Jan. 26, 1998	Clinton publicly denies relationship with Lewinsky.
April 1, 1998	Paula Jones case dismissed.
Aug. 6, 1998	Lewinsky begins testifying before grand jury.
Aug. 17, 1998	Clinton testifies before grand jury and gives a national public address, admitting a relationship with Lewinsky but denying any unlawful action.
Nov. 13, 1998	Clinton settles Paula Jones sexual harassment case by agreeing to pay $850,000.
Dec. 11, 1998	Judiciary Committee votes in favor of three articles of impeachment.
Dec. 18, 1998	House of Representatives votes to impeach Clinton.
Jan. 7, 1999	Clinton's impeachment trial begins.
Feb. 13, 1999	Clinton acquitted at impeachment trial.
April 13, 1999	Clinton found in contempt of court in the Paula Jones case.
July 30, 1999	Clinton fined $90,000 for lying under oath about Lewinsky affair.

CLINTON'S NATIONAL ADDRESS

On August 17, 1998, President Clinton testified before a grand jury about his relationship with Monica Lewinsky and his denial of that relationship under oath in the Paula Jones sexual harassment case. Later that day, he appeared on national television to address the public and inform them of his testimony. The House of Representatives did not vote in favor of an impeachment trial until three months later, so Clinton's speech appears in the context of uncertainty about his own political future. Try to determine the tone of Clinton's words. Does he seem sincerely apologetic and confessional or defensive and critical of his opponents? Or is he sending mixed messages? Do you find him convincing or sympathetic?

BILL CLINTON'S TELEVISED SPEECH
(*The Edmonton Journal*, August 18, 1998)

Good evening.

This afternoon in this room, from this chair, I testified before the Office of Independent Counsel and the grand jury.

I answered their questions truthfully, including questions about my private life, questions no American citizen would ever want to answer.

Still, I must take complete responsibility for all my actions, both public and private. And that is why I am speaking to you tonight.

As you know, in a deposition in January, I was asked questions about my relationship with Monica Lewinsky. While my answers were legally accurate, I did not volunteer information.

Indeed, I did have a relationship with Ms. Lewinsky that was not appropriate. In fact, it was wrong. It constituted a critical lapse in judgment and a personal failure on my part for which I am solely and completely responsible.

But I told the grand jury today and I say to you now that at no time did I ask anyone to lie, to hide or destroy evidence or to take any other unlawful action.

I know that my public comments and my silence about this matter gave a false impression. I misled people, including even my wife. I deeply regret that.

I can only tell you I was motivated by many factors. First, by a desire to protect myself from the embarrassment of my own conduct.

I was also very concerned about protecting my family. The fact that these questions were being asked in a politically inspired lawsuit, which has since been dismissed, was a consideration, too.

In addition, I had real and serious concerns about an independent counsel investigation that began with private business dealings 20 years ago, dealings, I might add, about which an independent federal agency found no evidence of any wrongdoing by me or my wife over two years ago.

The independent counsel investigation moved on to my staff and friends, then into my private life. And now the investigation itself is under investigation.

This has gone on too long, cost too much and hurt too many innocent people.

Now, this matter is between me, the two people I love most—my wife and our daughter—and our God. I must put it right, and I am prepared to do whatever it takes to do so.

Nothing is more important to me personally. But it is private, and I intend to reclaim my family life for my family. It's nobody's business but ours.

Even presidents have private lives. It is time to stop the pursuit of personal destruction and the prying into private lives and get on with our national life.

Our country has been distracted by this matter for too long, and I take my responsibility for my part in all of this. That is all I can do.

Now it is time—in fact, it is past time—to move on.

We have important work to do—real opportunities to seize, real problems to solve, real security matters to face.

And so tonight, I ask you to turn away from the spectacle of the past seven months, to repair the fabric of our national discourse, and to return our attention to all the challenges and all the promise of the next American century.

Thank you for watching. And good night.

CLINTON'S CREDIBILITY PROBLEM

The following newspaper editorial contemplates the effect of the Lewinsky scandal on Clinton's political leadership and suggests that the President should resign rather than drag himself, the government, and the public through impeachment proceedings. Coming a month after Clinton's televised address and two months before the House vote for a trial, this editorial raises concerns about Clinton's credibility based not on the immorality of his behavior but on his display of irresponsibility and recklessness. According to the editorialist, these latter weaknesses are the real issues threatening the President's ability to govern. Note how the writer connects the consequences of Clinton's private affair with his public actions, and forecasts the political costs of his relationship with Lewinsky. Pay attention to specific reasons that the writer finds fault not only with Clinton, but also with Lewinsky, Starr, and the Republicans. Try to put aside your knowledge of the trial's outcome, and consider whether these observations are thoughtful and convincing. Note that the editorial originates in a Canadian newspaper, *The Edmonton Journal*. Think about what political bias this non-American perspective presents or whether a Canadian viewpoint might allow for more emotional detachment than a similar American-based opinion piece.

"PRESIDENT CLINTON SHOULD RESIGN:
HE'S AN IRRESPONSIBLE RISK-TAKER"
(*The Edmonton Journal*, September 15, 1998)

U.S. President Bill Clinton has asked for an immediate meeting of international financial ministers to deal with the economic crisis in Asia and Russia, which he said is threatening to spread to Latin America and the rest of the developing world.

Clinton is urging the world's major industrial countries, including Canada, to "stand ready" to use $15 billion in emergency funds to keep the financial contagion from spreading.

Maybe Clinton's proposal has merit. But there is, of course, a problem: not many people are taking anything Bill Clinton has to say very seriously these days.

It's difficult to listen to his prescription for the world's economy when everyone is snickering over the details about his tacky affair with a young woman whose emotional balance was, how should we put this, suspect?

How can the world possibly consider taking the advice of a man who has so amply shown that he is an irresponsible risk-taker?

Clinton knew for four years that he was under the microscope, being pursued by Kenneth Starr, the independent counsel originally assigned to look into the president's involvement in possible misdealings in Whitewater.

Starr wasn't able to make that case but he continued to spend many millions of dollars on a very public hunt of the president. The results in all their lurid detail were released last week.

Knowing that he was being watched, Clinton still continued his politically suicidal dalliance with Monica Lewinsky. Remarkably, he continued to meet with Lewinsky and exchange gifts even after it was known she would be called by Starr as a witness in the Paula Jones case. Clinton could not have possibly been more reckless.

The report of the Lewinsky affair is filled with lurid but largely irrelevant detail that is obviously aimed at turning public opinion against Clinton. To underscore that point, Starr says his report looked into not only perjury and witness tampering, but also sexual harassment.

Readers of Starr's report may have trouble squaring that with the facts; Lewinsky was anything but unwilling. Clearly Starr was desperate to find the president guilty of something.

Legal experts in the U.S. say Clinton's lawyers are probably right when they argue there is not enough in Starr's report to merit an impeachment of the president. They say there is not sufficient evidence to prove Clinton obstructed justice and tampered with witnesses.

And as yet there is no groundswell from the American public to see the president impeached based on what they learned of Starr's report. Some 66 per cent of those surveyed in a weekend poll said Clinton should serve out the remainder of his term.

Impeachment is not the answer. That would only drag out this episode for years and serve to destabilize not only the United States but the whole world. As Clinton himself pointed out on Monday, the world is facing economic upheaval. And it is precisely because the world is in trouble that we cannot afford a lame-duck leader in the only remaining superpower.

Instead, Clinton should resign. His credibility problem isn't going to go away, at least not fast enough. It's a step he would take if he believed in the good of his country, as well as his own Democratic Party, which would then have Vice-President Al Gore well positioned for the next election.

He can take solace in knowing the step will backfire on his enemies: the American public still considers he is doing a good job. If he leaves, there's a good chance Americans will turn on Starr and the more rabid Republicans.

In resigning, Clinton will be able to prove that he was serious when he said he wanted to make amends to his family, especially his young daughter. In resigning, Clinton would also be able to show a sense of honour, something that neither he nor his political enemies have displayed so far.

RELIEF AND QUESTIONS FOLLOWING THE IMPEACHMENT TRIAL

This editorial offers a look backwards and forwards on the day after the Senate voted to acquit President Clinton in his impeachment trial. The writer expresses relief that the year-long investigation and legal proceedings are over but also speculates about the lasting consequences. What attitudes are expressed about "the public," party politics, and Bill Clinton? Can you determine the writer's moral and political position?

Note that the name "Svengali" near the end of the article refers to a sinister fictional character, a musician who exercised the mesmerizing influence of hypnosis over a female music student to advance his own career. The editorial's comparison of Clinton to Svengali likely implies a sinister angle on the President's relationship with Lewinsky and other women, and perhaps also suggests his ability to charm the public into accepting his political legitimacy in spite of his personal impropriety.

"PLEASE, LET THIS BE THE END OF IT:
U.S. SENATE ACCEPTS PUBLIC VERDICT"
(*The Edmonton Journal*, February 13, 1999)

It's safe to come out. The Clinton-Lewinsky scandal is really, finally over.

For the good and sufficient reason that the court of public opinion had already acquitted Americans' flawed but freely chosen president, the U.S. Senate killed two articles of impeachment against him Friday.

Someday, possibly as soon as the next the U.S. election in November 2000, disappointed Republicans will have cause to thank their Senate brethren for saving them from a terrible, indelible political blunder.

Many Americans—and many Canadians too—will draw the exact opposite conclusion. They will see the fundamentally political nature of the senators' decision as a moral disaster—one that signals tolerance for lies, lawbreaking and dishonourable sexual behaviour:

The most honest of them will take this horror to its logical conclusion, condemn "the public" for setting an amoral and dangerous precedent, and further lose faith in the masses' competence to rule themselves without proper guidance.

Except in the world of spin, however, the last thing the scandal, trial and verdict has been is a green light for licentious, dishonest behaviour: Acquittal or no, both Clinton and assorted accusers have paid a terrible price in ridicule and public disgust that will likely resonate in public and private life for decades.

The United States (and Canada, vicariously) has debated standards of suitable public behaviour as never before, and in the process, also examined and judged the sins of hypocrisy, demagoguery and political dishonesty.

Voters have balanced the sin of infidelity against the sin of being caught. They have been forced to look past the surface of their politicians, they have been forced to examine their priorities for political leadership.

And they have been forced to make a far more subtle, big-picture, *responsible* choice than congressional prosecutors pretended they faced in the attempt to whip up a hanging jury in public opinion.

Showing their contempt for the ordinary voter, Clinton's critics pretend the truth never got through to the public, or that it was falsely twisted along the way by the president's apologists.

On the contrary, it got through just fine, in exhausting, sickening detail, months ago. While Washington was huffing and puffing about idiotic definitions of sex and perjury, the public was quietly holding its own, rather more sophisticated, trial—and rendering a verdict that has been clear and unwavering for months.

Contradicting the prophets of moral doom, polls show a majority view Bill Clinton's lying, lawbreaking, adultery, dubious apologies and shabby treatment of assorted women with the distaste of a homeowner picking up a partially decomposed rodent.

The point is, they didn't hire him for those qualities, they don't think his actions reached the U.S. constitution's standard of "high crimes and misdemeanours," they have weighed the motives and political morality of his opponents, and most importantly, they find their Svengali has performed well in his public duties.

Republicans are lucky they failed to overrule the majority using constitutional cover they never applied to Ronald Reagan, and fought tooth-and-nail to resist in the case of Richard Nixon. Voters being voters, failure will largely be forgotten. Success would not have been.

While the affair's moral damage has been overstated, however, it's impossible to argue there has been no price.

Clinton and his accusers have further damaged the reputation of public servants and the attractiveness of public service.

They have made us even more skeptical than before of a politician's statements and motives.

And worse, by sanctimoniously shrieking "Wolf" on this particular scandal for so many months, they have probably made the body politic less sensitive to warnings of more serious wrongdoing involving affairs of state.

Perhaps those things ought to be impeachable offences.

QUESTIONS FOR WRITTEN AND ORAL DISCUSSION

1. In his national speech on August 17, 1998, President Clinton addressed the conflict and unclear boundaries between public office and private life. What association does he see between the two worlds

regarding his relationship with Lewinsky and his attempt to deny it? Discuss his statement, "Even presidents have private lives." To what extent do you think this statement *is* true and to what extent *should* it be true? Does the public properly respect the privacy of political figures? Do politicians expect too much if they believe their private lives should not be subject to public scrutiny? Provide specific examples to support your conclusions.

2. Like Clinton, Othello felt he could keep his public office and his domestic relationship separate. Find specific lines in the play that express this belief, and suggest reasons for Othello's failure to keep his military role and his marriage separate. Are deliberate choices or personalities the cause or do external circumstances and expectations make the separation impossible? Is Othello's idealism or naivete an issue? Explain.

3. One editorial in this section raises questions about Clinton's bad judgment and irresponsible risk-taking rather than about the immorality of his infidelity and deception. Do you agree that, from a perspective of public leadership, irresponsible behavior is more relevant than immoral behavior? Why or why not? What are the differences between irresponsibility and immorality? Give examples. Should immoral sexual conduct be a political concern? Why or why not? Is there a level of immorality that is tolerable and a point beyond which it becomes unacceptable? If so, where would you place Clinton's behavior on the scale?

4. Othello, like Clinton, can be accused of exercising bad judgment. Compare the circumstances and the outcomes for the two men. In what ways are they similar and how are they different? Consider how accurately the words "tragedy" and "scandal" describe their respective stories. Could you argue that there is an element of "scandal" to Othello's story or a degree of "tragedy" to Clinton's? As an imaginative exercise, write a newspaper editorial that takes one of these unconventional views.

5. The editorial that calls for Clinton's resignation concludes that stepping down from office would demonstrate "honor." Do you agree? Why or why not? "Honor" is an important word in Shakespeare's play. Othello refers to it in the final scene, asking, "But why should honor outlive honesty?" (5.2.242), and calling himself "An honorable murderer" (5.2.290). Does the word "honor" seem appropriate in discussing Othello's actions and motives? In comparing Clinton and Othello, does the word "honor" make them seem completely opposite or do they share some character traits?

6. Discuss the relationship between a familiar phrase in modern politics, "public image," and a word that is so thematically important in *Othello*, "reputation." Referring to details about the Clinton scandal or a recent election campaign or political issue, consider to what extent public image reflects truth or to what extent it tries to deflect or evade truth. Referring to two important dialogues about reputation or "good name" in *Othello*—between Cassio and Iago in 2.3.261–335 and between Iago and Othello in 3.3.144–171—discuss what reputation means to these three men and whether it is simply about public image or about deeper qualities of "character."

7. The editorial included in this section that assesses the Clinton scandal after the impeachment verdict draws clear distinctions between "the public" and the elected politicians involved in the President's trial. What are the major differences? According to the writer, what costs follow the impeachment process for the public, the politicians, and the political system? Which views in the editorial do you agree with and which would you question or dispute? Explain your position.

8. Research the impeachment process, its purpose, and its use in American history, and write your own opinion piece about its value and effectiveness, referring to Nixon's near impeachment and focusing especially on Bill Clinton's case. Does the standard, "high crimes and misdemeanors," seem to describe Clinton's actions? To what extent is party politics involved in the process, and do you think it should be?

9. As an imaginative exercise, compose a dialogue between Desdemona and Hilary Clinton, the President's wife, at a point when they are both aware of the way their husbands have mistreated them. Perhaps Desdemona appears in this conversation as a ghost after her death. Alternatively, compose a diary entry for Hilary in which she writes questions or reflections to Desdemona. Do the words express sympathy and understanding? Loyalty? Puzzlement and confusion?

10. Discuss the role of the media in Bill Clinton's scandal and the O. J. Simpson trial. Consider some of the following questions. Does the media inform or entertain? Does it tell stories or create them? Does it report public opinion or shape it? In addressing "the public right to know," does the media ever inappropriately cross over boundaries into private, personal matters? Does it engage in biased reporting? If so, to what effect? How might either of these news stories have developed differently if the media had not played such a prominent role?

11. Acting as an added character in *Othello*—a newspaper reporter looking for an interesting headline—write a series of articles that respond
to or record selected parts of Shakespeare's plot. What will capture
public interest? Are you committed to unbiased reporting of the facts
or are you willing to stretch the truth for the sake of a good story?

FROM THE STORYLINES

Connections with *Othello* can be made not only in recent historical events appearing in newspaper headlines, but also in storylines penned by other authors exploring expressions of love and hate, good and evil, appearance and reality. These timeless conflicts emerge again and again in fiction where characters and plots capture our imaginations, sometimes reflecting our own struggles and at other times drawing us into a world that magnifies conflict far beyond our own experience. We become engaged by what we recognize and by what we can hardly consider possible. Just as *Othello* is a tale of extreme emotions and responses, of outrageous behavior and its consequences, so, too, the poetry and stories discussed in this section recount extreme experiences that drive us to the edge of what we know, imagine, or believe and compel us to respond with some degree of fascination, horror, or dismay.

LOVE'S DARK SIDE

Love is typically the stuff of romance and comedy: boy meets girl and eventually they fall in love and live happily ever after. That general pattern seems to have endless appeal as it is refashioned into one novel, movie, or poem after another. Sometimes, however, love matches do not resolve happily, as *Othello* clearly illustrates. The passionate intensity of love as an emotion breeds internal and external conflicts such as jealousy and family disputes that become insurmountable and ultimately tragic or horrifying or both.

"My Last Duchess"

Robert Browning's nineteenth-century poem "My Last Duchess" visits this dark side of love. The poem's character, a nameless Italian Duke from a Renaissance city-state, Ferrara, speaks in a dramatic monologue about his former wife or "last Duchess." The Duke is clearly addressing a guest who appears to be present to negotiate the terms of a new marriage with a new Duchess, the daughter of a Count. That the Duke should devote virtually the entire one-sided conversation to reflections about his last Duchess and a painting of her is odd indeed. As readers, we become increasingly curious and uneasy about her absence and the Duke's apparent obsession with her past manners and her need to be "lessoned." It is impossible not to wonder what happened to the last Duchess when the Duke says, "I gave commands; / Then all smiles stopped together." Furthermore, the fact that he is telling the Count's servant this story implies that, directly or indirectly, the Duke is sending a caution or threat to his future wife about his expectations of her. Browning's poetic monologue is full of irony, for the Duke reveals far more than he actually says about himself and leaves impressions about his former wife that may be the opposite of what he intends.

The poem is sinister, to say the least. By choosing to set it in Renaissance Italy, Browning is appealing to popular views about that time and place where wealth and civility coincided with political intrigue and corruption. With a setting similar to *Othello*'s, "My Last Duchess" explores in a narrower, more limited context, a dark, unsettling vision of the relationship between corruption and courtesy, power and love, passion and cold, calculating reason.

ROBERT BROWNING, "MY LAST DUCHESS" (1842)
(The Poetical Works of Robert Browning, Vol. 4; London: Smith
Elder & Co., 1884)

FERRARA.

That's my last Duchess painted on the wall,
Looking as if she were alive. I call
That piece a wonder, now: Fra Pandolf's hands
Worked busily a day, and there she stands.
Will't please you sit and look at her? I said
"Fra Pandolf" by design, for never read
Strangers like you that pictured countenance,
The depth and passion of its earnest glance,
But to myself they turned (since none puts by
The curtain I have drawn for you, but I)
And seemed as they would ask me, if they durst,
How such a glance came there; so, not the first
Are you to turn and ask thus. Sir, 't was not
Her husband's presence only, called that spot

Of joy into the Duchess' cheek: perhaps
Fra Pandolf chanced to say "Her mantle laps
"Over my lady's wrist too much," or "Paint
"Must never hope to reproduce the faint
"Half-flush that dies along her throat:" such stuff
Was courtesy, she thought, and cause enough
For calling up that spot of joy. She had
A heart—how shall I say?—too soon made glad,
Too easily impressed; she liked whate'er
She looked on, and her looks went everywhere.
Sir, 't was all one! My favour at her breast,
The dropping of the daylight in the West,
The bough of cherries some officious fool
Broke in the orchard for her, the white mule
She rode with round the terrace—all and each
Would draw from her alike the approving speech,
Or blush, at least. She thanked men,—good! but thanked
Somehow—I know not how—as if she ranked
My gift of a nine-hundred-years-old name
With anybody's gift. Who'd stoop to blame
This sort of trifling? Even had you skill
In speech—(which I have not)—to make your will
Quite clear to such an one, and say, "Just this
"Or that in you disgusts me; here you miss,
"Or there exceed the mark"—and if she let
Herself be lessoned so, nor plainly set
Her wits to yours, forsooth, and made excuse,
—E'en then would be some stooping; and I choose
Never to stoop. Oh sir, she smiled, no doubt,
When'er I passed her; but who passed without
Much the same smile? This grew; I gave commands;
Then all smiles stopped together. There she stands
As if alive. Will 't please you rise? We'll meet
The company below, then. I repeat,
The Count your master's known munificence
Is ample warrant that no just pretence
Of mine for dowry will be disallowed;
Though his fair daughter's self, as I avowed
At starting, is my object. Nay, we'll go
Together down, sir. Notice Neptune, though,
Taming a sea-horse, thought a rarity,
Which Claus of Innsbruck cast in bronze for me! (150–152)

"A Rose for Emily"

William Faulkner's twentieth-century short story "A Rose for Emily" portrays a relationship between a man and a woman that reaches such a bizarre and grotesque conclusion that we might even question how the word "love" could possibly apply. Faulkner's story is set in America's Deep South following the Civil War, at a time when tensions between North and South and between the established aristocracy and the new generation were still very evident. The plot, with its episodic lack of chronological order, reads like a mystery story, raising questions and dropping clues along the way. The townspeople observe the life of aristocratic Emily Grierson from a distance as they gossip about her short-lived relationship with the Northerner Homer Barron, his sudden disappearance, and her subsequent years of eccentric seclusion until her death finally allows the community to pay their respects and uncover her frightful secrets. The closing revelation suggests, as does Browning's "My Last Duchess," that the exterior courtesy and civility of aristocracy can mask some extremely appalling human behavior. The story, as a whole, explores some of the same issues as *Othello*, such as the relationship between romance and madness, between love and control. And although questions about what Emily did or did not do are never explicitly answered, all the evidence is available for readers to make reasonable assumptions. The excerpt below comes from the story's concluding section, where the townspeople enter an upstairs room in Emily's house that no one has seen for years.

FROM WILLIAM FAULKNER, "A ROSE FOR EMILY" (1931)
(*Collected Stories of William Faulkner*,
New York: Random House, 1950)

The violence of breaking down the door seemed to fill this room with pervading dust. A thin, acrid pall as of the tomb seemed to lie everywhere upon this room decked and furnished as for a bridal. . . .

The man himself lay in the bed.

For a long while we just stood there, looking down at the profound and fleshless grin. The body had apparently once lain in the attitude of an embrace, but now the long sleep that outlasts love, that conquers even the grimace of love, had cuckolded him. (129–130)

QUESTIONS FOR WRITTEN AND ORAL DISCUSSION

1. In "My Last Duchess," what does the Duke's monologue reveal about his character? Consider the effect of irony and suggest where or how the Duke may say more than he realizes. Identify his complaints about his former Duchess and discuss whether they seem like faults to you. If so, why? And if not, why does the Duke think so?

2. Compose another monologue spoken by the Duke's guest when he returns to give a report to his master, the Count, whose daughter the Duke next intends to marry. What information and impressions will this messenger convey?

3. What parallels can you identify between the events revealed within "My Last Duchess" and the plot of *Othello*, especially related to love, marriage, and the end results? Make a list of similarities, and then create a list of significant differences. Discuss whether and how this exercise affects your perceptions or feelings about each work. Do you like the poem or the play better, and, if so, for what reasons?

4. Compare Browning's Duke with Othello and Iago. With which of Shakespeare's two characters does he seem to share the most similarities? Provide specific examples, considering not only his social and marital status, but his values, intentions, and actions.

5. Compare the Duchess—as the Duke describes her and as you understand her—with Desdemona. What do they have in common? Are they innocent victims or not? Are they sympathetic characters? What part do you think politics or power plays in their respective marriages and the outcomes?

6. Rather than simply comparing characters, as the two previous questions suggest, compose an imaginary dialogue between the Duchess and Desdemona or between the Duke and Othello or Iago. What might these fictional characters have to say to one another? Would they offer advice, express sympathy, openly confess motives and actions, respond with feigned civility or genuine honesty? What effect might the shared Italian Renaissance context have on their conversations?

7. Consider whether and how the word "evil" or "jealousy" applies to Browning's poem. Compare or contrast the significance of one of these words with its relevance in *Othello*.

8. Discuss the conflict between passion and reason in Browning's poem and Shakespeare's play. Consider why love and hate, as passionate emotional responses, can become so closely related while seeming to be such obvious opposites. Is it possible to feel passionately but

to react with the calm logic of reason? Are there characters who do so? Explain and give evidence.

9. Read the entire story "A Rose for Emily" in an anthology or short story collection. Identify some external barriers to a healthy relationship and potentially happy marriage that Emily and Homer face. Can you also find suggestions in the narrative that Emily and Homer simply are not personally suited for each other? Discuss the significance of social and family expectations, as well as character traits, and indicate which of these factors you think are most influential in the bizarre development of the plot.

10. Are there victims in "A Rose for Emily"? If so, who and victims of what? Does the relationship between love or romance and victims invite you to see similarities or differences between Faulkner's short story and *Othello*? Provide specific examples.

11. Compare "My Last Duchess" and "A Rose for Emily" as fictional portrayals of the dark side of love. What makes the poem and the story dark or sinister, what does each say about love—as a true or false feeling—and why do you suppose both authors compel their readers to draw conclusions without directly providing the relevant information? How does the element of mystery affect your response to the central characters?

12. Discuss whether you think the word "tragedy" applies to either "My Last Duchess" or "A Rose for Emily." Is a plot that is horrifying, disturbing, or grotesque necessarily tragic? Why or why not? Consider how the development of the characters, the point of view (i.e., the speaker), and your emotional response influence your observations and conclusions. Suggest whether these reflections on tragedy lead you to see similarities or differences between the poem or the story and *Othello*.

THE PROBLEM OF EVIL

Evil is a problem not simply because it often manifests itself in destructive behavior. It is a problem because it reflects a side of humanity that disturbs us. Either we can hardly comprehend it or we can, with even greater discomfort, identify in our own experience temptations to similar behavior—more or less extreme—even if we choose not to respond to those temptations. Evil is a problem because sometimes it fascinates us as much as it disturbs us, a paradox that is also uncomfortable. And evil is a problem because the very word implies a moral judgment and a standard of acceptable or "good" behavior that is not easily defined or upheld and may not be universally accepted. When we encounter representations of what might be considered evil in literature, we can perhaps attempt to dismiss the horrors because they are not "real." But when the stories are well-told or effectively dramatized, they do engage us in spite of ourselves. People want to—and even do—stand up in a performance of *Othello* and shout, "Stop!" or "Don't do it!" Other stories invite similar involvement and compel us to reflect on our own responses of horror and fascination, of judgment against what repels us but what may also reveal something of ourselves.

"The Cask of Amontillado"

Edgar Allan Poe's nineteenth-century short story "The Cask of Amontillado" unfolds a plot of intrigue and deception initiated by one man's vow of revenge against another. Montresor, the narrator and scheming main character, draws us into a dark underworld both literally and figuratively. As he guides his companion into the damp catacombs beneath his home with the false request to inspect a cask of wine, he takes us—the readers—inside a mind that is both calculating and consumed by a passion on the edge of madness. While he systematically buries his victim alive, we read on, perhaps with a sense of being trapped ourselves and with an uneasy, suffocating realization that the "joke"—as Montresor calls his murderous plot—is also on us because we have not been able to escape or prevent the dreadful conclusion. The vaguely defined Italian Renaissance setting Poe chooses for his story conjures up the same notions of corruption, deceit, and immorality—of stereotypical Machiavellianism—that Browning appeals to in "My Last Duchess" and that Shakespeare adopted several centuries earlier for *Othello*. If Iago has sometimes been regarded as a machiavel or as "evil" personified, Poe's Montresor invites a similar evaluation for his monstrous actions and apparent delight at his success. The excerpt below comes from the beginning of the story.

FROM EDGAR ALLAN POE, "THE CASK OF AMONTILLADO" (1846)
(The Complete Works of Edgar Allan Poe, Ed. James A. Harrison, Vol. VI; New York: Society of English and French Literature, 1902)

The thousand injuries of Fortunato I had borne as I best could, but when he ventured upon insult I vowed revenge. You, who so well know the nature of my soul, will not suppose, however, that I gave utterance to a threat. *At length* I would be avenged; this was a point definitely settled—but the very definitiveness with which it was resolved precluded the idea of risk. I must not only punish but punish with impunity. A wrong is unredressed when retribution overtakes its redresser. It is equally unredressed when the avenger fails to make himself felt as such to him who has done the wrong.

It must be understood that neither by word nor deed had I given Fortunato cause to doubt my good will. I continued, as was my wont, to smile in his face, and he did not perceive that my smile *now* was at the thought of his immolation.

He had a weak point—this Fortunato—although in other regards he was a man to be respected and even feared. He prided himself on his connoisseurship in wine. Few Italians have the true virtuoso spirit. For the most part their enthusiasm is adopted to suit the time and opportunity, to practise imposture upon the British and Austrian *millionaires*. In painting and gemmary, Fortunato, like his countrymen, was a quack, but in the matter of old wines he was sincere. In this respect I did not differ from him materially;—I was skilful in the Italian vintages myself, and bought largely whenever I could.

It was about dusk, one evening during the supreme madness of the carnival season, that I encountered my friend. He accosted me with excessive warmth, for he had been drinking much. The man wore motley. He had on a tight-fitting parti-striped dress, and his head was surmounted by the conical cap and bells. I was so pleased to see him that I thought I should never have done wringing his hand.

I said to him—"My dear Fortunato, you are luckily met. How remarkably well you are looking to-day. But I have received a pipe of what passes for Amontillado, and I have my doubts."

"How?" said he. "Amontillado? A pipe? Impossible? And in the middle of the carnival!"

"I have my doubts," I replied; "and I was silly enough to pay the full Amontillado price without consulting you in the matter. You were not to be found, and I was fearful of losing a bargain."

"Amontillado!"

"I have my doubts."

"Amontillado!"

"And I must satisfy them."

"Amontillado!"

"As you are engaged, I am on my way to Luchresi. If any one has a critical turn it is he. He will tell me——"

"Luchresi cannot tell Amontillado from Sherry."

"And yet some fools will have it that his taste is a match for your own."

"Come, let us go."

"Whither?"

"To your vaults."

"My friend, no; I will not impose upon your good nature. I perceive you have an engagement. Luchresi——"

"I have no engagement;—come."

"My friend, no. It is not the engagement, but the severe cold with which I perceive you are afflicted. The vaults are insufferably damp. They are encrusted with nitre."

"Let us go, nevertheless. The cold is merely nothing. Amontillado! You have been imposed upon. And as for Luchresi, he cannot distinguish Sherry from Amontillado."

Thus speaking, Fortunato possessed himself of my arm; and putting on a mask of black silk and drawing a *roquelaire* closely about my person, I suffered him to hurry me to my palazzo. (167–169)

Lord of the Flies

William Golding's twentieth-century novel *Lord of the Flies* addresses the contrast between human civility and depravity when individuals are pushed to the edge of survival in a context that requires them to depend on each other. The story describes what happens to a group of British schoolboys marooned on an uninhabited island while waiting and hoping to be rescued. Initially, they attempt to establish some form of social order based on their experience of civilization back home. Ralph, a natural leader, receives authority to direct each day's activities, organized by the need for food and shelter and for signaling potential rescuers. Before long, however, order begins to crumble. Jack, another strong character, undermines Ralph's leadership and lures boys into his camp by appealing to their sense of adventure, fear, and superstition. They paint their faces, sharpen wooden spears, and hunt wild boars—a source of food and a symbol of dark savage power. Soon the savagery manifests itself in the boys' treatment of each other. Two are brutally killed, and when the story concludes, Ralph is a solitary outcast fighting a losing battle for his life just as a British naval officer arrives on the beach as part of a rescue mission.

Golding's story raises many questions about the foundations of civilized behavior, about what separates the human race from beasts, what savage impulses lie buried in human hearts, and what draws these impulses to the surface. *Lord of the Flies* suggests, as *Othello* does, that corruption comes not from without but from within, from people who belong in society as Iago does, and from suspicions and passions that need little encouragement to erupt into actions as violent as Othello's. In the excerpt below, from the end of the novel, the rescuing officer asks his initial questions only half-seriously until he realizes Ralph's answers are true. The situation is more appalling than the officer can easily apprehend, and in his civilized presence, Ralph, too, is finally overwhelmed—with relief and horror.

FROM WILLIAM GOLDING, *LORD OF THE FLIES*
(London: Faber and Faber, 1954)

"We saw your smoke. What have you been doing? Having a war or something?"

Ralph nodded. . . .

"Nobody killed, I hope? Any dead bodies?"

"Only two, and they've gone."

"Two? Killed?"

Ralph nodded again. Behind him, the whole island was shuddering with flame. The officer knew, as a rule, when people were telling the truth. He whistled softly. . . .

"I should have thought," said the officer as he visualized the search before him, "I should have thought that a pack of British boys—you're all British aren't you?—would have been able to put up a better show than that—I mean—"

"It was like that at first," said Ralph, "before things—". . . .

Ralph looked at him dumbly. For a moment he had a fleeting picture of the strange glamour that had once invested the beaches. But the island was scorched up like dead wood—Simon was dead—and Jack had. . . . The tears began to flow and sobs shook him. He gave himself up to them now for the first time on the island; great, shuddering spasms of grief that seemed to wrench his whole body. His voice rose under the black smoke before the burning wreckage of the island; and infected by that emotion, the other little boys began to shake and sob too. And in the middle of them, with filthy body, matted hair, and unwiped nose, Ralph wept for the end of innocence, the darkness of man's heart, and the fall through the air of the true, wise friend called Piggy.

The officer, surrounded by these noises, was moved and a little embarrassed. He turned away to give them time to pull themselves together; and waited, allowing his eyes to rest on the trim cruiser in the distance. (221–223)

QUESTIONS FOR WRITTEN AND ORAL DISCUSSION

1. "The Cask of Amontillado" begins with Montresor's stated purpose: revenge. Why is he seeking revenge? Are his reasons vague or specific? Do his motives fit his actions? If so, how, and if not, then what explains why he does what he does? Does revenge require reasons or can it be a response of passion that lies beyond reason?

2. Read the first two paragraphs of Poe's story with Shakespeare's Iago in mind, especially his early speeches in 1.1 of *Othello*. What comparisons can you make between Montresor and Iago and between the way the two plots begin? Can you imagine Iago speaking Montresor's initial lines about Othello rather than Fortunato? How does that possibility affect your comparison?

3. Irony is an important technique in Poe's story—both verbally in the contrast between what Montresor says and what he intends, and dramatically in the contrast between what readers know and what Fortunato knows. Find examples of irony. Then discuss why Montresor chooses to deceive Fortunato in this deliberate fashion, and what effect irony has on the story's atmosphere and on your involvement as a reader.

4. Compare the use of verbal and dramatic irony in "The Cask of Amontillado" and *Othello*, especially in the portion of the story's dialogue included in this chapter and in the dialogue between Iago and Othello in 3.3, sometimes called the "temptation scene." What similarities can you discover? What do these similarities suggest to you about the

relationship between appearance and reality and good and evil in the story and the play? Do Fortunato and Othello demonstrate their own weaknesses or do they appear as innocent victims?

5. Write a personal response about your emotional reaction to Poe's story. Are you horrified, fascinated, intrigued, or dismayed by it? Do you find it suspenseful? Do you identify with one character or the other? How do you think your reaction might be different if the narrator were not Montresor but Fortunato or a third-person narrative voice? You might want to consider rewriting the story's beginning from a perspective outside of Montresor's mind and reflect on how the point of view (i.e., narrator's voice) affects your response to the story.

6. Discuss whether "madness" and "evil" are appropriate words to describe what happens in "The Cask of Amontillado" and/or "A Rose for Emily." Are the two words related in either story or does one word seem more relevant than the other?

7. In *Lord of the Flies*, Ralph and Jack begin as friends and end as enemies. Similarly, Othello and Iago share at least the appearance of friendship, but conclude with Othello attempting to murder Iago. Discuss these two relationships, considering the balance of power and authority between them, the role that passion and reason or ambition and jealousy play, and the motives and reasons for the change between the characters. How might the words "control" and "out of control" describe their circumstances and their connections to each other?

8. Consider the significance of animals and animal imagery in *Lord of the Flies* and *Othello*. What similarities and differences can you identify in their contribution to plot, character, and tone?

9. Discuss the use of setting in *Othello* and *Lord of the Flies*. How do Shakespeare's "warlike isle" of Cyprus and Golding's uninhabited island contribute to the atmosphere and conflict in each plot? How significant is a military, warlike context in either the play or the story?

10. Ralph weeps for "the end of innocence, the darkness of man's heart." Write a short response about what destroys innocence in the novel and what defines the darkness.

11. Evil is both an individual and a social phenomenon. Discuss whether it appears to be manifest more at an individual or social level in *Lord of the Flies*, providing specific examples to support your position. What happens when individuals lose their identity in a group or mob? What happens when one person has leadership skills without a moral purpose or conscience? Compare *Lord of the Flies* with *Othello*, con-

sidering how evil is portrayed in both plots and what each invites us
to conclude about good and evil within ourselves.

SUGGESTED READINGS

Faulkner, William. "A Rose for Emily." Found in numerous anthologies
     or collections of Faulkner's fiction.
Golding, William. *Lord of the Flies*. London: Faber and Faber, 1954.
Olsen, Kirstin. *Understanding* Lord of the Flies: *A Student Casebook to
     Issues, Sources, and Historical Documents*. Westport, CT: Green-
     wood Press, 2000.
Poe, Edgar Allan. "The Cask of Amontillado." Found in numerous an-
     thologies or collections of Poe's fiction.

Index

About the Author

FAITH NOSTBAKKEN has taught literature at the college level. Her research focuses on Shakespeare and Renaissance drama, particularly the historical contexts. She is the author of *Understanding* Macbeth: *A Student Casebook to Issues, Sources, and Historical Documents* (Greenwood 1997).